State and Revolution in Cuba

ENVISIONING CUBA

Louis A. Pérez Jr., editor

State
and Revolution
in Cuba

Mass Mobilization and Political Change, 1920–1940

ROBERT WHITNEY

The University of North Carolina Press   *Chapel Hill and London*

© 2001 The University of North Carolina Press
All rights reserved

Set in Cycles and Arepo typefaces
by Tseng Information Systems, Inc.
Manufactured in the United States of America

∞ The paper in this book meets the guidelines
for permanence and durability of the Committee
on Production Guidelines for Book Longevity of
the Council on Library Resources.

Library of Congress Cataloging-in-Publication Data
Whitney, Robert (Robert W.)
State and revolution in Cuba: mass mobilization
and political change, 1920-1940 / Robert Whitney.
p.   cm. — (Envisioning Cuba)
Includes bibliographical references and index.
ISBN 0-8078-2611-1 (cloth: alk. paper)—
ISBN 0-8078-4925-1 (pbk.: alk. paper)
1. Cuba—Politics and government—1909-1933.
2. Cuba—Politics and government—1933-1959.
3. Government, Resistance to—Cuba—History—20th century.
4. Oligarchy—Cuba—History—20th century.
5. Political participation—Cuba—History—20th century.
6. Democracy—Cuba—History—20th century.
I. Title. II. Series.
F1787 .W58   2001
972.9106—dc21
00-051205

05 04 03 02 01   5 4 3 2 1

Contents

Acknowledgments

I am grateful to Catherine LeGrand for her help and encouragement through-out the writing of this book. She is an exemplary scholar and teacher and a wonderful person. Her insightful and constructive criticisms helped me sharpen my arguments and correct my habit of tripping over my own words.

In Cuba I owe a special kind of recognition to Dr. José Tabares del Real of the University of Havana. The endnotes and the bibliography of this book attest to his scholarly contribution to the study of Cuban history. What these references cannot communicate is how honored I am to have felt his gener-osity and personal warmth. Not only did he facilitate my access to archives, arrange interviews with historians and other knowledgable people, and pro-vide me with documentation hitherto unavailable to academics, but he also introduced a foreigner into the murky history of Cuban revolutionary poli-tics. Pepe Tabares could do this because his credentials as a writer of history are matched only by his reputation as someone who helped change history. By sharing this aspect of his life with me, he has given me something that no "pure" academic can give, and for that I am deeply grateful.

I would like to thank the Cuban Institute of History for sponsoring my research trips to Cuba between 1990 and 1994. In particular, the institute's late president, Jorge Mendoza, gave me full access to institute archives. His successor, Manuel López, has shown the same kindness in recent years. My research at the institute would not have been possible if it were not for Sergia Martínez, formally of the institute's International Relations Department. Sergia did all the work no one sees and few appreciate: she arranged visas, wrote letters of introduction, confirmed airplane tickets, fought with bu-reaucrats, and arranged transportation to and from archives. These tasks, of course, were part of her normal job, but much of my research was carried out at a time when life in Cuba was far from normal. My academic visits to Cuba coincided with the worst years of the "Special Period" (1990–94): power failures were common, transportation was nearly nonexistent, food was in short supply, water often stopped running, and the telephones rarely worked. Somehow, Sergia managed to get everything done with her usual professionalism and with a warm smile. I do not how she did it all, and she tells me she does not know, either. I cannot imagine having written this book without her.

Similar professionalism and personal warmth was exhibited by the librarians and archivists of the Instituto de Historia, the Cuban National Archives, and by the staff of the Biblioteca Nacional José Martí. Their country was a mess and their personal lives and routines in turmoil, yet they always provided me with more information than I asked for, most of which appears in the sources for this book.

Several Cuban scholars helped me clarify my ideas, and they generously gave of their time, experience, and hospitality. Jorge Ibarra, Oscar Zanetti, Alejandro García, Pedro Pablo Rodríguez, Ana Cairo Ballester, Graciella Chailloux Laffita, Carlos del Toro, José Cantón Navarro, Rosa López Oceguera, Rafael Hernández, Newton Briones Montoto, Rafael Soler, and the late Ramón de Armas have set a very high standard for historians of Cuba, and I am very grateful for their advice, friendship, and support. All of these people generously shared private research sources with me and they let me read many of their unpublished works. I am proud to be permanently in their debt. I would also like to thank Enrique de la Osa and Segundo Curti for sharing their personal experiences of the events covered in this book. Both men were important participants in Cuban political life between the 1920s and the 1940s, and their insights into the times brought life to the primary sources I was reading. Both men passed away during the final stages of writing this work. I will always remember their kindness, eloquence, and dignity.

John Kirk from Dalhousie University and Barry Carr of La Trobe University were kind enough to read and comment on earlier drafts of this book. Both scholars know Cuba and Cuban history well, and I am grateful for their support and encouragement. In the late stages of writing this book the sound advice and guidance of Louis Pérez Jr. and Harold Sims was decisive. Both the content and the form of this book has been made stronger and more coherent thanks to these four eminent scholars.

Two people who have influenced me greatly over the years are David Johnson and Fred Judson, both of the University of Alberta. I can only hope that this book has come close to what they would expect. At Queen's University

David Eltis, David Parker, and Robert Malcolmson made constructive criticisms which tightened the central arguments of the book. Sam Noumoff of McGill's political science department shared his considerable knowledge of the history of the communist movement in general and the Comintern in particular. I would also like to thank Claude Morin and Karen Robert for their constructive criticisms.

Important segments of the research for this book would not have been possible if it were not for the generosity of Susan Fernández at the University of South Florida. She welcomed a stranger into her home and introduced me to the wonderful Cuban collections in Tampa and Gainesville. It is also thanks to her that I met Robert and Delia Lauriault, who in turn pointed me in the direction of Carl Van Ness of the University of Florida's archives. Without Carl's incredible knowledge of the Braga Brothers' Collection this book could not have been written. I am deeply appreciative of their kindness and for the pleasant evenings I spent in the company of Susan, Robert, and Delia.

I am very grateful to Elaine Maisner of the University of North Carolina Press for her effort and encouragement. Her guidance and interest in Cuba made the final stages of writing and editing a pleasure. At an early stage of editing, Viki Marcok and Gaspar Quintana Alberni were more helpful than they give themselves credit for.

On a more personal note I would like to express my gratitude to Cuban friends who opened their doors to me while I worked in Cuba. Year and after year Clara Alberni, Gaspar Quintana, and Maricel Bauzá gave me a home away from home. Hard times can forge strong friendships, and the constant blackouts, water shortages, the lack of food, and the general malaise and chaos of living in Cuba during the 1990s have created personal bonds that words cannot describe. They, like the vast majority of Cubans, survived (as they do today) on their wits, inventiveness, creativity and good humor. Not only did I benefit from their capacity to resolve the endless problems of day-to-day existence, but I feel part of a family, which is truly an honor. In the same spirit I must mention the friendship of Marité López Tamargo. Marité, along with her father, mother, and brother, gave me a place to go when I was tired of talking about history and politics (though, of course, we still *did* discuss history and politics—who doesn't in Cuba?). I am privileged to know each of these wonderful individuals.

This book would not have seen the light of day if it were not for my wife, Debbie Payne. She witnessed my various existential crises, and I am glad she did not take them too seriously, for both our sakes.

I would like to dedicate this book to the memory of Richard Frucht. Though I had been involved with Cuba for a long time before I entered the academic world, Richard was the first scholar to inspire me to study Cuba and Latin America. His courses in the social and cultural anthropology of the Caribbean are still fresh in my mind, even though more than twenty years have passed. Because of his infectious love for the people and the region, I will always be an anthropologist at heart.

Abbreviations

ABC	ABC Revolutionary Society
Ala	Ala Izquierda Estudiantil (Student Left Wing)
APRA	Alianza Popular Revolucionaria Americana (American Popular Revolutionary Alliance)
APRA-Cuba	Alianza Popular Revolucionaria Americana-Cuba (American Popular Revolutionary Alliance-Cuba)
CIO	American Confederation of Industrial Organizations
CNOC	Confederación Nacional Obrera de Cuba (National Confederation of Cuban Workers)
CP	Partido Comunista de Cuba (Communist Party of Cuba)
CTC	Confederación de Trabajadores de Cuba (Cuban Confederation of Workers)
CTM	Mexican Confederation of Workers
DEU	Directorio Estudiantil Universitario (University Student Directorate)
FEU	Federación de Estudiantes Universitarios (Federation of University Students)
FOH	Federación Obrera de la Habana (Havana Federation of Labor)
IR	Izquierda Revolucionaria (Revolutionary Left)
JC	Joven Cuba (Young Cuba)
NCOS	Non-Commissioned Officers
OCRR	Organización Celular Reforma Revolucionaria
ORCA	Organización Revolucionaria Cubana Anti-imperialista (Cuban Anti-imperialist Revolutionary Organization)
PAN	Partido Agrario Nacional (National Agrarian Party)

PIC	Partido Independiente de Color (Independent Party of Color)
PPC	Partido Popular Cubano (Cuban Popular Party)
PRC-A	Partido Revolucionario Cubano (Auténtico) (Cuban Revolutionary Party-Authentic)
SNOIA	Sindicato Nacional de Obreros de la Industria Azucarera (National Union of Sugar Industry Workers)
UN	Unión Nacionalista (Nationalist Union)
UNIA	United Negro Improvement Association
UR	Unión Revolucionaria (Revolutionary Union)

State and Revolution in Cuba

Introduction

Between the 1920s and the early 1940s the combined pressures of mass mobilization, revolution, economic crisis, and the threat of foreign intervention from the United States compelled Cuban politicians from across the ideological spectrum to come to terms with the *clases populares* (popular social classes) as a factor in national and international politics. In 1920 an oligarchy of wealthy landowners, professional politicians, merchants, bankers, and sugar mill owners had a tight grip over national politics, and the idea that the state should be "popular" was an anathema to the ruling groups. By the early 1930s, however, social protest from the *clases populares* became so widespread that the established mechanisms of social and political control no longer functioned. Yet at the time, it was by no means clear how "the masses" were to be incorporated into the political process. It was one thing for political elites to recognize that the popular sectors were a force to be reckoned with; it was quite another matter to create new political institutions and discourses that could harness their energy. Before anyone could accustom themselves to the idea of "the masses" as political actors, in the summer of 1933 Cuba exploded in social revolution.

For the eight years prior to 1933 Cuba, had been ruled by Gerardo Machado y Morales. Between 1925 and 1930 Machado's rule faced no serious opposition. By 1929, however, the economic crisis sparked by the world depression threw the established political and economic order into chaos. All factions of the Cuban elite were increasingly besieged by social forces that were outside the traditional political circles. Prior to 1933 the occasional student march or worker's strike was violently and sometimes easily suppressed by the police or the rural guard. From the late 1890s to the 1920s the Cuban population was too socially and economically fragmented to present a sustained threat to the ruling elite. By early 1933 the intensity of popular protest had reached unprecedented levels. Machado was increasingly isolated from other sectors of the political elite, and economic crisis and labor unrest challenged the political and social order.

With the revolution of 1933, the young and relatively inexperienced revolutionaries found themselves pushed into the halls of state power by worker and peasant mobilizations. Between September 1933 and January 1934, a loose coalition of radical activists, students, middle-class intellectuals, and disgruntled lower-rank soldiers formed a Provisional Revolutionary Government. This coalition was directed by a popular university professor, Dr. Ramón Grau San Martín. The Grau government promised a "new Cuba" with social justice for all classes and the abrogation of the Platt Amendment.[1] While the revolutionary leaders certainly wanted diplomatic recognition by Washington, they believed their legitimacy stemmed from the popular rebellion that brought them to power and not from the approval of the U.S. Department of State. To this end, throughout the fall of 1933 the government decreed a dramatic series of reforms. The Platt Amendment was unilaterally abrogated, and all the political parties of the *machadato* were dissolved.[2] The Provisional Government granted autonomy to the university, women obtained the right to vote, the eight-hour workday was decreed, a minimum wage was established for cane cutters, and compulsory arbitration was promoted. The government created a Ministry of Labor, and a law was passed establishing that 50 percent of all workers in agriculture, commerce, and industry had to be Cuban citizens. The Grau regime set agrarian reform as a priority, promising peasants legal title to their lands. For the first time in Cuban history the country was governed by people who did not negotiate the terms of political power with Spain (before 1898) or with the United States (after 1898).

The Provisional Government survived until January 1934, when it was overthrown by an equally loose antigovernment coalition of right-wing civilian and military elements. Led by a young sergeant, Fulgencio Batista y Zaldívar, this movement was supported by the U.S. State Department. To many Cubans at the time, it appeared that the country would revert to traditional methods of state domination. Previously, whenever the struggle for state power got out of hand, U.S. diplomats brokered a compromise among competing factions: there was no indication that anything would be different this time around.

Yet Cuba after 1933 was a very different country from what it had been only a few years earlier. The experiences of revolutionary struggle and mass mobilization became a part of the Cuban political landscape. The revolution of 1933 politicized Cuban society in fundamentally new ways. Between 1934 and 1940 a new political and economic consensus based on authoritarian and reformist principles emerged. After the revolution of 1933 most political groups in Cuba—from the far right to the communists—drew the conclusion that a new and modern state should intervene in society to modernize the country's political and economic structures. This reformist impulse culminated in 1940 when a new constitution proclaimed political democracy, the rights of urban and rural laborers, limitations on the size of sugar plantations and the need for systematic state intervention in the economy, while preserving the supreme role of private property.[3] Ironically, many of the demands of 1933 became the constitutional edicts of 1940. The 1940 Constitution signified a collective acknowledgment by the economic and political elite, the middle class and the working class, the army led by Batista, and the United States, that they had to live together, no matter how much they disliked this fact. Although Cuba had several civilian presidents from 1935 to 1940, it was clear to all that "the strong man [Batista] was the ruler of Cuba while the shadows flitted across the political stage in his direction."[4] Following seven years of controlling Cuban politics from behind the scenes, Batista became president of Cuba in 1940. Batista supervised Cuba's transition from a military dictatorship in 1934 to a nominal constitutional democracy in 1940.[5] This book will examine how and why this remarkable transformation in the Cuban political process came about.

Ideas of Social Class in Early-Twentieth-Century Cuba:
Workers, the Middle Class, and Oligarchs

In this book I want to explore the major developments within Cuban class structures, especially the expanding middle class and the working class. I will accomplish this task by examining the formation of social classes within the context of mass mobilization, government corruption, political dictatorship, economic crisis, and American policy toward Cuba. The problem, of course, is that we must be reasonably clear about what is meant by "social class," as well as more specific terms such as "oligarchy," "middle class," and "working class." In the case of Cuba, and Latin America generally, any discussion of the meaning of social class must first acknowledge that class formation was a very uneven process and that the middle and working classes were highly fragmented social groupings.[6] If class identity is defined in reference to a group's social relation to the means of production, then in Cuba between 1900 and 1940 such identity was highly unstable. Mass unemployment and underemployment, periodic economic crisis, combined with the large scale importation of migrant labor, served to undermine any long-term or stable access to jobs, land, education, and financial stability.

In early-twentieth-century Cuba, journalists, politicians, and social commentators dealt with the problem of naming social classes by using the terms *clases populares* (popular classes) and *clases económicas* (economic classes) to describe the two main social groups within society. The *clases populares* comprised all social sectors outside the political elite and large sugar, commercial, and industrial sectors. The *clases populares* were the urban and rural wage laborers, peasants, the lower-middle-class groups of students, government employees, and those involved in petty-commerce.[7] The *clases económicas* were made up by the professional politicians who dominated the traditional political parties (Liberal, Conservative, and Popular Parties), as well sugar-mill owners, large-scale sugar growers, and Cuban and resident Spanish commercial and banking interests. For the purposes of this work, and especially in the first four chapters, I will use the term *clases populares* in the sense just outlined, with the important proviso that when I use the term "working class," I will be referring specifically to manual wage laborers, both urban and rural. One of the important features of class formation in Cuba was that by the 1940s a stronger sense of *working class* identity did develop. After 1933 politicians and the press began to drop the use of the term *clases populares* and replace it with "working class." The Confederación de Trabajadores de Cuba (CTC) was formed in 1939, and the CTC grouped together the largest and most important unions in the country. The Cuban population as a whole numbered just over 5 million in 1945, and the total number of organized workers was around 500,000.[8] In the 1940s and 1950s Cuban workers were organized as never before, and though trade union life was wracked with sectarianism and violence, the Cuban working class was a political force to be reckoned with by all national politicians.

In a similar way, just as the notion of *clases populares* had incorporated lower-level white-collar employees in banks, retail stores, import-export firms, insurance companies, students, or small-scale business people, after 1933 the term "middle class" was increasingly used to describe people working in these areas of the economy. This change was certainly influenced by the rapid growth of the middle class between the 1930s and 1950s. Between 1931 and 1953, the number of government, commercial, and service employees grew to represent some 50 percent of the middle class, with the other half made up of self-employed small business owners and small-scale proprietors. The amorphous makeup of the middle classes meant that scholars and census takers in the 1940s and 1950s had classified as much as half the Cuban population as belonging to the broad category of the "middle classes."[9]

Which brings me to the issue of what it meant to be "middle class" in Cuba between 1920 and 1940. In the ever-changing world of export capitalism, the middle classes found themselves in a constant struggle to locate themselves, both socially and economically, between the extremes of the very rich and the very poor.[10] Office clerks, bank tellers, salespeople, printers, junior army officers, schoolteachers, mid-level town officials and lawyers, medium-sized farmers, small-scale landlords, and journalists worried that they could all too easily "descend" into the ranks of the popular classes. Once again, before 1933 the vague term *clases populares* included at its upper limits people we might call "lower middle class" Cubans; "upper middle class" Cubans, on the other hand, could more easily claim membership in the lower limits of the *clases económicas*. It was precisely this vagueness and insecurity of middle-class identity that underlay their collective desire for better and more practical education in the sciences, technology, medicine, law, and commerce. They wanted the state to create the conditions where their class position would be secure. At the same time middle-class people aspired to be economically secure, they tried to distance themselves socially from the *clases populares* by being *culto* ("cultured") and *gente decente*. Consequently middle-class political leaders came to believe that Cuba urgently needed a modern and democratic state which would serve as a buffer against the volatile forces of unrestrained export capitalism and class polarization. This reification of the modern state and of "culture" tended to make the middle classes see themselves as the best representatives of national culture and of modern economic development.

Yet the day-to-day reality was different: classifying oneself as being "upper middle class" or "lower middle class" had much less to do with a person's qualifications for any given job than it had to do with successfully cultivating personal ties with influential employers. The best and most secure employers were often American businesses, since these tended to be less vulnerable to the vicissitudes of the export economy. A clerk working at a large American-owned sugar mill or bank had more chances of keeping his or her job than a clerk in a small Cuban-owned retail store. Young professionals who could speak and write English had far more employment options open to them than did unilingual Cubans. Skills mattered, but competition for reasonably secure jobs was fierce, so the better you knew people in the right places, the better were your chances of getting and keeping a job. Such personalistic ties were a way to obtain some measure of security, and along with security came the possibility of maintaining an "upper middle class" life-style, as opposed to those semiproletarianized employees living in constant fear of losing their jobs. Typically, a middle-class lifestyle meant being proud to be a white Cuban and admiring and acquiring things North American.[11] Yet image and reality would often clash. Landing a job through "friendship" and "loyalty" could just as easily be seen by those denied employment as "corruption" and "cronyism." At another level, working for a large and modern American business could be seen as either seizing a rare opportunity for personal and professional advancement, or as turning one's back on building Cuban-owned and -run businesses. For middle-class Cubans in the 1920s and 1930s, personal choices could easily have political consequences, whether intended or not. Both the ideas of middle-class and of working-class identity were social constructs forged in the political and economic struggles of early-twentieth-century Cuba.

One of the central points made in this book is that the revolution of 1933 undermined the institutions and coercive structures of the oligarchic state. What was the "oligarchic state," and which people made up the "oligarchy" and the *clases económicas?* Following Laurence Whitehead, I define the "oligarchic state" as a state "in which such public authority as existed was broadly at the service of a restricted sector of the population, which derived its coherence from the various nonstate sources of social power, such as land ownership, family lineage or a position of advantage in international trade and finance."[12] For the purposes of this study, within the Cuban context, "oligarchy" refers to the Cuban political and sugar-growing elite and not to foreign capitalists resident in Cuba. Alternately, I will use the terms "upper classes" and "elites" to refer to Cubans who were professional politicians from the traditional parties, the large-scale sugar growers (*hacendados*), large-scale commercial and import-export capitalists, and factory owners. What about a Cuban bourgeoisie? As with the *clases populares* and the middle classes, before the 1940s the *clases económicas* were too divided among themselves to be a coherent and self-conscious social class. Certainly there were Cuban commercial capitalists, factory owners, and agrarian capitalists who struggled to gain a solid foothold within the shifting fortunes of the Cuban sugar economy. But they were unable to establish any significant independent presence until after 1940.[13] The dominant *economic* class in Cuba was made up of North American capitalists who used their ties with the United States to maintain American hegemony. The Cuban political class, on the other hand, used both their clientist networks of followers and the mechanisms of the Plattist state to accumulate wealth and exercise power.

By doing so, the Cuban political classes threatened, but without success, to become a rival bourgeoisie that could challenge or compete with foreign capitalists.[14]

The term "oligarchy" might give the impression that this group was socially homogeneous and clearly separate from "nonoligarchic" sectors. They were neither, and we should be wary to not see oligarchies as a monolithic social class or as an abstract historical category. Sugar planters, large-scale urban capitalists, import-export merchants, bankers, professional politicians, regional and local power-holders, and high-level army officers had distinct interests, and each group often promoted policies that were at odds with other members of the dominant classes, or even with the United States. There is a tendency in much of the scholarship dealing with Latin American political elites to lump all these groups together as if they were members of one social class with common interests.[15] As Louis Pérez Jr. has pointed out, there was no economically dominant *national* class in Cuba during the early Republic.[16] American capitalists dominated the all-important export sector. In the pages to follow I hope to give some indication of just how complex Cuban oligarchic political economy was, though we still need much more information on exactly who the upper classes were and how their clientistic networks functioned. It will nonetheless be clear from the Cuban case that oligarchic rule was far more resilient than we have given it credit for. One objective of this study is to highlight in greater detail what the goals and interests of the dominant groups were and how they influenced policy decisions at certain critical moments of the country's history.

Despite these internal differences within the Cuban upper classes, I will retain the terms "oligarchy," "oligarchic power," and "oligarchic capitalism" as broadly descriptive concepts that stand in contrast to the politics of the modern state. Oligarchic power in Cuba was not *nationally* based. What made the state oligarchic was that ruling groups appealed to real or fictitious bloodlines and kin ties as the source of their status and authority. Political power was therefore not centered at any particular group or institution; rather, power was defused in a complex hierarchy of national, regional, and local networks of *caciques* and *caudillos*. The power of these *caciques* and *caudillos* derived from their ability to provide their followers with access to state revenues and to distribute local resources, both human and material. Oligarchic capitalism, in other words, was capitalist in the sense that relations of production in Cuba were increasingly characterized by the proletarianization of rural and urban labor; it was oligarchic in the sense that the allocation and distribution of wage labor often relied upon precapitalist and highly localized mechanisms of social control. *Caudillos* and *caciques* did own land and capital and were often very entrepreneurial; yet their power was also extraeconomic in that their ability to distribute wealth, jobs, land, market access, and political office derived from their careful cultivation of personal authority, reputation, and loyalty. In Cuba this meant that political leaders required a close relationship with the largely foreign-controlled sugar companies because it was the sugar economy that generated most state and nonstate revenue. While it was true that after 1898 the Cuban economic and political elite were denied direct control over most of the *production* of national wealth, it was equally true that the *caciques* and *caudillos* who manned the different layers of political society proved to be very effective at the *redistribution* of wealth for both economic gain and political influence. In contrast to the defuse nature of oligarchic power, the idea of the "modern state" rested on the principle that the whole population should be mobilized by state leaders in the cause of the nation.[17] While oligarchic rule was arbitrary, the modern state existed to implement and legitimize the principles of democracy and nationhood. The privileged status of the nation merged and became identical with the idea of the state, and the state became the collective patrimony of society. These were the main sentiments behind the constitutional consensus of 1940.

Mass Mobilization and Political Change

The main argument of the book is that the transition from oligarchic rule to the modern state came about primarily because of the mass mobilization by the *clases populares* against oligarchic capitalism. To be sure, the modern state in Cuba, as in many other formerly colonial countries, never had a strong foundation. While it is true that the 1940 constitutional consensus reflected a significant change in Cuban political culture, it was still the product of a unique set of international and national events. The combined factors of the world economic depression in the 1930s, the coming war in Europe, the rise of antifascist popular frontism, the growth of leftist and rightist populist and corporatist movements in Latin America, and Cuba's own revolution of 1933 set the terms of state formation in Cuba between 1930 and 1940. After 1940, however, the war and postwar economic boom, the defeat of fascism, and the emergence of cold-war geopolitics redefined the character of political discourse and practice in Cuba and in the rest of Latin America.[18] Throughout the continent, the left-leaning populism of the 1930s gave way to an anticommunist conservatism in the 1940s and 1950s.

In Cuba, while it was true that Batista gave cabinet portfolios to two communists in the early 1940s, after 1944 it was no longer convenient for Cuban governments to be too close to the Communist Party (CP). Soon gangsterism, violence, and corruption were far more effective political tools than were the high-minded statutes of the constitution. Despite this disappointing outcome there was a widespread and popular consensus that a "modern state" needed to be established in Cuba. From the 1920s to the 1940s politicians and political activists were bitterly divided over what "popular" and "modern" state power meant: mass participation and democracy meant very different things to different people. Yet no politician, regardless of his location on the political spectrum, could ignore the powerful idea that a modern state *should* produce a new and democratic Cuba. *Caudillismo* and *caciquismo* continued to plague Cuban politics, but they were no longer the only political mechanisms available to Cubans. Party politics, mass meetings, electoral campaigns, and constitutional legitimacy also mattered.

In the broadest sense, then, what changed between 1920 and 1940 was Cuban political culture. I use the term "political culture" in a broadly anthropological sense and not in the way used by modernization theorists. For the modernization school, and one might add for present-day neoliberals, political culture refers to rather abstract values, beliefs, and traditions that either positively or negatively influence a people's ability to attain liberal democratic (modern) "civic values" or "civil society."[19] The explicit or implicit assumption is that some societies and social classes "have" more political culture than do others and that the reference points for being "modern," "democratic," and "politically cultured" are Western capitalist political values. In contrast, I take the view that political culture is about the ability and *the power* to bestow meanings on things, people, social relations of production, and ideas within specific historical contexts and social struggles. This power to bestow meanings, in turn, is often realized within the context of historically specific collective action and mass mobilization. In other words, political culture is not defined *exclusively* by its relation to the modern capitalist state. Political culture refers to the living collective memories, struggles, and values of social groups who create their own identities and political meanings not only to resist dominant political discourses and practices but also to create alternative ways of living.[20] To use the modern state as the only standard by which to measure political culture ignores the reality that there are a whole range of human practices and discourses not covered by the material reality of state power. Popular political culture cannot be completely contained by state power because no one has ever agreed about who "the people" are and which sectors of the people should have full (if any) political rights. State leaders aspire to be left in peace to mold citizens into "responsible" and "rational" subjects who accept the rules of political and economic power. This form of political and social engineering is carried out just as much by liberal democratic states as it is by more authoritarian forms of government. The problem was (and is) that those who are denied a political voice and/or economic power occasionally refuse to be quiet, and by their refusal they simultaneously undermine and transform the meaning of politics.[21] Political culture is about the way people make sense of their day-to-day struggles. The importance of the revolutionary upheavals of the 1930s and the 1940 constitutional consensus was that they represented an attempt to make sense of the changing balance of power in Cuba.

The Historiography

Historians usually view the events of 1933 as part of Cuba's "long revolution" for independence and social justice.[22] This long revolution "began" with the independence wars against Spain in 1868–78 and 1895–98, continued through the "frustrated" revolution of 1933, and "culminated" in the revolution of 1959.[23] Scholars hold varied opinions about how the revolution of 1933 fits into this longer historical process, but there is a general consensus that the 1933 revolution is important because it set into motion a political process that would eventually—perhaps inevitably?—lead to Castro's victory.

For example, one group of historians views 1933 as a frustrated liberal democratic revolution that, had it been successful, would have preempted the more radical socialist revolution of 1959.[24] Grau was not a radical politician. On the contrary, the Cuban press often referred to Grau as the "Roosevelt of Cuba" who simply wanted a "new Cuba" controlled by Cubans and not by foreign capitalists. Though deeply nationalistic, Grau and his followers were far from anti-American. They were, however, anti-interventionist. From the perspective of many Cuban nationalists, a clear distinction could be made between, on the one hand, the avaricious capitalist "trusts" of Wall Street, and, on the other hand, the fair-minded New Deal liberalism of president F. D. Roosevelt. Ever since the U.S. military intervention in Cuba in 1898, the "trusts" of large sugar companies, banks, land companies, and other private interests did more or less what they pleased in Cuba. In early 1933, however, the recently elected American president promised that the United States would be a "good neighbor" and respect the sovereignty of Latin American nations. This shift in direction by U.S. policy-makers seemed to bode well for Cuba's future. Grau and his backers found much to admire in the state-sponsored social policies of the New Deal administration, and they saw no reason why the United States would not recognize the new government in Havana. So when the United States failed to recognize Grau, and when Ambassador Sumner Welles backed Batista's coup in January 1934, it seemed to many Cubans as if the Wall Street "trusts" had once again determined U.S. policy in Cuba. Reformist optimism was shattered. An additional reason why the revolutionary regime collapsed was that it did not have a political party which could channel popular support in an effective way. Instead, factionalism and indecision undermined the government's ability to rule. At the same time, the Communist Party and its trade-union cadre vehemently opposed the government. Meanwhile, the army was being reorganized by Batista without cabinet control. The government was a house of cards ready to collapse.

The explicit or implicit perspective of these historians is that the defeat of 1933 "frustrated" Cuban nationalist sentiments and Fidel Castro would eventually exploit this sense of frustration in the 1950s. For example, Luis Aguilar, in the concluding chapter of his book on the 1933 revolution, sees the link between 1933 and 1959 as "obvious." After the frustration of the corrupt and violent 1940s and 1950s, Castro "spoke the language people wanted to hear"; in the early 1960s, however, he shifted direction and took Cuba in an "unexpected" and "tragic" direction.[25] Ramón Bonachea and Marta San Martín introduce their book on the Cuban insurrection of 1952–59 by saying that the generation of the 1950s had essentially the same ideology as the frustrated generation of the 1930s, but this time Castro and his followers were more determined and better led.[26] In a similar way, Andrés Suárez states that Castro's success can be explained by his crass manipulation of the "atmosphere of tragic frustration" dating back to the defeat of 1934.[27] Castro's success was therefore not so much of his own making as it was due to the inability of reform-minded Cubans to succeed during and after 1933.

A closely related position on the events of 1933 places greater emphasis on the unwillingness or inability of the United States to understand the implications of the 1933 revolution. Had the United States supported Grau's moderate government, subsequent Cuban history might have taken a very different turn. American policy, however, was locked into a short-sighted vision of maintaining Cuban stability at any cost. Even though Grau and his Partido Revolucionario Cubano (Auténtico) (PRC-A) became noticeably more moderate after 1933, U.S. diplomats felt that they could not fully trust the Auténticos to maintain order and protect American investments. Despite the fact that the Platt Amendment was abrogated in 1934, Cuban sovereignty continued to be limited by American hegemony. While this problem was nothing new to Cubans, after the dramatic upheavals of 1933, Cubans as a whole were far more hostile to U.S. intervention in their internal affairs. Accordingly, American policy should have adapted to Cuban nationalism, but it failed to do so. This failure by Washington to adapt meant that another confrontation between the insurgent forces of Cuban nationalism and the United States was inevitable. A young Fidel Castro would take up the challenge in 1952.

Another group of historians does not see the revolution of 1959 as a negative or tragic result of the failures of 1933. Rather, they interpret the events of 1933 as a "prerevolution" or a "prologue" in a positive sense to the Castro revolution. The revolution of 1933 becomes a kind of dress rehearsal for the revolution of 1959, even though the "objective" and "subjective" conditions for victory did not exist in 1933. According to this perspective, "objectively" the balance of social and class forces in 1933 was not propitious for a successful social (and socialist) revolution; "subjectively" the radicals of 1933 were too divided among themselves and too ideologically immature to develop a clear political strategy to seize power. As a result, the desire of the Cuban people for national liberation could not be realized at that time. Much of this writing, especially by Cuban scholars, contrasts the political weaknesses of radicals in 1933 with the leadership of Castro in the 1950s. The failure of the 1933 revolution proved that reforming the neocolonial system was impossible and that only socialist revolution could bring freedom to Cuba. The political chaos and corruption in Cuba between 1933 and 1959 was therefore symptomatic of the unresolved crisis of neocolonial rule. The line between 1933 and 1959 is a direct one, and the events of 1933 become part of the historical narrative of 1959.[28]

While this brief overview of the literature does not do justice to the important insights of individual authors and the subtleties of their interpretations, all of the writing on the 1933 revolution shares the central idea that its significance is found largely in reference to what happened (or failed to happen) in the 1950s. On the whole, I see nothing wrong with this position: if our objective is to understand the origins of the 1959 revolution then we must come to terms with the legacy of 1933. My objective, however, is different. I start from an earlier vantage point, the political and economic conjuncture of 1920, and I use a different and more immediate outcome, the constitutional consensus of 1940. It is important to recognize that our choice of historical outcomes does determine the way we construct our narrative; by doing so, the sequence and relative importance of events changes significantly. We gain a heightened appreciation of how people saw their country change in more concrete and immediate ways. The fact that Cubans in the 1950s felt their political hopes and expectations had been betrayed tells us little about how their sentiments were raised and encouraged in the first place. If we focus too much on the failures and disappointments of the 1940–59 period we risk underestimating what actually did change in Cuba between 1920 and 1940. I conclude the narrative in 1940 because thereafter a new phase of Cuban political history begins. Between 1940 and 1959, political adversaries and a new generation of radicalized youth would use the constitution's edicts and principles as ideological weapons against one another, and they would constantly attack each other for betraying the popular aspirations of the past decade; they did these things not to overthrow the modern state but rather to improve the state and make it more representative of the popular will.

It is important to point out that noticeable advances have been made in the historiography in recent years. For example, research on the complexities of worker and peasant mobilization before and after 1933 have shed more light on how popular political activity engaged Cuban capitalism and U.S. imperialism in qualitatively and quantitatively new ways.[29] In a similar way, historians and social scientists writing on the process of state formation in Latin America have made important observations about the connections between popular insurgency and the social and historical foundations of political power.[30] The state is increasingly viewed by scholars as more than a set of reified institutions "above society," and revolutions are more than a series of dramatic "events" that undermine state power. Instead, both states and revolutions should be studied as socially and historically constructed *processes* through which people struggle over issues of political, economic, and cultural power. This way of seeing the state, and, one might add, of politics and culture in general, seeks to avoid reducing the state (and politics and culture) to economic determinants, simplistic class analysis, or teleological models of social and economic development.[31] In the words of political scientist Joel Migdal, I want to investigate "the transformation of people as they adopt the symbols of the state and the transformation of the state as it incorporates symbols from society."[32] This study is an initial attempt to take up this challenge for Republican Cuba. By incorporating many of the important insights of this new scholarship, I hope to shed more light on the complex interactions between popular mobilization in Cuba and the process of state formation between 1920 and 1940.[33]

In Chapter 1, I lay out a social map of how politics functioned under the oligarchic state in Cuba circa 1920. Then I will discuss a specific example of how a popular rebellion challenged the oligarchic state. This rebellion, known as the Veterans' and Patriots' Movement, occurred between 1923 and 1924. Its objective was for the "moral regeneration" of Cuban politics and for political and economic reform within existing state structures. The Veterans' movement failed to achieve its objective, but, as we will see, it was precisely because the movement failed that many of its younger participants began to rethink the relationship between society and the state and to increasingly question the meaning of the political process within the context of Cuba's neocolonial condition. A new generation of radical students, workers, and middle-class Cubans increasingly looked to newer political doctrines and ideas, such as socialism, populism, and fascism, as alternatives to oligarchic politics. To be sure, Cuban radical's knowledge of these ideologies was often vague and impressionistic, but they certainly knew enough to appreciate that they were part of a worldwide movement for social and political change.

Chapter 2 continues the narrative from the previous chapter by focusing on the ideological crisis provoked by the defeat of the Veterans' movement. From 1924 until the end of the decade, there was a wide-ranging debate about what many viewed as the cultural and political crisis of Cuban and Latin American modernity. In particular, a new generation of Cubans tried to come to terms with the political implications of capitalist modernity and how to respond to the "masses" as a social, political, and economic force. The political existence of the masses was a recent phenomenon for everyone on the ideological spectrum. No one really knew who the masses were, though many leaders claimed to articulate their interests. The basic questions about the social composition and inclusiveness of "the people" or "the masses" could not be answered with precision because the interwoven processes of class, state, and national formation outpaced people's ability to explain what was happening around them. It should not be surprising, therefore, that the ideological implications of mass politics were rarely laid out in detail. This chapter will examine how Cuban radicals grappled with these issues in the 1920s. These debates would also set the tone for similar controversies in the years to come.

Chapter 3 is concerned with the growing crisis of oligarchic rule in Cuba between 1929 and 1932. This chapter demonstrates how a combination of economic and political crisis fueled mass insurgency against the oligarchic state. By 1932 the Cuban political class was besieged by a population in revolt. These experiences would prove decisive in forming the political consciousness of large sectors of the *clases populares,* as well as providing the formative political experiences for a new generation of activists from across the ideological spectrum.

Chapter 4 deals with how new and nationalist visions of the modern state emerged within the context of the crisis of oligarchic capitalism between 1930 and 1933. Middle-class political groups formulated new conceptions of the state that were intended to be truly national and therefore capable of providing an alternative to oligarchic capitalism. At the same time, communists, trade unionists, and independent leftists tried to harness the insurgent energy of the *clases populares* for more radical objectives, yet they, too, were as much the products of mass mobilization as they were its leaders. Of course, ideas about what should replace the oligarchic state varied considerably: those on the political left of center thought "the people" should lead the revolutionary democratic political process, while those on the right developed corporatist and paternalistic conceptions of the state that were designed to contain the popular sectors. But within the context of mass insurgency the difference between these two conceptions of state formation was not as clear as might be supposed.

Chapter 5 focuses on the revolution of 1933. The emphasis here will be on how mass mobilization undermined oligarchic rule and placed a revolutionary government in power. The organizational weakness of the popular sectors, combined with factionalism among middle-class and leftist radicals, undermined the strength of this short-lived government. The revolutionaries were forced to take power before they had a chance to systematically work out what "taking power" meant. The revolution had unleashed forces that the regime could not control. What took place was less a transfer of power than a transfer of crisis. Yet, as this chapter will show, the dramatic experience of the prolonged revolutionary struggles of 1930–33 succeeded in shifting the balance of political power away from the oligarchy and toward other social classes. Cuba would never be the same.

Chapter 6 discusses the situation after the revolution of 1933. What at first appeared to be a restoration of oligarchic rule was in reality a continuation in the process of postrevolutionary state formation. This chapter follows the emergence of Fulgencio Batista. Batista's political ideas fit nicely into a corporatist vision common to many Latin American leaders during these years. In order to understand the early Batista, however, it is necessary to take him at his word when he said he was continuing the revolution of 1933. After all, the colonel's former allies in the Grau government of 1933 accused Batista of "betraying" the revolution: one has to be first part of the revolution in order to "betray" it, and from Batista's perspective he was bringing "order" to the revolution, not betraying it. Before Batista could implement his ideas, however, he first had to use the army and police to "discipline" the insurgent *clases populares* and the "idealistic" and "impractical" elements encouraging "chaos." This chapter will argue that it is impossible to understand Cuba's evolution to a nominal democracy between 1937 and 1940 without taking into account state violence. This state violence had the effect of destroying, at least in the short term, any political and organizational autonomy the *clases populares* had managed to win during the recent social and class struggles. The masses would have to be "disciplined" before they would be ready to be a part of what Batista called an "organic" and "renovated democracy."

Chapter 7 focuses on how Batista changed from a shadowy military figure with conventional corporatist ideas into a very public political leader with populist pretensions.[34] The colonel wanted to be a legitimate president of a democratic Cuba, and he succeeded in 1940. Batista employed a populist political style and strategy to obtain his objective. Populism arose as a political and economic response to the growth of a mass work force that had been released from traditional personalistic and clientist ties of bondage and dependence. Populists acknowledged the reality that the masses were a new force in society and that "the people" were at the center of the nation and the state. Populist discourse, in other words, functioned to construct "the people" out of fragmented and scattered populations.[35] Batista was very aware that in order to rule Cuba, he had to appeal to the people and to the revolutionary sentiments of 1933. This chapter will examine how Batista made the transition from a military dictator to a populist leader between 1937 and 1940.

The conclusion will provide an overview of the main themes discussed in the book and make some suggestions about areas and themes for future research on this period of Cuban history.

CHAPTER ONE

Oligarchic Rule and the Practice of Politics in Cuba, 1901–1924

An Overview

Cuban history is usually divided into three broad phases: the Spanish colonial period (1509–1898), the republic (1901–58), and the socialist revolutionary phase (1959 to the present). We know that each phase underwent many complex changes and transformations. In the literature dealing with the republican period, the word "republic" is typically preceded by adjectives such as "neocolonial," "dependent," "semisovereign," "semi-independent," and "Plattist." Whichever adjective is used, however, the meaning is essentially the same: after the American occupation of Cuba in 1898 the sovereignty of the Cuban Republic was sharply restricted by the shifting policies and priorities of successive administrations in Washington.[1]

The cornerstone of American neocolonial control over Cuba was the Platt Amendment, which the United States had imposed on the Cuban Constitutional Assembly of 1901.[2] The imposition of this amendment meant that if Cubans wanted independence, they would have to give the United States the constitutional right under the *Cuban* constitution to intervene in their internal affairs to preserve political order and protect private property. It was mediated sovereignty, or no sovereignty at all. With the rapid expansion of American investment in Cuba after World War I, Cuban political factions lost direct control over the economic direction of the country. The state became truncated from the economy and from much of society generally. As long as the Cuban political classes did not destabilize the economic life of the country, the United States permitted them to use state revenues to obtain and distribute wealth or to provide jobs and income for loyal followers. For large numbers of Cubans without stable employment in agriculture or industry, access to the state became a means to accumulate capital and obtain employment.

It will become apparent in the following pages that there are good reasons why the word "republic" should not stand alone. At the same time, by adding a qualifier we are no closer to understanding the complexity of political life during the republican years. However we label the republican political system, we must take care not to turn complex and multilayered experiences into one-dimensional, predictable, and lifeless events. In our rush to explain the structures of domination and subordination we can ignore the creativity of resistance, survival, and adaptation.[3] We therefore need to sharpen our focus on how people responded to the immediate circumstances around them. Accordingly, this chapter will focus on the first major crisis of the republican system, which occurred between 1920 and 1924. Before highlighting this four-year period, it is necessary to outline what is meant by "oligarchic rule."

What made political practice "oligarchic" was that ruling groups appealed to real or fictitious bloodlines and kin ties as the source of their status and authority. Political power was not centered on any particular group or institution; rather, power was in the hands of regional and local networks of *caciques* and *caudillos*. Within the Cuban context, *caciques* and *caudillos* were people whose authority stemmed from their past roles (real, imagined, or invented) in the independence war of 1895–98. *Caciquismo* was based on strong regional and ethnic loyalties and dependencies that crossed the boundaries of social class. *Caciques* commanded the loyalty of their followers by promising them land, work, and personal contacts which might provide some degree of security within the incessant ebb and flow of inter-elite rivalries and the volatile sugar economy. Businesses received concessions and contracts, and political leaders obtained kickbacks and favors. Mill owners used *caciquismo* to prevent or break union organizing. Conversely, *caudillos* and *caciques* could and did threaten mill owners with work stoppages or violence if workers loyal to the *caudillo* were not treated properly.

The most powerful figures had direct access to state revenues, the national lottery, local and regional government subsidies, and military and policing positions. *Caciques* and *caudillos* used their patronage networks to gain access to wealth and political positions. Many became sugar-mill owners or small- or large-scale *colonos*.[4] A few became national politicians, and two became presidents of the republic. But oligarchic power was not *nationally* based. On the contrary, national leaders needed to command the loyalty of locally based *caciques* and *caudillos* if they were to have influence outside of the larger urban centers. One of the legacies of the war of 1895–98 was that *caciques* could and did tap into popular aspirations and address local grievances by strategically using carefully cultivated and long-standing ties of loyalty and friendship. Skillful local leaders could exploit these networks to either support or challenge Havana-based politicians, the sugar companies, *colonos,* or even the United States if necessary. In this way "nonpolitical" issues such as access to jobs, land, credit, debt, and loans could easily be converted into political capital when the moment was right.

The most meaningful politics were personal and local politics. Indeed, the highly personalistic networks so characteristic of *caudillismo* and *caciquismo* were based on the strong loyalties forged during the war of 1895–98 and before. Some 50,000 poor and destitute army veterans desperately needed land and employment, yet there were no institutional structures in existence that could satisfy these needs. At the same time, thousands of Cubans, many of them professionals and educated people, had spent years in exile in the United States and other countries; they returned to Cuba with high expectations that their skills, political connections, and often their command of English would open the door to appointments to neocolonial state structures. By 1905 the two groups within the independence movement had evolved into two political alignments, the Conservatives under Tomás Estrada Palma and the Liberals under José Miguel Gómez. The Conservative base was in the civilian wing of the Cuban independence movement, whereas Liberal support was especially strong among soldiers who had once been workers and peasants. This difference between the two "parties" was exacerbated by long-standing class and racial tensions which had always been present in the independence struggle.[5] It was within this context of wartime loyalties, social and economic dislocation, and racial and class tensions that people chose their allies and benefactors. The old command structures of the Liberation Army evolved into the political affiliations of the early republic. Conservatives could and did use their connections with American officials, as well as their social and economic status, to occupy national, provincial, and municipal government positions. The *miguelistas* claimed that their military sacrifices proved that they—and not those who had left the field of battle for a safe exile—were the best representatives of an independent Cuba. As we will see, these loyalties were strong and would last for decades to come.[6]

Between 1905 and 1918 this divided Cuban political class grouped themselves into either the Liberal or the Conservative Parties. After 1918 the Popular Party was formed by dissident members of the other two parties. Despite their social and class differences, the Liberal network of *caciques* under President José Miguel Gómez functioned in much the same way as the Conservatives under Mario Menocal, who had replaced Estrada Palma as party leader.

José Miguel Gómez (1858–1921) had fought in the second war for independence and served as governor of Santa Clara province, where he had a strong personal power base. Known as *tiburón* (the shark), Gómez became famous for his ability to protect loyal family and friends. It was under Gómez that the national lottery became a major source of state patronage.[7] The social base of *miguelismo* was in the rural areas, especially among cattle ranchers, small-scale *colonos*, Spanish commercial and milling interests, veterans, the reorganized army, and the dependent workers in these sectors. José Miguel promised to protect his followers from losing their lands and positions, especially in the face of the expansion of sugar *latifundios*.[8]

José Miguel's arch rival, Mario Menocal (1866–1941), grew up in Mexico and was educated in New York and at Cornell University, where he graduated in 1888. In the early 1890s he worked on engineering research for a proposed trans-isthmus Nicaraguan canal. Menocal fought in the war of 1895, obtaining the rank of general. From 1906 to 1908, under the first U.S. intervention government of Charles Magoon, he was head of the National Police. He constructed and managed the sugar mill at Chaparra, in Oriente province, one of the largest mills in the world at the time. The *menocalistas* were closely tied to foreign capital and the sugar companies, especially from the United States. It was during Menocal's term that the large sugar companies obtained the best concessions: the Cuba American Sugar Company, Manatí Cuba Company, Punte Alegre Sugar Company, the United Fruit Company, and the Cuba Cane Company, to name some of the more prominent examples, received cheap land and tariff concessions. Menocal ran against General Machado in the presidential elections of 1924 and was defeated. He continued to play an important role in Cuban politics until his death in 1941.[9]

One example of how *caudillista* politics functioned was after 1907, when Afro-Cuban artisans, skilled workers, traders, and peasants organized the Partido Independiente de Color (PIC). The PIC was created to help promote Afro-Cuban social, economic, and political rights. Afro-Cubans had fought in two wars for independence and for an end to racial injustice, only to see racial tensions intensify with the American occupations of 1899–1902 and 1906–9. The black population had been hit particularly hard by the postwar crisis and the expansion of the sugar economy: with no or tenuous legal title over the lands they occupied, many black veterans were pushed aside by the sugar companies and their allies in the judicial system and the newly formed rural guard. By 1912, at the end of the Gómez government, Afro-Cubans supporting the PIC rebelled. They demanded land, increased access to public office, free education, better working conditions, and an end to racial discrimination.[10] The rebellion was brutally suppressed by Gómez, with more than three thousand Afro-Cubans killed in Oriente province alone.[11] Menocal exploited the fact that Gómez oversaw the severe repression of the movement, and for years to come he patronized Afro-Cuban clubs and associations. Both parties used the personalistic loyalties and economic dependencies of their followers to take advantage of access to the state or resist the power of the state if one's adversaries held power. The lack of any institutional connections between the state and society was the leitmotif of oligarchic capitalism.

This kind of political behavior proved to be remarkably adaptable to the needs and priorities of U.S. policy after 1898. But, if Cuban independence was a fiction, Cuban obedience had its limits. Much of the political activity of the oligarchy was intended to provoke the United States into implementing the Platt Amendment. Virtually every inter-elite conflict between 1901 and 1933 was characterized by political factions trying to curry favor with the United States while blaming their adversaries for political chaos. In this way, victory was attained when the U.S. embassy finally backed one side over the other. Elite factions could gain access to the state and patronage networks without threatening American hegemony. The political activity of the Cuban elite was oriented more to negotiating the terms of American hegemony than to challenging it head-on. Victory was attained when the U.S. embassy finally backed one side over the other. Jorge Mañach, one of Cuba's prominent intellectuals, explained the problem in the following manner:

> Whether the Platt Amendment limits Cuban sovereignty or not has been much discussed in Cuba. The discussion is merely technical. The important point is, not whether the Platt Amendment limits sovereignty itself, but the national sentiment of sovereignty. And on this point doubt is scarcely possible. The paternal and perspicacious prudence of the American Congress resulted in crushing the Cuban sentiment for self-determination, when it imposed express limits on the exercise of the collective will. The most serious consequence was the weakening of those organic defenses of the new state which would have safe guarded its democratic health and vitality. Feeling the threat of potential intervention, the Cubans' sense of responsibility was undermined and with it his power of self-correction. . . . Tutelage favored the growth of general civic indolence, a tepid indifference to national dangers. Should the nation be threatened, the intervention of Washington was always there as a last recourse, or last hope.[12]

American diplomats frequently complained about this state of affairs, but they had set the rules of the game and they had no choice but to play.[13] Sooner or later the United States would have to remind the quarreling political factions who had the final say. A Havana-based British diplomat described the U.S.-Cuban relationship in blunt terms: "The Government has been made to understand that they retain power only by the consent of Washington, and the Government is accordingly duly obedient."[14]

An additional factor in explaining the willingness of many Cuban politicians to accept American hegemony was that upper-class opinion was usually skeptical about the ability of Cubans to be a sovereign people. This attitude was not new: for most of the nineteenth century the idea of independence took third place to those supporting some form of autonomy within the Spanish orbit or outright annexation to the United States.[15] Even during Cuba's two wars for independence there was significant disagreement among the independence forces about the exact meaning and implications of independence. In large measure these disagreements were fueled by the internal class and racial divisions among the anti-Spanish sectors, as well as by the positivist and social Darwinist thinking so common in late-nineteenth-century Latin American (and American) political and intellectual circles. For the Cuban political class, the United States was the epitome of modernity, progress, and freedom. Spain was decadent, backward, and authoritarian. Cuba was literally caught in the middle and had to choose which historical direction it would take. Typically, the Cuban political class expressed the hope that one day Cuba would or should be independent, but this would take time. Cubans were not "morally," "psychologically," and "intellectually" ready to assume nationhood. The Cuban population was too racially mixed, and years of war had made Cubans unruly, violent, and irresponsible. Cuban "high culture" was not sufficiently developed to lead the nation out of this "uncivilized" condition. Accordingly, Cuba would have to be supervised out of its backwardness. This reasoning was behind why so many nominally pro-independence leaders accepted the Platt Amendment: mediated sovereignty, they often argued, was a step toward full independence.

This was the social and political backdrop to the presidential elections of 1920. By that year the infighting among the oligarchy reached crisis proportions. The United States watched helplessly as corruption and fraud by the government of the day provoked the opposition to threaten armed rebellion. In 1919, at the urging of the U.S. State Department, General Menocal's government promised electoral reform to help remove the constant threat of inter-elite civil war. Meanwhile, the Liberals under Gómez claimed that they could better guarantee political stability and honest government. Gómez's chances to become president of Cuba for a second time were set back when his rival for the party leadership, Alfredo Zayas, formed the Partido Popular Cubano (PPC). Zayas's party promptly joined with Menocal's Conservatives to form the Liga Nacional. Zayas became the presidential candidate of the Liga, whereas Gómez ran under the Liberal banner. When elections were over in November 1920, both candidates claimed victory.

With the country once again on the brink of another political crisis, the United States sent General Enoch Crowder to find a solution to the crisis. The Cuban treasury was empty, and the United States was not about to authorize more loans until there was stability. At the same time, isolationist sentiment within the United States would not permit all-out American intervention in Cuban affairs. Crowder's job was to find a solution to the Cuban crisis without resorting to military intervention. Finally, in June 1922, Crowder forced a reorganization of the cabinet, appointing people he felt would encourage confidence within Cuba and in the United States. The so-called Honest Cabinet was set to rule Cuba until the electoral system could be safely left to the Cubans themselves. The Cuban state was in shambles, and it was the job of the United States to bring order to the chaos.[16]

While Cuban politicians and American diplomats were busy testing the boundaries of the Platt Amendment, the Cuban economy became ever more dependent on foreign capital. If the state became the source of wealth for the Cuban elite, the land and labor of Cubans became the source of wealth for the large sugar companies. The story of the post-1898 expansion of the sugar industry has been told often and does not need to be repeated in detail here.[17] A few compelling statistics will illustrate the dimension and growth of the sugar industry during the first twenty years of the century. The United States–Cuba Reciprocity Treaty of 1903 and the Permanent Treaty of 1903 stimulated the production and marketing of Cuban sugar toward the U.S. market. Cuba became increasingly dependent on U.S. manufactured goods.[18] Consequently, American investment in Cuba skyrocketed. By 1903 there were 37 American-owned land companies in Cuba: 10 in Havana province, 6 in Matanzas, 4 in Santa Clara, 8 in Camagüey, and 9 near Santiago de Cuba, in Oriente province.[19] The total value of American property holdings in 1911 reached over $220 million: $50 million was invested in sugar mills; $30 million went into the public debt; $100 million was invested in railways, mining, mercantile, and manufacturing activity; and a further $20 million each went to mortgages and credits and to public utilities. The remainder was invested in nonsugar agricultural production, shipping, and banking.[20]

World War I precipitated the collapse of European sugar beet production, leaving the market open for Cuban sugar. Between 1914 and 1920, thirty-eight sugar mills were constructed, the majority in the eastern provinces of Camagüey and Oriente. By 1920 these previously underpopulated and economically backward provinces became the major sugar-producing regions of the island. In Camagüey, between 1901 and 1922, the production of sugar doubled every five years. In 1902 the two provinces produced 15 percent of Cuba's sugar; by 1922 they accounted for 55 percent. In 1904 Cuban sugar production exceeded one million tons. With the reduction of the U.S. tariff on Cuban sugar in 1913, followed by the huge wartime demand from the U.S. market, sugar production rose from 2,597,732 tons in 1914 to 4,009,734 tons in 1919.[21] By 1919 Cuban sugar production amounted to 25 percent of world production, with 77 percent of the Cuban crop going to the United States.[22] In that same year, 49 percent of Cuban sugar was ground in American-owned mills: American control of sugar production through shares in Cuban-owned companies increased U.S. control over sugar production to above 50 percent.[23] By 1924 U.S. investment had reached $1,200 million.[24]

To facilitate the expansion of the sugar industry, small-scale rural producers were pushed off the land. Peasants became proletarians or were forced into complete destitution and/or banditry.[25] Many of these displaced people had occupied lands without title since the war of 1895–98 or before; with the expansion of the sugar *latifundios,* they were forced off the land. At the same time, in the early years of the century American-owned sugar companies brought in hundreds of thousands of Haitian and Jamaican workers for the sugar harvest (*zafra*); these workers were later shipped back to their countries of origin, at the Cuban government's expense, once the harvest was over. Of course many workers remained in Cuba illegally, with large numbers making their way to the increasingly congested Havana shanty towns.[26] Between 1892 and 1894, nearly 300,000 Spaniards emigrated to Cuba; from 1902 to 1929, an average of 27,000 Spaniards arrived in Cuba annually.[27] Though many of these new immigrants were shopkeepers, merchants, soldiers, and farmers, many others were seasonal laborers, craftsmen, factory workers, and construction workers. Overall, between 1902 and 1919, 700,000 immigrants arrived in Cuba.[28] While it should be kept in mind that many Spaniards returned to Spain after a few months or years, the Cuban labor market was nonetheless significantly influenced by Spanish migrant labor.[29]

The wartime boom in the demand and production of sugar was matched by prices. In 1919 the price of sugar was around 6.5 cents per pound. By February 1920 the price had risen to 9.5 cents; in April 1920 it reached 17.5 cents, and by May the price reached a high point of 22.5 cents per pound.[30] However, the production of sugar throughout the world had increased, and subsequently the price of sugar dropped precipitously: by the end of 1920 the price had fallen to 3.25 cents per pound.[31] Given such volatile conditions, the Cuban economy was subject to overproduction, widespread financial speculation, and the overextension of credit. Banks folded, depositors withdrew their accounts, large amounts of sugar could not be sold, and cash and credit were in short supply. Many Cuban sugar mills had to be sold, most of them to Americans. The *colono* system of sugar production, which had developed with the post-1898 sugar expansion and which was made up of mainly Cuban producers, experienced a profound and prolonged crisis. Traditional planters either lost their land or became the dependent sugar growers (*colonos*) for large mechanized American mills. Between 1921 and 1933 18,000 of an estimated 50,000 *colonos* lost their land, largely to foreign mill owners.[32] The crisis occurred at a time when Cuban dependence on the United States increased: by the mid-1920s 60 percent of the Cuban sugar industry was controlled by American capitalists, and 95 percent of the crop went to the U.S. market.[33] Meanwhile, Cuban producers were being eliminated or marginalized.

Within Havana itself, the industrial working class was small and fragmented. Small-scale artisan production dominated light industry. According to the 1925 Cuban Commission of Statistics, there were 703 "factories" in Cuba, with an average of 5.2 workers per factory. In Havana there was one factory with more than 600 workers, 8 factories with between 100 and 200 laborers, and 240 factories between 10 and 20 workers, while 180 factories had fewer than 10 workers.[34] Unlike the wartime economic boom in sugar production, the tobacco industry was hurt by the cancellation of export contracts. As a result, layoffs and factory closures were common.[35] In 1907, workers in industry, construction, and electrical power made up 6.15 percent of the total population; in 1919, 6.57 percent; and in 1931, 8.94 percent.[36] Because of its fragmented nature, the Cuban working class before the 1920s was politically weak and divided.[37]

By 1920 the general response to this situation of economic and social dislocation was an upsurge in Cuban social protest and nationalist sentiment. On one level, Cuban capitalists, both rural and urban, demanded that the state implement protective policies for Cuban businesses. Cuban light industry had experienced modest growth during World War I, but the postwar crisis threatened to erase any gains.[38] On May 4, 1923, the Association of Hacendados and Colonos of Cuba, which represented the leading sugar refiners and growers in Cuba, declared that "[Cubans] were obliged to import from the United States the necessities of life, as well as other articles, at war prices which were highly onerous, the outcome of this situation being that when in 1920 an economic crisis occurred throughout the world, the sugar producers and merchants of Cuba found themselves indebted to American exporters and bankers in excess of $300,000,000, a sum which represented for Cuba the fabulous burden of $100.00 per inhabitant." [39] Cuban *hacendados* and *colonos* pressured the government for protection against free-market forces and especially from foreclosures and buyouts by large, foreign-owned sugar-milling companies. After 1920, many sugar millers and producers advocated that the Cuban state should set limits on sugar production in order to stabilize prices. Within the context of sharp competition from producers in the Philippines, Java, the southern United States, and from the beet-sugar producers in Europe, Cuban producers increasingly looked to the state for protection. Too many sugar growers—particularly *colonos*—were vulnerable to erratic price fluctuations, especially if they were carrying a heavy debt load, as many were. Cuban sugar producers demanded credit relief, and the creation of an agricultural bank was proposed. Railway tariffs were too high, transport facilities required expansion and improvement, and the Cuban government should seek out more markets for sugar in order to lessen dependence on the U.S. market. [40]

At the same time, there was a rise in labor unrest in both the cities and the countryside. As early as 1918, there was widespread concern about working-class agitation. The British naval attaché in Havana reported to the Foreign Office that "the labouring classes are dissatisfied owing to the suppression of any attempt on their part at securing unity of organization. . . . In the cafés where the labourers congregate there is open talk of the intention to destroy all foreign, and especially American, sugar mills and property. . . . The revolution that seems imminent will be a protest against the whole system of government." [41]

Skilled and semiskilled workers in Havana had a long tradition of organizing, especially among tobacco workers, dock workers, railwaymen, woodworkers, painters, shoemakers, and other workers in small industry. Worker organizations usually took the form of craft associations. Typically, skilled workers and craftsmen resisted intrusion into their ranks by unskilled labor and they opposed mechanization in the labor process when it threatened their employment. Skills tended to be passed down through family or personalistic ties of apprenticeship. Ideologically, anarcho-syndicalist and socialist ideas gained ground among some Cuban workers. [42] But while it is true that anarcho-syndicalist ideas sometimes came from first- or second-generation Spaniards, it should not be forgotten that between the 1860s and the 1930s anarchist or proto-anarchist movements emerged in most countries. Anarchism arose as one response to the rapid expansion of industrial relations of production; the growth of commercialized agriculture in Latin America, Asia, and Africa; the proliferation and growth of urban centers and enclave economies; and the consequent emergence of a mass workforce increasingly dependent on wage labor. Anarchism, with its stress on non-authoritarian and cooperative organization, appealed to many people who had recently lost their land and ties to a stable community. Cuba was undergoing these same transformations, and Cuban workers did not require foreigners to inject them with political consciousness.[43] It should also be noted that the majority of Spanish emigrants who went to Cuba came from north or northwest Spain, where anarchism did not have a large following.[44] As with most anarcho-syndicalists of the time, Cuban syndicalists tended to be hostile to any form of "politics" and nationalism, both of which they viewed as synonymous with corrupt behavior, elitism, breaking working-class unity, and the exploitation of the "honest laborer."[45] Syndicalists saw their role as defenders of the immediate interests of the workers. Typically, urban workers demanded better wages, job security, improved working conditions, and recognition of their unions.[46] Yet, as we shall see, the apolitical or antipolitical inclinations of the anarcho-syndicalists clashed with the popular nationalism of many Cubans, especially during and after the War of 1895–98. Though "politics" continued to be associated with corrupt behavior for years to come, working-class Cubans increasingly played a self-conscious political role in mass mobilizations in the early part of the century.[47]

Despite the often elitist, urban, and craft-based nature of many unions and associations, new forms of worker mobilization and organization developed in the countryside and in the smaller urban centers. From Oriente province, through Camagüey, and right across the island, associations of mill workers were founded. Sometimes these associations were created with the help of organizers from the cities, but spontaneously formed ad hoc committees were the norm. These committees usually developed in response to local problems at individual mills. Very few of these "unions" survived longer than the harvesting season: once workers were discharged after the *zafra*, they left the mills and plantations to find employment wherever possible.[48] Workers not involved in the upkeep and maintenance of the mills were let go, and they often drifted to the cities and towns looking for work or they returned to their villages and farms. With the end of the *vacas gordas* (the "fat cow," or boom years) in 1920, worker migration and destitution reached crisis proportions. Prior to 1920, mill owners often complained that the expansion of the sugar economy was occurring faster than the labor supply. As a result, laborers could take advantage of the situation by demanding that mill owners or *colonos* provide higher wages, access to food plots, and cleaner living conditions in and around the *bateyes*.[49] After the crisis of 1920, however, both field hands and machinists lost much of their bargaining power. With few options open to them, hungry workers were forced to accept low wages and appalling working conditions.[50] Workers organized petitions and strikes, only to have the strikes broken by the rural guard or their demands ignored by company management. Workers' demands usually included a minimum wage of eighty cents to a dollar a day, the right to form a union, payment in money wages instead of *vales* (scrip) from the plantation stores, and the right to cultivate a small plot of land for subsistence during the "dead season."[51]

By 1924 working-class mobilization reached dramatic proportions. In that year thirty sugar *centrales* (mills) were shut down by striking workers, with railway laborers supporting the mill hands.[52] In November of the same year the *Heraldo de Cuba* reported that strikes were particularly disruptive in the eastern provinces. Destitute workers in Oriente, Camagüey, and Las Villas seized vacant lands owned by the sugar estates. The crisis in the sugar sector had caused mill owners and *colonos* to discharge workers: without employment these workers were faced with the choice of moving to increasingly congested urban centers or finding a plot of land to eke out a subsistence. Cane fields were set alight by strikers. Hungry laborers attacked and burned company stores that charged high prices for basic items such as food and clothes. It was common for workers to receive their wages in the form of vouchers instead of cash. These vouchers could be cashed in at the company store, with the amount of the purchases docked from the worker's wages at the end of the month. Workers consistently demanded that this practice be abolished. Money wages, when paid, were often lower than ten cents per day. These demands and actions by plantation workers were met by determined intransigence by the sugar companies. On November 24, 1924, the Association of Hacendados and Colonos expressed "grave concern about the revolutionary character of the strikes" and demanded military action be taken against the strikers.[53] The Havana Federation of Workers threatened a general strike in support of the mill hands. Starvation in the rural areas was common, and workers often labored for more than twelve hours a day.[54]

In February 1924 a group of Havana-based railway workers issued a manifesto that defined the attitude of the growing numbers of politicized workers. After lamenting the increased foreign domination over Cuba, the manifesto linked the workers' struggles of the day to the independence wars of the nineteenth century. Cuban workers were fighting "for national survival and against national slavery." The document went on to say that "the workers of Cuba and the entire people clamor for liberty and justice, two words which represent the best qualities of our people. We will make a revolution if the government does not fulfil [*sic*] its obligations to respect these two basic principles of our society." [55]

There were also signs of growing discontent from the students at the University of Havana and other educational institutions. One of the earliest manifestations of growing student discontent took the form of sports clubs made up of students from the nonaristocratic social classes. With the costs of living and education getting out of hand, many students became overtly political. They demanded better public education and the reform of university curriculum to meet the needs of modern professional and technical skills.[56] By 1923 university students had formed the Federación Estudiantil Universitaria (FEU) to promote students' rights and their fight for educational reform. In October of that year the National Revolutionary Congress of Students, which was attended by 138 delegates from across the island, debated issues of university reform as well as the need for students from all over Latin America to unite against "Yanqui imperialism" in Cuba and throughout the continent. Forty-nine educational institutions were represented at the congress, and the delegates demanded that students be represented in the governing bodies of all institutions, that faculty be subject to more stringent professional guidelines, and that the national government increase spending on education.[57]

Students were especially interested in obtaining a modern and technically oriented education that would better prepare them for the rapidly changing and industrializing world. In the early 1920s university education emphasized law and the medical sciences. In the academic year for 1920–21, for example, 2,166 students graduated from the University of Havana: 1,417 graduated from the Faculty of Medicine and Pharmacy, 409 from the Faculty of Law, and 340 from the Faculty of Literature and Science. There was a total of 234 professors: 71 were full professors, 45 were assistant professors, and the remaining 118 were contracted to teach on a term-by-term basis. Students complained that many of these professors did virtually no work and were given their positions through political patronage. An examination of the student-professor ratio, broken down by individual schools, shows some striking examples of university mismanagement: In the School of Science there were 4.8 students for each professor; the School of Literature and Philosophy had 5 students for each professor; and, in the School of Public Law there were 4 professors for every 5 students. Professors' salaries amounted to 76.8 percent of the total university budget.[58] From 1922 through to 1925 these and other concerns dominated life in and around the university and in intellectual circles generally.

The rise of student politics in 1923 and 1924 established the university as a potential thorn in the side of the government. In response to student concerns, in May 1923 President Zayas established a body of ninety faculty, students, and alumni with the mandate to recommend university and educational reform. This move served to pacify the majority of students. As a result, the Zayas plan managed to undercut student activism, at least for the short term.

Clearly, then, in the early 1920s political discontent among factions of the political class and mass mobilization from the *clases populares* were placing new pressures on the neocolonial state. We know in hindsight that these early conflicts were the opening rounds in a prolonged offensive against oligarchic rule that would continue for another decade. Yet the dramatic increase of subaltern protest in the early 1920s could not hide the fact that most Cubans lived in compartmentalized worlds. It was one thing for a new generation of politicized Cubans to recognize that the popular sectors were a force to be reckoned with; it was quite another matter to modify and create new political institutions and discourses that could harness the energy of the subordinate classes. This problem, of course, was not new. At least since Cuba's first war for independence from 1868 to 1878 and until the end of the second war in 1898, Cubans were sharply divided over the meanings of *cubanidad, la patria,* and *ciudadanía.*[59] It should be no surprise, therefore, that in the midst of the boom-and-bust atmosphere of the early 1920s, a new generation of Cubans would raise these issues again with renewed vigor.

In response to the political and economic crisis of the early 1920s, a wide range of new "civic organizations" of industrialists, *hacendados* and *colonos,* intellectuals, students, and workers were founded. They issued manifestos, wrote articles, and organized conferences, all with the purpose of dissecting the national crisis and suggesting solutions. The language used in these documents and meetings was strikingly similar: people wanted "moral rectification," "national regeneration," and the "modernization" of Cuban society as a whole. The "decadence" of the Cuban colonial mentality was decried.[60] The Platt Amendment, foreign domination of the economy, and the legacy of Spanish colonialism were typically singled out as the causes of Cuba's appalling condition, but some documents pointed to foreign immigrants and the Afro-Cuban population as contributing factors for Cuban "backwardness." Those who came of age after 1898 became adults in a country that appeared to be unraveling around them. This anxiety about Cuba's ability to survive as a nation became one of the dominant themes of the country's intellectual and political discourse for decades to come.[61] Many of the organizations that issued these protests eventually threw their support behind a movement which came to represent a broad spectrum of Cubans resentful of Cuba's neocolonial political and economic condition. This movement, known as the Veterans' and Patriots' Movement, was formed in 1923 and lasted until the end of 1924.

The Veterans' and Patriots' Movement, 1923-1924

Cuban veterans of the wars of independence had long been dissatisfied with their treatment after 1898. Cubans fought for an independent country, but their victory was denied by the invading Americans. Instead, Cuba's second war for independence was converted into the "Spanish American War." Many had fought for the right to possess land, but the land went to foreign sugar companies. Pensions were in arrears; Afro-Cuban veterans were the victims of racism and discrimination by the occupying forces and often by members of their own liberation army. Generally, most veterans felt that their patriotic sacrifices and reputations were not sufficiently recognized by the Cuban state and by the American army.[62] Before 1920 the struggle for recognition of veteran's rights had lost much of its steam, but with the political and economic crisis fueling popular protest, the aging veterans added their voice to the concerns expressed by the generation born after 1898. For younger Cubans the concerns and humiliations of the veterans legitimized their nationalist feelings and resentment of corrupt politics and foreign control: old and young alike were denied a place in their own country.

As a consequence of the merging of the two generations, the leadership of the revitalized veterans' movement included a cross section of the veteran leaders of 1895 and younger upper- and middle-class Cubans. General Carlos García Vélez, son of the famous general of the independence wars, Calixto García Íñiguez, was the president of the Supreme Council of the Veterans' and Patriots' Association. General Manuel Sanguily, another important leader from the independence wars and a close collaborator of Cuba's independence hero José Martí, helped revitalize the association. Fifteen other generals, eight colonels, two commanders, and four prominent doctors made up part of the Supreme Council. Other members of the Supreme Council included Carlos Alzugaray, president of the Commercial Association of Havana; Alejo Carreño, president of the National Association of Hacendados and Colonos; Manuel Despaigne, a prominent veteran and former member of Crowder's "Honest Cabinet"; and Dr. Enrique José Varona, the single most important intellectual in early-twentieth-century Cuba and a formative influence on successive generations of nationalists. Younger members of the Supreme Council were Julio Antonio Mella, representative of the Federation of University Students; Rubén Martínez Villena, a poet and the director of the Falange de Acción Cubana, a group of nationalist intellectuals; and Dr. Juan Marinello, a rising literary critic.[63] Other names that appeared on the Veterans' manifestos were Carlos Mendieta, Ramón Grau San Martín, Carlos E. Finlay, Porfirio Franca, and Federico Laredo Bru. As we will observe in following chapters, these and other participants in the Veterans' Movement were to play important roles in Cuban politics in the years to come.

One sees, then, that newer demands for social and economic reform surfaced alongside the historic concerns of the generation of the 1890s. The political program of the Veterans' Movement, released at the end of August 1923, declared that they wanted "nothing more than to purify the government and the moral rectification of those in government by Cuban means and among Cubans themselves."[64] The Veterans' program frequently used the words "rectification," "regeneration," and "moralization" to describe what they wanted from the state. The government should rectify itself, or there would be revolution. While the program emphasized that the Veterans were independent of any of the existing political parties, they hastened to add that members of all parties were invited to support the movement. At the same time, the new association recognized the legitimacy of existing republican institutions. In this sense, the Veterans' and Patriots' Movement was reformist. They did not want to transform or overthrow the Cuban state; rather, the Veterans wanted to "purify," "renovate," and "rectify" the government by placing "honest" people in office.[65] This position permitted the Veterans to assume an ambivalent stance toward Crowder's intervention in Cuban affairs. The association's main objection to Crowder's visit was that Cubans—not an American general—should be solving the problems of corruption and political instability. The Veterans disliked the messenger, not the message.

The new association was opposed to American domination of the sugar industry, especially through the banks. They wanted a free and fair press. Women's political rights were supported, though the exact contents of these rights was not spelled out. The corruption of the lottery system was condemned because it went against "the economic and cultural interest of the nation by discouraging education and work as the legitimate means of self improvement." Illiteracy needed to be eradicated because those couldn't read could be manipulated by corrupt politicians. A major demand of the Veterans was for the abrogation of the Tarafa Law, a measure that restricted the access of sugar producers to only a few ports, thus leaving the producers vulnerable to foreign railway monopolies and the railway lines of the big mills.[66] Such a demand is hardly surprising, as many of the signatories of the Veterans' program had the designated title "*colono*" or "*hacendado*" after their names. Both groups were resentful of the high freight costs they had to pay to get their sugar to the mills and ports.[67] The misery and hunger of Cuban workers was noted, and their displacement by foreign labor was condemned as a national scandal. The program demanded that modern labor-capital legislation be introduced, though the documents are not specific as to what this meant. At the General Assembly of the association on August 29, 1923, one delegate from the workers' associations, Alfredo Padrón, a furniture maker, spoke about the terrible class inequality in Cuba and the harm done to the nation by the importation of cheap foreign labor. Padrón went on to say that "workers want, before the granting of their own demands, the realization of the Cuban national personality."[68] For the Veterans, the realization of the "national personality" meant that Cubans must gain control over their economy and politics. Cuba, the program concluded, was becoming a haven for rich foreign capitalists and American tourists, while the Zayas government "plays with Cuban nationality."[69]

The immediate spark that set off the Veterans' protest was their conflict with President Alfredo Zayas (1920–24) over the issue of pensions. For a very brief period, the Zayas government was "popular" among the elite factions because Menocal left office with virtually no public support. Zayas, at least, was a change, or so many hoped. Within the first year of his mandate, the new president found himself in a precarious situation. Whatever good-will Zayas had managed to garner disappeared when the same patterns of graft and corruption surfaced within his government. The British minister in Havana reported that "[Zayas] finds himself called upon to face a situation which could hardly be more difficult. . . . [He] must find room for a host of place seekers who have been disbarred for the last eight years from the sweets of office. Somehow or other he must keep the machine going and stave off a crisis."[70] Indeed, part of the crisis Zayas faced was the issue of the nonpayment of pensions to the veterans by the government. This issue, combined with the larger economic and political problems of the day, helped fuel an already volatile situation.[71] By August 1923 the veterans were organizing a series of meetings with the intention of broadening their movement and increasing the pressure on the Zayas government.[72] No sooner had the Supreme Council of the Veterans' and Patriots' Association been established, however, when the Zayas government declared the group's activities to be seditious and rebellious.[73]

The Veterans' Movement was caught completely off guard by the government's response. Veteran protests became haphazard and lacked coordination. Throughout the autumn of 1923, rumors about armed uprisings were widespread, and newspapers carried reports of pending civil war.[74] An attempt to organize a coordinated armed uprising in April 1924 fell apart due to the lack of communication among the organizers, the successful infiltration of the movement by government informants, and the assistance of American officials who provided Zayas with information about the Veterans' arms purchases in Florida. No serious armed confrontation between the Veterans and the government took place. There was no mass uprising from the *clases populares* in support of the Veterans' demands for the "rectification of the state." Indeed, there is no evidence that the Veterans' leadership seriously encouraged mass insurrection: true to the Plattist political tradition, they threatened the Zayas government with rebellion, hoping that the government would either comply with their demands or resign and let others make the necessary reforms. By the summer of 1924, most leaders of the movement were either in jail or in exile. Others accepted Zayas' promises for amnesty on the condition that they withdraw from political activity.[75]

The failure of the Veterans' and Patriots' Movement proved to be a bitter pill for many participants. Particularly for the younger generation, there was a generalized sentiment that their patriotic sentiments had been betrayed and manipulated by traditional *caudillos*. What had started as a movement for the regeneration of Cuba ended in humiliating disarray. As we will see in the next chapter, the experience of the Veterans' Movement provoked a profound intellectual and ideological crisis among many members of the younger generation. Younger Cubans were deeply disappointed in the veteran leaders, who, they concluded, had abused their status as independence fighters. For the first time, some Cubans—and especially young people—began to question not simply the moral authority of some of the older leaders, but the very nature of the neocolonial state itself. The fact that so many of the leaders of the Veterans' Movement quietly and easily re-integrated themselves back into the patronage networks of the Plattist state proved that sweeping changes in both the state and society were necessary if Cuba was to move forward.

The Veterans' revolt brought to the fore a central contradiction within Cuban society in the 1920s. On the one hand, the problem of *caudillismo* and *caciquismo* would continue to plague Cuban politics for years to come; on the other hand, after 1924, a younger generation of Cubans began to formulate new ideas about how to change Cuba's neocolonial status. As we will see shortly, what was at issue for the new generation of political activists in the 1920s and 1930s was how to forge new cultural values within a society they saw as decaying and hopelessly backward. Despite the failure of the Veterans' Movement, the dramatic political and social changes taking place in Latin America and in the rest of the world seemed to provide a wide range of alternatives. The 1920s was a time of crisis and transformation and hope and despair. For many younger people, the fiasco of the Veterans' and Patriots' Movement was the start of a political journey that would lead them toward a new conception of politics and society.

CHAPTER TWO

To Scratch Away the Scab of Colonialism

Radical Nationalist Politics, 1924–1928

The easy suppression of the Veterans' and Patriots' Movement by the Zayas government provoked a deep moral and political crisis among many of its younger supporters. For more seasoned politicians and *caudillos*, the Veterans' Movement had always been nothing more than a pressure tactic to push for change within the Plattist system. Younger participants, on the other hand, had hoped to challenge the entire system of oligarchic rule. The bitter disappointment of the Veterans' Movement compelled some members of new generation to draw increasingly radical conclusions concerning the nature of neocolonial rule as well as possible alternatives to oligarchic rule. Students, writers and journalists, intellectuals, and artists began to express what one scholar appropriately describes as the "aggrieved sense of inauthenticity that plays itself out in a typical colonial experience."[1]

What made these people "radical" was that they set themselves against the values of oligarchic rule; they wanted to break with the political traditions of *caudillismo* and *caciquismo* and build a "modern" world where reason, science, technology, and a democratic state administration would serve the Cuban people and the entire nation. The "radicalism" of the new generation, as this and the next chapter will show, was not so much a question of ideology as it was of attitude and sentiment. Following Eric Wolf, I see ideology as "unified schemes or configurations developed to underwrite or manifest power."[2] Radical sentiment, however, was too defuse and vague to be converted into programs in the struggle for power. To be sure, by the late 1920s and early 1930s radicals looked to the new ideologies such as socialism, fascism, populism, and American New Deal liberalism as alternatives to oligarchic rule. But in the early and mid-1920s the ideological implications of mass politics were not clear, and opposition to the Plattist state was expressed in moral and ethical terms. What was at the root of this ethical, moral, and indeed cultural critique of oligarchic capitalism was the denial of, and the struggle for, *citizenship*. Citizenship, in the broadest sense, refers to both membership in a nation state and some popular sense of social rights and obligations associated with this membership. Above all, citizenship implies a sense of community, of belonging to a nation, and of having a state that helps make the national community coherent and meaningful. Cuba, however, was not a nation state, nor did the population as a whole share a social and political vision of what a Cuban "imagined community" should be like.[3] Moreover, issues of citizenship, national identity, and popular rebellion were further complicated by neocolonialist domination, anti-imperialist struggle, race, and revolutionary upheavals in Latin America and the rest of the world.[4]

Young Cubans were very concerned with these issues, and, as we will see in later chapters, the 1920s proved to be formative years for the political leaders and activists of the 1930s and 1940s. In this chapter I want to do two things. First, I will outline the general contours of radical nationalist discourse during the 1920s. Second, I will focus on the ideas and activity of two young radicals who came to play a decisive role in the formulation of a specifically leftist critique of Cuban neocolonial political economy. Rubén Martínez Villena and Julio Antonio Mella had joined the Veterans' Movement with the hope of improving the national condition. They were to be bitterly disappointed by the experience, and, as a result, they concluded that socialism was the only possible solution for Cuba's lamentable condition. Martínez Villena and Mella were not typical representatives of their generation; they proved to be far too radical for most of their compatriots. Most nationalists, whether radical or reformist, rejected Marxism as having little if any relevance to Cuban reality. Both men also died young, so we cannot know how they might have influenced events had they lived longer, especially during and after the revolution of 1933. Rather, what was significant about the ideas and activities of Martínez Villena and Mella was that they played a decisive role in creating a Marxist and radical leftist subcurrent within the larger stream of Cuban radical nationalism. Martínez Villena and Mella were, among many other things, early leaders of the Communist Party of Cuba (CP), and though the CP would undergo radical shifts in its strategy and tactics, a significant number of Cuban radicals, whether party members or not, came to take Marxism seriously as *one* source of ideological inspiration in their struggle for a new Cuba.[5]

In the aftermath of World War I, the contradictions of capitalist modernity dominated much of the intellectual and political discourse. The industrial economy was changing the way people worked and where they lived. Urbanization and rural-urban migration were transforming the human landscape. Because of improvements in transportation and communication, people were more aware than ever of the gap between rich and poor nations. Ideas about social space and the meaning of history and social change were being questioned as never before. The trauma of the First World War, combined with the revolutions in Russia, Mexico, and China, encouraged the belief that there was more than one path to modernity and human progress.[6] For Latin America the experience of modernity had been wrenching and painful. Indeed, Latin Americans seemed to be the *object* of an externally imposed modernity and not the agents of their own destiny. History and progress were out of their control, and Latin American cultures were often characterized as backward, traditional, and, at best, exotic. Capitalist modernity seemed to be more a fate to be endured than an optimistic hope for human progress and development. In response to this colonialist modernity, Latin American intellectuals and radicals in the 1920s struggled to formulate their own ideas about what progress and modernity should mean for the continent. These wide-ranging debates and discussions centered on the meaning of, and the struggle for, *culture.* "Culture," as one scholar aptly phrases it, "can seem like a substitute for politics, a way of posing imaginary solutions to real problems, but under other circumstances, culture can become a rehearsal for politics, trying out values and beliefs permissible in art but forbidden in social life."[7] Young intellectuals were under growing pressure to decide whether they would withdraw from the world and seek refuge in reified artistic creation "outside" time and social struggle, or whether they would become militants in the fight for cultural and political liberation.[8] Especially for Cubans, who had experienced twenty-five years of dramatic changes that were not of their own making, the notion that people could—and should—seize control of their own destiny was a powerful impulse.

Following the Veterans' defeat, the amorphous coalition of forces that made up the movement fragmented. By fall 1924, each member organization went its own way. For some of the groups within the Veterans' Movement, the demise of the rebellion had no long-term importance. The election of the Liberal Party candidate Gerardo Machado y Morales in May 1925 signaled a new phase in the evolution of the Plattist state. From 1925 until the end of the decade, the Machado government promoted moderate nationalist policies. Tariffs protected Cuban light industry, and many of the demands made by the Veterans' and Patriots' Movement were met by the early Machado regime.[9] As a consequence, many Cubans were optimistic that they could put the worst abuses of the Plattist state behind them.[10]

The main forum of expression for nationalist debate was in the major intellectual journals of the period. Magazines such as *Social* (1916–36), *Carteles*, *Juventud* (1923–25), *Revista de Avance* (1927–30), *Cuba Contemporánea* (1913–27), *Venezuela Libre* (1921–25), and *Atuei* (1927–28) were the outlets for a wide variety of political and cultural ideas. The journals *Social*, *Carteles*, and *Cuba Contemporánea* were not specifically on the left of the political spectrum, but they did provide a forum for a wide range of views, including those of the Cuban and Latin American left. The *Revista de Avance*, though more literary in tone, published articles by Cuban radicals and the writings of prominent Spanish intellectuals, including Miguel de Unamuno, Fernando de los Ríos, and Luis Araquistaín.[11] The works of the French writers Henri Barbusse and Anatole France also appeared. Friedrich Nietzche's writings were popular, and excerpts from Oswald Spengler's *Decline of the West* were published. Peruvians Víctor Raúl Haya de la Torre and José Carlos Mariátegui were other, frequent contributors to these publications. The evolving debate between Haya's non-Marxist populism and Mariátegui's Latin Americanist Marxism was closely followed by Cuban radicals. Haya de la Torre was the founder of the Popular American Revolutionary Alliance (APRA). The Apristas advocated Latin American unity, anti-imperialism, nationalization of all essential industries and land, solidarity with all oppressed classes, and a multiclass alliance of intellectuals and manual workers to fight for a progressive form of Latin American capitalism, free from imperialist domination. *Atuei* was the magazine published by Cuban Apristas. The Apristas, as we will see shortly, though of little consequence numerically speaking, were at the center of a political debate which was to have lasting consequences for the radical left in Cuba. The magazines *Juventud* and *Venezuela Libre* were explicitly left wing, with Mella and Martínez Villena serving as editors and contributors to both journals.

The widespread anti-imperialist sentiment, repression, and sense of cultural crisis of the times challenged intellectuals to make a greater political commitment to the struggles they wrote about. One of Haya de la Torre's most enduring concepts was the notion of the intellectual as worker and the need for an alliance between intellectuals and manual workers. The pages of the *Revista de Avance*, *Social*, *Juventud*, *Venezuela Libre*, and *Atuei* contained numerous references to the idea of "the United Front of Intellectuals and Workers."[12]

One of the first expressions of a clearly articulated anti-imperialist argument appeared in the August 1922 issue of *Social*. The magazine's literary editor, Emilio Roig de Leuchsenring, wrote a series of articles about the historic significance of the Russian Revolution for Latin America.[13] In the first installment, Roig argued that the Russian Revolution was a decisive moment in the progressive path of human progress. One did not have to be a Russian to be a Bolshevik because to be a Bolshevik meant to "reorganize humanity." Roig went on to say that if people "serenely study history," it might still be possible to prevent violent revolutions. But, he emphasized, whether through reform or revolution, change was inevitable; Russia's revolution showed the path to the future and Latin America would follow its example.[14] By 1926 Roig would be more precise when discussing the significance of the Russian Revolution: capitalism was failing, its so-called democracy was giving away to dictatorship and fascism, and a "modern and technocratic Russia" was providing a new definition of modernity.[15]

In general, much of the writing on the Russian Revolution was short on specifics and long on interpretation. There were few references to Lenin and his work, and there was little information available in Cuba about the policies of the revolutionary government. Nonetheless, the symbolic importance of the Russian Revolution was a powerful force. When the Russian events were combined with the Mexican Revolution and with other Latin American struggles, the legitimacy of revolutionary struggle as a way to enter the modern world was clearly established. Enrique José Varona, when interviewed by *Juventud* in March 1924, declared that "with respect to the Russian Revolution, it has greatly advanced our understanding of modern societies. It is an extraordinary social and human advance, equal to the French Revolution before it. . . . And Mexico is another victim of the lack of understanding by powerful external forces. . . . As for Lenin, well, I don't know much about him, but he strikes me as an extraordinary man, who while having the power of a Napoleon in his hands, is using his power to serve his ideals."[16] There was nothing radical or revolutionary about Varona's perspective on the Russian events. As a neopositivist philosopher, and like his contemporaries José Vasconcelos in Mexico and José Ingenieros in Argentina, Varona could easily see the Russian Revolution in light of the "inevitable progress of humanity." These three thinkers played an important role in encouraging Cuban and Latin American youth in the belief that for once history and progress were on their side. This optimistic interpretation of these philosophers' works often overlooked their racist and social Darwinist musings about how Latin Americans of Indian or African dissent were to blame for the cultural "backwardness" of the continent.[17] Thus another young writer, Rubén Martínez Villena, could write on the occasion of the death of Ingenieros in 1925 that the Argentine philosopher expounded an "admirable doctrine and dynamic concept of infinite perfectibility, of endless optimism. . . . [He was] a teacher for the New America, the America of Ariel, Our America which is still being born, and will soon be born in twenty new peoples of the New Humanity." [18]

Such vague but powerful sentiments lay behind the nationalist sentiment of most young artists and writers, young businessmen, women's groups, and students. These heterogeneous social groups, however, were far from united about what the alternative to oligarchic rule should be. As we will see in the next chapter, many activists in the mid- to late 1920s found themselves engaging in revolutionary struggle not out of political principle, but rather because the increasingly dictatorial regime of General Machado left them no other option. *Moral* and *ethical* indignation about dictatorship certainly fuelled the radicalism of an entire generation; but most opposition groups lacked any long term strategic vision of what a post-Machado Cuba would look like. There were others, however, who developed more ideologically based critiques of Cuban politics and society. Two of the young participants in the Veterans' and Patriots' Movement, Rubén Martínez Villena and Julio Antonio Mella, illustrate this tendency. Both men came to the conclusion that Marxism was the best guide for political action.

Rubén Martínez Villena (1899–1934) came from a middle-class Havana family. His father was a university professor of philosophy and literature at the University of Havana. He graduated from law school in 1917 but spent most of the time working as a journalist for *El Heraldo* newspaper. Later, he worked as the personal secretary for the famous Cuban social scientist Fernando Ortiz.[19] In the early 1920s Martínez Villena participated in literary *tertulias,* or discussion groups, with other artists and writers. These gatherings debated issues of culture, politics, and the meaning of national literature within a rapidly changing world. Meanwhile he was making a name for himself as a poet and journalist. These informal networks of writers and artists tended to be sympathetic to the nationalist demands of the Veterans' Movement. After the failure of the movement, he collaborated with Julio Antonio Mella in the José Martí Popular University, as well as taking on other new initiatives. In 1927 he joined the recently founded Communist Party of Cuba, becoming a member of the Central Committee in 1928. Soon thereafter, he abandoned his literary career to work full time on party activity. From 1927 until 1931, he spent considerable time writing party manifestos and articles for the communist press. Martínez Villena suffered from tuberculosis, and in 1931 the party sent him to Moscow to recuperate. He returned to Cuba in the spring of 1933 and played an active role in the revolution of that year. Martínez Villena died of tuberculosis in Havana in January 1934.[20]

Julio Antonio Mella (1903–1929) also came from a middle-class Havana family. His mother was Irish and his father was from the Dominican Republic. In the early 1920s Mella studied at the University of Havana, but most of his time was taken up with student politics and sports. In 1923 he was already familiar with the works of the Peruvian thinkers José Carlos Mariátegui and Víctor Raúl Haya de la Torre. That same year he spent considerable effort organizing the José Martí Popular University, which, as we will see shortly, was part of a continental movement of popular universities. In 1925 he helped found the Communist Party of Cuba, the Anti-Imperialist League, and the Anti-Clerical League. Mella wrote a great deal, especially for student publications, and he produced several polemical essays on revolutionary theory and practice in Cuba. By late 1926 the increasingly dictatorial regime of General Machado had exiled Mella to Mexico. While in exile in Mexico, Mella became a member of the Mexican Party's Central Committee. In 1927 he went to Moscow and on his return to Mexico became embroiled in factional fights within the Mexican Party. He was assassinated on January 10, 1929, by Machado's agents.[21]

As we saw in the previous chapter, both Martínez Villena and Mella helped found the revitalized Veteran's Movement in 1923. Though both Martínez Villena and Mella eventually became Marxists, their political evolution was largely determined by their sharply different personalities and temperaments. Martínez Villena was a leading member of Cuba's new literary vanguard of writers and poets.[22] It was in this capacity that in the spring of 1923 he participated in the "Protest of the Thirteen": thirteen prominent intellectuals and poets denounced government corruption and the abuse of republican institutions by Plattist state officials.[23] Soon after, he wholeheartedly threw himself into working for the Veterans' cause.

The failure of the Veteran's insurrection was a terrible blow for Martínez Villena. In June 1924, in a letter written from Tampa, Florida, to fellow poet and activist Enrique Serpa, Martínez Villena expressed his deep humiliation and despair about the Veterans' experience:

> I only have a scrap of dignity left. It is ridiculous to have been defeated before the struggle started. It is hard to face up to. . . . Public opinion is of no interest to me any more. It's my opinion of myself, and it's a miserable one that I have to live with. Should I return to Cuba?

Should I return now? Should I wait until I get over all this? These are the questions I ask myself. What others think is not important; but I am not prepared to be part of a sick and cowardly joke and pretend that I can hide myself in the pretence of "friendships." The bourgeoisie has had their revenge by pretending to be false prophets. . . . And before history? Aren't we the most ridiculous? Especially those like me who have a sense of historical responsibility, who believed in the promises, who really felt the indignation and wanted to rid our country of all the shame. Is it possible that all this will end in a "Cuban" way—with the bowing and scraping by the "honorably defeated" and those who take the easy but corrupt path to political positions. I know that I am not one to be broken, to give up. My opinion about the situation in Cuba is known, it is written down and I still hold to it. And if I would be of use in Cuba I would go . . . but unfortunately it is clear, I am of no use there now.[24]

As it turned out, Martínez Villena did return to Cuba in August 1924.[25] His personal and political crisis persisted throughout the remainder of the year, which was to prove one of his most productive years from the literary perspective. Politically speaking, he began to raise questions about how a popular movement for social change should be organized. In an interview granted to the *Heraldo de Cuba* on October 3, 1924, he gave his overall evaluation of the Veterans' Movement. He argued that the association should reorganize itself because its program was still relevant and should be put into practice. He went on to say that the association "should be the vehicle of popular aspirations in order to take public power; not of professional politicians but of organized public and civic opinion representing the values of social justice." If this was not accomplished, there was a real danger that "civilization would arrive in Cuba at the point of the Yankee boot." By "civic and revolutionary action" Martínez Villena meant "intense cultural campaigns to prepare the people to exercise their legal rights and public duties." This cultural preparation would be a long-term process, and "it is useless to ask the government to do this." Still, the struggle for reforms should continue. As for the leadership of the reorganized movement, Martínez Villena came out firmly against *caudillismo:* when asked who the leaders of the movement should be, he answered that "anonymous workers are the ones who carry out great tasks."[26]

There was a mixed message here. On the one hand, Martínez Villena was suggesting that the rank and file of any reorganized movement should hold the political initiative, not the leaders; on the other hand, he implied that an unidentified intellectual elite should "prepare the people" culturally and politically. Martínez Villena was addressing the same issues as his older neopositivist contemporaries Enrique José Varona (Cuba),[27] José Ingenieros (Argentina), and José Vasconcelos (Mexico): these philosophers argued that "culture" should be brought to the masses by an intellectual elite. At the same time, Martínez Villena raised one of the central problems of modern politics: how were radical intellectuals to relate to the masses? Prior to 1924, very few Cuban intellectuals asked this question, but the failure of the Veterans' Movement brought this issue to the forefront. Martínez Villena was concerned about how to develop new ways of mobilizing the masses. With the Cuban popular groups asserting their presence in the political arena, the practical problem of how to establish an "organic" connection between radical intellectuals and the *clases populares* needed to be addressed. But, in 1924, Martínez Villena still clung to the hope that a new veterans' movement might come about if it was reorganized from the bottom up.

A reorganized veteran's movement was, however, not to be. With the movement dead, in early 1925 Martínez Villena joined Julio Antonio Mella to work for the José Martí Popular University, which functioned from 1923 to 1927. Before examining the popular university movement, however, it is worthwhile to examine how Mella reacted to the Veterans' experience. All indications are that Mella was not as deeply committed to the Veterans' Movement as was Martínez Villena. While there is no statement by Mella explaining this position, an examination of his writings and speeches throughout 1923 and 1924 indicates that he was already more radical than Martínez Villena. Like many students at the time, Mella participated in the struggle for university reform and autonomy that was sweeping Latin America and Cuba. The purpose of this movement was to fight for educational reform that stressed the practical skills required for a modern capitalist society. Students wanted less emphasis on law and philosophy and more attention paid to science and economics. They also demanded that the state not interfere in the day-to-day running of the university.[28] By 1923 the university reform movement was continent-wide, and the students at the University of Havana were very much a part of this wave of student protest.[29] As we will see, Mella was quick to link the student struggle with the larger social and anti-imperialist struggles of the day, particularly those taking place in Mexico, Peru, Venezuela, Russia, and China.

Immediately after the demise of the Veterans' Movement, Mella wrote a scathing article entitled "The Last Farce of the Politicians and the 'Patriots.'" The Veterans' Movement, Mella argued, "never gained the support of the people, the true people, those who work." There were no true leaders because there were no great ideals. These ideals, he went on to say, "are for the liberation of an enslaved people. History has taught us that for a real and just transformation the economic system has to be destroyed. . . . [W]e do not simply rebel, we are revolutionaries." Mella concluded his article saying that the real fight was between capital and labor, the clergy against culture.[30]

Mella's article was written in May 1924. While Martínez Villena was still struggling to keep the Veteran's Movement alive, Mella's break with the movement was decisive and he quickly turned his energies to the popular university movement. The formation of the José Martí Popular University in 1923 provides an example of how radical students and intellectuals attempted to intervene in the cultural life of the working class. These ideas were not unique to Cuba: the influence of the Córdoba university reform movement in Argentina in 1918, the popular university initiatives in Peru, and the visit of the Peruvian radical Víctor Raúl Haya de la Torre to Havana in November of 1923 were defining movements for the student left.[31]

As with all of the popular universities in Latin America during the 1920s, the José Martí Popular University existed to challenge what Mella called the "false values of colonialism."[32] It had some five hundred students, most of whom were urban workers from Havana. Classes were usually convened in the evening to make attendance easier for workers. Sympathetic professors and students from the University of Havana gave classes on Cuban history, the legal rights of workers, and the latest political and philosophical ideas. Important international events such as the Russian and Mexican Revolutions, the struggles in China and Ireland, and the policies of the U.S. government toward Cuba and Latin America were discussed in classes. Exiled professors from Peru, strongly influenced by Haya de la Torre and Aprismo, taught at the Popular University in Cuba.[33]

For those who worked at the popular university, education had to have a strong ethical and socially conscious content. According to Mella, the teacher must replace the priest as the one who should "form the character of the student" and the teacher must set a high moral standard for students. A new spirit of rebelliousness was encouraged to provide the basis for "true education, which is the religion of new men." This "true education" was intended to counter what Mella termed "the disorientation of the spirit" caused by colonialism. The goal was "to revolutionize the consciousness of the people so as to build a new society." "Culture," Mella declared, "is the only true and final guarantee for the emancipation of a people." In addition, the new education must be modern, scientific, and technical to allow

Cubans, from the cane-cutter up, to reconquer the productive forces of the country from foreign hands.[34] The Popular University "must promote culture, but not bourgeois culture."[35] The role of the popular university was to support workers "at those moments when the Cuban worker is carrying out the most important battles for their [sic] own organization, which, in turn, is the battle for progress."[36] The enemies of this struggle for progress were "yanqui imperialism" which "had converted the nation into a factory," and the corrupt Cuban governments which were unable to defend Cuban sovereignty.[37] The role of the popular university was to create revolutionaries. According to Mella, workers made the best revolutionaries because, while middle-class students could be bought off with government jobs, the workers continued to be exploited by native and foreign capitalists alike. Only "the most radical elements, the extreme Left, the conscious proletariat" would push the national struggle to the stage of social revolution.[38]

As innovative as the popular university was, it faced serious obstacles. The most obvious problem was government repression. As the Machado regime became increasingly dictatorial after 1926, the popular university was forced to shift locations and interrupt classes.[39] Machado had promised the U.S. government that he would not permit labor unrest. He failed to fulfill that promise, but from 1926 to 1929 he did manage to keep the opposition on the defensive. Mella recognized this problem, and in September 1926 he described the situation in Cuba as "difficult"; Cuba, he concluded, was not ready for revolutionary agitation. Mass mobilization during these years was at a low ebb in comparison to 1923–24. As a result, the popular university was "a university for revolutionaries in a country where there was not the environment to create them."[40]

Another problem with the popular university stemmed from the complex social and political situation for urban workers and the *clases populares* generally. Workers often attended classes expecting to receive practical instruction in mechanics, mathematics, and literacy. Moreover, attracting workers from outside the Havana area proved to be nearly impossible. There was virtually no contact between the popular university and sugar workers. The popular university tended to attract craft workers, most of whom were under the influence of syndicalist ideology. As a consequence, the antipolitical and antinationalist orientation of anarcho-syndicalism made many workers suspicious of some of the ideas promoted by the popular university.[41]

Then there was the issue of Mella himself. His charismatic personality so dominated the popular university that without his presence the political orientation of the university changed. Mella insisted on the class-based and anti-imperialist orientation of the university. But the popular university was only one of several projects that occupied the young leader.[42] Not only was it impossible for Mella to be everywhere at once, but he tended to dominate any group he participated in. This was not a new phenomenon: as early as 1922 many students in the student federation identified themselves first and foremost as *mellistas*.[43] This characteristic was a double-edged sword for the fledgling Cuban left: on the one hand, the fact that Mella could attract people to his projects by sheer dint of personality helped recruit followers to the cause; on the other hand, the personalist nature of the relationship between Mella and his followers undermined any attempt to strengthen a group's collective and organizational structure. More often than not, when Mella was not present for any length of time, the leftist positions of the groups left with him. Whatever projects Mella became involved in, he attracted strong personal loyalties and enmities.

As the limitations of the popular university became evident to Mella, he put more energy into other projects. His experience in the popular university, coupled with his analysis of the Cuban and Latin American situation during the 1920s, pushed Mella further to the left. Anti-imperialist struggle, he concluded, was the appropriate strategic orientation.[44] Mella was far from alone in this assessment. The so-called national question, and the meaning of national liberation generally, became subjects of considerable debate among young politicized Latin Americans. Sandino's fight against American Marines in Nicaragua, the continuing debates about the Mexican Revolution and the Russian Revolution, the anticolonialist movement in China, and the formation of anti-imperialist leagues throughout Latin and North America focused people's attention on the international dimensions of the struggle.

The centrality of the anti-imperialist struggle for nationalist radicals stemmed from their conclusion that anti-imperialist sentiment had the greatest potential to unify the *clases populares*. In 1926 Mella wrote that "we have to present the 'national problem' to some, and the 'social problem' to others—but anti-imperialism to everyone." In the same document he admitted that there were many ambiguities in this formulation, but he expressed confidence that in the course of the struggle issues would define themselves. "The most important thing," he concluded, "is to do things, to act, to fight."[45] Martínez Villena, writing in the same year, spoke about how U.S. capitalist imperialism is the enemy of all of Latin America and that the oppressed of "Our America" are carrying out a "spiritual revolution" in the process of national and continental liberation.[46] By 1926 Martínez Villena, like Mella before him, was taking the more radical position that it was the working class of Cuba and of all Latin America that should lead the anti-imperialist struggle. The problem, however, was that the social and class nature of the anti-imperialist struggle was far from clear. Who was to lead this struggle? The working class? Or should it be the new nationalist bourgeoisies of Latin America? These were the larger questions which preoccupied Cuban and Latin American radicals in the 1920s.

Mella's view that the working class should lead the anti-imperialist forces became the central point of contention between Marxism and Aprista populism in Cuba and Latin America.[47] Haya de la Torre's new Aprista movement was gaining strength in the 1920s. By the late 1920s there were Aprista parties in most Latin American countries, including Cuba. Moreover, though the actual size of most Aprista groups was small, and though they rarely had much of a direct impact on the broader social struggles around them, Aprismo as an ideology gained considerable influence among prominent intellectuals throughout the continent. In this sense, and especially for Cuba, the importance of Aprismo was that it provided a broad intellectual and political framework from which to view the complex reality of Cuban social relations. Haya de la Torre and the Apristas argued that the nationalist middle classes of Latin American should lead the anti-imperialist movement. Haya's argument was that Latin America needed to find its own path to capitalist modernity. This goal, he understood, would almost inevitably lead to a clash with the imperialist nations of the world since they had interests to defend in Latin America. The Aprista political vision was that Latin America must go through the equivalent of the French Revolution of 1789: the young nations of Latin America required their own bourgeois democratic revolutions, which, Haya maintained, should be supported by a multiclass coalition of middle-class and working-class Latin Americans. Accordingly, Haya and his followers saw the Mexican Revolution as one phase of this continent-wide bourgeois anti-imperialist revolution. What added ideological confusion to these claims was that in his early writings Haya claimed that Aprismo was a new and distinctly Latin American interpretation of Marxism.[48] As a consequence, at mid-decade Latin American leftists were trying to sort out how their struggles fit into the larger worldwide pattern of anti-imperialist struggle, in both symbolic and theoretical terms. As it turned out, by the late 1920s the ideological divide between Apristas and Marxists widened, with Julio Antonio Mella playing a critical role in clarifying the differences between the two strategic conceptions of political change.[49]

Before we examine Mella's critique of Aprismo, however, it is worthwhile to focus on the wider intellectual environment that influenced the thinking of Cuban radicals. Between 1924 and 1929, when both Aprismo and Marxism were new to Latin Americans, both ideologies did indeed seem to be complimentary. Marxism, and specifically Soviet Marxism, was still in the early phases of becoming "orthodox." Most European-based Marxists knew little about Latin America, and what they thought they knew was usually mistaken. As a result, Latin American leftists were essentially on their own to formulate revolutionary strategies appropriate to specific national conditions. Of course the powerful imagery and symbolism of the Russian Revolution, and therefore of Marxism, was almost impossible to resist.[50] But what had greater relevance for Latin Americans were the events in their own region, where Marxism had practically no influence. Understandably, within this context there was much to debate. Especially for Cubans, where the contradictions of capitalism, neocolonialism, and mass mobilization were more stark than ever, these larger political issues were immediate and relevant.

For his part, Julio Antonio Mella characteristically drew radical conclusions from world events. The Russian Revolution, and Marxism, were the revolutionary expression of a new humanistic modernism. The First World War had exposed "the false work of civilization . . . a civilization barbarically industrialized by the bourgeoisie."[51] The revolutionary struggles in Russia, China, and India were bringing an end to this barbarous social order in the "old world." It was now the responsibility of Latin Americans to do the same for their continent. Cuba and Latin America, Mella believed, were reaching the stage where the utopian vision of José Martí and Simón Bolívar could be realized in the near future.[52] For Mella it was imperative that revolutionaries have the "faith to make utopia a reality of today."[53]

Mella made one of his clearest statements on the need for a truly national Cuban Marxism when the news of Lenin's death reached Cuba in early 1924. After discussing how the Russian Revolution was an important step in the progress of humanity, Mella went on to state that "we do not pretend to implement in our situation simplistic copies of other revolutions made by other peoples. On some points we do not understand some transformations; on other points our thinking is more advanced. . . . We do not expect that everyone hold to the same doctrine—this is not the most important thing at this moment. What is most important is that people act according to their own thinking and not because of what people have reasoned in far away places. We want people, not sheep."[54] Later that same year, in an article entitled "The New Liberators," Mella was more specific about the nature of the struggle: "The cause of the proletariat *is* the national cause. It is the only existing force with the capacity to struggle for the real triumph of our ideals at the present moment. . . . The cause of socialism is the cause of the times in Cuba, in Russia, in India, in the United States, and in China. The only obstacle is to know how to adapt it [socialism] to the given environment." [55]

It was the events surrounding the Mexican Revolution and the struggle against the dictatorship of Juan Vicente Gómez in Venezuela that helped bring this utopian vision down to earth. *Social,* the *Revista de Avance, Atuei,* and the journal *Venezuela Libre* devoted a great deal of attention to Mexican and Latin American events. A common theme was the idea that the Mexican Revolution symbolized a great unfolding historical drama of a people breaking the chains of colonial oppression. In contrast to the view from Washington, which saw the Mexican upheaval as subversive, anarchic, and little more than mass banditry, Cuban and Latin American journalists saw the Mexican people claiming their rightful place in the modern world.[56] Mexican workers and peasants were the driving force of the revolution, not the corrupt landed classes and capitalists. Spanish colonialism, followed by capitalist imperialism, had turned Mexico into a nation of primary producers: now it was the producers themselves who initiated "the great revolutionary experiment." It was true that the revolution had its failings, but at least they were Mexico's own failings. The Mexican Revolution filled all Latin America with the hope that utopia was not a pointless dream but something that could be created on earth through struggle and sacrifice.[57]

Dictatorship and repression in Venezuela generated the same intense feelings. A group of Venezuelan exiles living in Cuba, with the support of Cuban radical intellectuals and activists, founded the magazine *Venezuela Libre* in 1921. Both Mella and Martínez Villena worked on this journal. The purpose of *Venezuela Libre* was to combat the dictatorship of Juan Vicente Gómez.[58] The fight against Gómez was part of a worldwide struggle of the poor and the hungry from China, India, Africa, and Latin America to "escape from under the boot of the colonizer."[59] Europe was violent and decadent, and the United States, once the hope of humanity, "had sold its soul for money and riches." Both centers of colonial power backed the Gómez government: they, too, had blood on their hands. The only way to resist these "anaemic Old World societies" was to forge Latin American unity on the basis of social justice for the poor and against colonialism and racism.[60]

Cuba's place in the anti-imperialist mosaic was seen very much in the same light. Julio Antonio Mella's article, entitled "Where Is Cuba Going?" was written to address this issue. In the article Mella argued that Cuba was "at a crossroads in its history." Cubans were involved in a simultaneous struggle for social justice and against imperialism. But, Mella argued, imperialism cannot function without internal allies. In Cuba, General Machado played this role. Mella pointed out that nationalist movements almost always had two tendencies, one that tried to reach a compromise with the colonizer and another that more directly challenged imperialism. Machado represented the former, as did the main leaders of the Veterans' rebellion. Nationalism is, therefore, only one element in the national liberation struggle. Indeed, nationalism could accommodate itself to the overall interests of imperialism. It is worth quoting Mella at length on this issue:

> It is the nationalist movement and the workers movement which are able to raise the hopes of the entire nation. The first movement mobilizes the entire people with its demands. They are anxious to get the practical job done of getting rid of despotism, which might require violence. But the majority within the nationalist leadership maintains the idea that things should be done legally. They hope that the government will not 'place itself outside the law.' The real division within the nationalist movement is between those who want to defeat Machado through legal means and those who respond to violence with violence. Included in this last group are nationalist university students; the other important movement is the workers.[61]

Mella went on to outline what made the Latin American anti-imperialist struggle unique: "In our countries, more so than in Europe, the development of social classes and nations is determined by the violent penetration of imperialism. This meant that the periodic insurrections have not been just simple movements of *caudillos* but movements of the masses as well. The working classes are therefore compelled to participate in these struggles even though they know it is possible that at later stages the Moncadas [the Nicaraguan president] or the Chang Kai Sheks [the Chinese nationalist leader] might emerge. This is not important. Mexico is an example of what can be achieved by the masses."[62]

Mella wanted to highlight Cuba's own history of anticolonialist insurrections, including the internal contradictions of its own nationalist experience. Every president of Cuba since 1901 claimed political legitimacy from his real or imagined role in the independence wars, yet each one and together all had overseen the increasing imperialist domination of Cuba. The veteran *caudillos* of the independence wars had likewise encouraged nationalist agitation in 1923–24, only to turn their backs on the masses. Machado, Mella said, was no exception: he, too, was a veteran of 1895; he, too, claimed to be a nationalist; and still he was a servant of U.S. imperialism. If imperialism continued to dominate Cuba, Mella asked, then what future was there for Cuba? "There is only one answer possible: to move in the direction of becoming a formal colony of the United States . . . *toward the destruction of all the constituent elements of national identity.*"[63]

Mella's attempt to link political struggle with national identity runs parallel to his contemporaries Antonio Gramsci and José Carlos Mariátegui. Whether it is Mella's call to "make utopia the reality of today," or Gramsci's argument for the "creation of a concrete fantasy which acts on a dispersed and shattered people to arouse and organize its collective will," the point is that for socialism to have meaning for the oppressed it must bring utopia to earth through national liberation.[64] Mariátegui, in an article published in *Social* in 1928, elaborated on the difference between the reactionary utopianism of positivists such as Vasconcelos and the new form of revolutionary utopianism: "Our destiny is more to struggle than it is to contemplate. This might be the great limitation of the times we live in, but we do not have time to discuss it. . . . [The utopia of Vasconcelos] is further away than our utopia. For him, 'pessimism in reality, optimism in the ideal.' It should be, 'pessimism in reality, optimism in action.' . . . It is not enough to condemn reality, we have to change it. This might oblige us to reduce our ideal, but it shows us how to realize it."[65]

Mella would certainly have agreed. He would have also concurred with another one of Mariátegui's maxims: "I struggle, therefore I exist."[66] Mella's Marxism was clearly within the tradition of his Italian and Peruvian contemporaries. Unlike Mariátegui and Gramsci, however, Mella did not have the opportunity to carry out a full polemic with the Comintern about the Cuban and Latin American revolutionary process; but, had he lived, there is no reason to believe that he would not have done so. As with Mariátegui's early death in Peru and Gramsci's death in prison, Mella's untimely death robbed the Cuban Marxist movement of its best and most independent "organic intellectual."

We saw earlier that Mella had helped found the Communist Party of Cuba and that Martínez Villena joined the party in 1927. Between 1925 and 1930, however, the Communist Party remained a small sect, isolated from the working class and from rural Cuba.[67] The party was founded at a low point of the social and class struggles in Cuba: the years from 1925 to 1929, as Mella pointed out, were not propitious for revolutionary struggle. At its founding congress the party claimed to have some eighty members in all, with only ten to thirteen delegates present then.[68] Prior to 1931, the party had no significant impact on Cuban politics. Both the Communist Party and the National Confederation of Cuban Workers (CNOC), also founded in 1925, experienced considerable internal conflicts. To add to the party's isolation, the Comintern's decision in 1928 to reject any alliances with reformist or noncommunist groups encouraged loyal party followers to turn their isolation into a virtue. Following the political line of the Comintern, the party entered an ultra-leftist phase where they denied any difference between what theoreticians called "bourgeois democracy" and "fascism." The choice was between socialism or fascism, with no middle ground. This rigid political dichotomy would isolate the party from the majority of radical activists and skew its analysis of Cuban social and political reality. As we will see in the next chapters, this sectarian policy would have disastrous implications for the party and for Cuban politics generally.

As for the few communists within CNOC, their early years in the federation involved conflicts with apolitical craft unions or with anarchists.[69] General Machado had assured the United States that Cuba was a safe place to invest, and that labor unrest would be dealt with by his government in a swift and decisive matter. And indeed it was: strikes by sugar and textile workers were repressed by the government, with union organizers arrested and the unions outlawed. The publications of the Havana Federation of Labor (FOH) were banned, and the short-lived Sindicato de la Industria Fabril was forced underground. At the same time, Machado worked with the American Embassy and with the American Federation of Labor to organize a progovernment union, La Federación Cubana de Trabajo.[70] The police and the army broke strikes, expelled workers who occupied factories, and protected sugar mills from attacks by striking workers. Machado's agents assassinated the popular and charismatic CNOC anarchist leader, Alfredo López.[71] These measures against organized labor and the students were successful in the short term. With little money, a weak and scattered workforce, and constant government surveillance and repression, workers and students were on the defensive. To be sure, the Communist Party and CNOC would play a significant role in future struggles. After the collapse of the world trading system in 1929 and the consequent economic and political crisis in Cuba, these and other radical organizations would become major players in Cuban politics.

What was immediately significant about the years 1924 to 1929 was that the level of debate and analysis about Cuba's colonial condition was raised to new levels. While it is true that most of the writing and discussions in the journals and meetings were carried on in isolation from the day-to-day struggles of the *clases populares,* these debates shaped the thinking of a generation of radical and reformist activists and leaders. The often vague, utopian, but powerful ideas and sentiments that were articulated in the 1920s provided a broad conceptual framework for Cuban nationalism in the 1930s and 1940s. The project of nation building—and that is what the radicals of the 1920s saw themselves as doing—involves, first, acts of imagining a national community, and second, acts of political struggle to make these images real.[72] Nationalism, as one scholar on the subject points out, should be viewed as "a broad vision for organizing society, a project for collective identity based on the premise of citizenship—available to all, with individual membership beginning from the assumption of legal equality." Nationalism is therefore "a series of competing discourses in constant formation and negotiation."[73] In other words, there is no one nationalism, there are only nationalisms.[74] In Cuba during the 1920s, the wide-ranging discussions about Cuba's colonial condition generated competing visions of what kind of imagined community Cuba should be. As we have seen, these often reified musings were filtered through a kaleidoscope of neopositivist, populist, Marxist, utopian, and anarchist ideas. As we will see in the next chapter, however, Cubans involved in these debates would soon be confronted with a social and economic crisis that would make the upheaval of 1920–24 pale in comparison.

CHAPTER THREE

The Crisis of the Plattist State, 1927-1932

W hen General Gerardo Machado assumed power in May 1925, Cuba appeared to be on the path to political and economic recovery. The 1925 elections were relatively honest. Machado took advantage of the nationalist upsurge of the early 1920s. He promised to lead Cuba into an era of modern capitalist economic development. Indeed, in contrast to the situation prior to 1924, Machado's election seemed to indicate that a new era of peaceful political competition was in store for Cuba. Machado's first two years in power seemed to confirm that expectation. Most of the demands of the Veterans' and Patriots' Movement were met. The new president promised to protect the small sugar growers (*colonos*), institute protective tariffs for Cuba's light industry, build public works and improve the urban environment, and regulate the sugar industry by setting production quotas to control prices. Machado stated that he would diversify agriculture. He declared that his government would not take out any new foreign loans. Finally, he made the commitment to serve as president for only one term of four years.[1]

In 1926 there was no serious opposition to Machado. So united was elite political sentiment behind the new president that by the fall of that year the political parties of the elite—the Conservative, Popular, and Machado's own Liberal Party—established an arrangement known as *cooperativismo* to jointly support Machado until the next elections.[2] With no viable opposition to challenge him, and with the firm belief that he had more to accomplish, Machado viewed the upcoming 1928 presidential election as an inconvenience. Yet Machado himself had promised he would serve only one term. In his presidential campaign he had condemned reelectionism as the source of Cuba's political turmoil. Machado's solution to this problem was to amend the Constitution of the Republic, stipulating that he could rule until 1934. This move antagonized those members of the political class who felt that reelection violated the redistributive nature of Cuban elite politics. The *machadista* consensus quickly fell apart. There was no doubt that Machado would be reelected, but after 1928 his power would increasingly depend upon bribery, corruption, and repression. For all but his most loyal supporters, Machado's reelection meant four more years of exclusion from access to state revenues and offices.

Initially, opposition to Machado's extension of powers came from within the oligarchy. As early as 1927, some prominent politicians broke with Machado to form the Unión Nacionalista (UN), a loose coalition of anti-reelection forces.[3] Traditional politicians from both the Liberal and Conservative Parties formed the UN around the demands for Machado's resignation and a rejection of his extension of term. Unión Nacionalista leaders such as Carlos Mendieta, Mario Menocal, Carlos de la Torriente, and Roberto Méndez Peñate were skilled practitioners at Plattist politics. Accepting the principle that the United States determined the legitimacy of any given Cuban government, they spent considerable effort trying to convince American officials that the United States should withdraw support from Machado. With the exception of Menocal, all the UN leaders participated in the Veterans' and Patriots' Movement.

The UN claimed that Machado's authoritarian tendencies were a threat to the established political order, and that if the United States wanted to prevent more aggressive intervention in Cuban affairs at a later date, then Machado should be removed as soon as possible.[4] Carlos Mendieta and Mario Menocal, the two principal UN leaders, had maintained contacts with the American embassy since 1927, and though their preference was to have Machado pushed out by the Americans, they were always willing to use the old tactics of mobilizing their supporters to provoke American intervention. In an editorial about Machado's visit to Washington in May 1927, the UN made its position on the Platt Amendment clear:

> We must say that if among the matters which prompted General Machado to go north was the idea of obtaining abolition of the Platt Amendment, we must state that such an intention was not convenient and the moment untimely . . . because Cuba is going through an acute crisis, its wealth destroyed, its commerce ruined, faith in its institutions lost, and political tyranny prevailing, it is to be doubted that the government of the American nation is going to suppress the Amend-

ment under these circumstances, when the Amendment is held as the best guarantee of the large American capitals invested here.[5]

The Unión Nacionalista was acting in accordance with the rules of the Plattist state: they were opposed to Machado, but not to the neocolonial state.

American support for Machado, however, was as strong as ever. The U.S. ambassador, Harry F. Guggenheim, felt that Machado was the best man to defend United States' interests on the island. Guggenheim met with Machado to encourage him to compromise with the Unión Nacionalista; at the same time the U.S. ambassador did not want to press Machado too hard for fear of embarrassing and undermining his authority.[6] Echoing these sentiments, the British embassy in Havana reported to the Foreign Office that "the President's rule in Cuba assumes everyday more and more the role of a dictatorship," but the opposition was too weak to present a viable alternative. The embassy dispatch continued that Machado still enjoyed the firm support of the U.S. embassy and the American Chamber of Commerce in Havana because he protected American (and British) property. The British concluded that while Machado's dictatorial measures were lamentable, "the Machado Government is better than anything the country has known before."[7] Machado had little to fear, domestically or internationally.

Still, as early as 1926 the university had once again become the focus of opposition activity. Not only were students concerned about Machado's extension of term, but in November of that year Machado abolished the body established by Zayas to oversee educational reform. He then appointed a close friend as rector of the university, thus returning to the personalistic practices of the pre-1923 period.[8] On October 14 1927, students tore down a sign with Machado's name on it, and as a result several students were expelled from the university for between one to fifteen years. For those seeking to reform the system, the situation was bleak.

Machado could act with impunity and the only response was passivity and submissiveness. An editorial in the UN newspaper noted that while a few idealistic students maintained a rebellious spirit, "the nation, culture, science and art are held prisoner within the university ivory tower."[9] Just over a week later, the recently formed Directorio Estudiantil Universitario (DEU) issued a manifesto that reflected the same anger and frustration: "You [Machado] accuse us of being political, Bolsheviks, impulsive, immature, etc. If to oppose the dictatorship is to be a Bolshevik, then we are Bolsheviks. If by opposing the prolongation of powers we are being impulsive, then we are impulsive. And, if we are being immature by demanding a truly sovereign and free republic, then, we are immature." [10] Machado closed the university during the Pan American Conference in 1928, and when it was reopened in April of that year soldiers were stationed throughout the campus. Protests continued throughout 1928, but there was little antigovernment agitation outside the university. Little had changed by 1929. On November 27 students from the faculties of medicine, dentistry, law, pharmacy, science, and litera- ture held a demonstration and issued a manifesto against Machado's repres- sive measures and the extension of his term. The manifesto stated, "We are protesting alone, there are no workers or opposition politicians with us." [11]

This downturn in radical struggle, however, proved to be the calm be- fore the storm. Two things happened to bring about a change in the political atmosphere. First, from 1929 to 1934 an economic crisis drove hundreds of thousands of Cubans to the point of ruin and starvation. Second, this eco- nomic crisis fueled a variety of insurrectionary movements across the island. From 1929 on, Cuba was to enter a prolonged crisis of oligarchic rule. The old patterns of *caudillista* and *cacique* social control were now under intense pres- sure of mass mobilization from the *clases populares* and growing numbers of middle-class youth. To be sure, old patterns of social control and resistance did not end quickly. As we will see, it would take years before the forces of the "old Cuba" would give way to new ways of ruling the country, and, even then, some *caudillos* and *caciques* showed remarkable flexibility in the face of the emergence of modern state politics. But this is to anticipate: in the late 1920s and early 1930s the political problem for the Cuban political class was centered on the question of how to respond to a growing and increasingly politically conscious population. There was nothing in their political history or experience to help guide them through the coming social and economic turmoil.

The Economic Crisis, 1929–1932

The world depression of 1929 hit Cuba hard. Sugar production, the measure of the Cuban economy, dropped a full 60 percent between 1929 and 1933.[12] After thirty years the Cuban sugar boom came to an end. Cuban sugar pro- duction had, since the early twentieth century, been increasingly exposed to the danger of the closure of the U.S. market. American beet sugar producers had long opposed the entrance of low-priced Cuban sugar on the U.S. mar- ket, and with the onslaught of the depression, they won their battle. The Hawley-Smoot Tariff of 1930 raised the duty on Cuba sugar to two cents per pound. Cuban sugar producers saw the price of their product fall to less than half the price received by American producers.[13] The Cuban share of the U.S. sugar market dropped from 49.4 percent in 1930 to 25.3 percent in 1933.[14] In 1924, total Cuban exports to the United States were valued at $434 million; by 1932 they stood at $80 million. Imports from the United States showed a similar decline during the same period with a drop from $290 million to $51.2 million. Cuban government revenues fell from around $90 million in 1928 to $47 million in 1931–32. By the end of the fiscal year of June 30, 1933, the Cuban government owed its employees $9 million in back wages, which amounted to one-fifth of the national budget.[15] Cuba's second major export, tobacco, experienced a similar decline: between 1929 and 1933 the export value of leaf tobacco fell 68 percent.[16] The tobacco industry had been in decline well before the depression, a decline precipitated by the transfer of cigar factories to the United States, the elimination of tobacco labor due to new technology, and the growing popularity of cigarettes over cigars. The tobacco industry, as one report phrased it in 1929, "was in a state of complete decay and had an uncertain future."[17]

In response to this crisis, Cuban sugar growers attempted to reduce sugar production to counter the drop in prices. Yet world sugar production remained high and prices continued to fall despite the efforts of Cuban producers. In the spring of 1931, Cuba, along with six other nations, signed the Chadbourne Plan, an initiative intended to coordinate the restriction of world sugar production.[18] Cuba agreed to reduce its output by 36.5 percent, Java agreed to a 10.42 percent reduction, and the European beet-sugar producers accepted 15 percent.[19] Despite these measures, the price of sugar fell by 60 percent: in 1925 the price was 2.25 cents a pound; in 1929 it was 1.72 cents. In 1933 sugar prices bottomed out at 0.97 cents.[20]

The social consequences of the agreement to restrict sugar production proved disastrous, especially for labor and small-scale sugar growers. In the first place, the Chadbourne Plan was impossible to enforce. Larger producers, who could absorb the cut in production, supported the plan. But many indebted *colonos* could not survive a cut in production. Most *colonos* rented their land from large milling companies, and they paid this rent either in the form of a percentage of their crop, in cash, or in some combination of the two. The loss of revenue from the restriction meant that many *colonos* could not pay rents and their accumulated debts; nor could they pay their laborers.[21] In August 1927, thirty-two *colonos* from Camagüey wrote to the Eastern Cuba Sugar Corporation, a subsidiary of Cuba Cane Corporation, complaining that the corporation would not reduce its rents, despite the loss of revenue from the crop restriction. "With the present system followed by the Company," the *colonos* argued, "there is only one thing for the *colono* to do: to keep away from the *fincas,* contrary to his will, working at something else that will permit him to live until better times and higher prices arrive."[22]

Earlier in 1927, Gerard Smith, the Havana-based executive vice president of the Cuba Cane Corporation, wrote to his New York office about the uncertainty of when the harvest would begin. Smith was concerned about the reaction of *hacendados* to the crop restriction, not to mention the reaction of the workers to the ensuing hardships. After noting that the *zafra* would probably begin on January 1, 1928, Smith explained, "I talked with Dr. Viriato Gutiérrez [Machado's secretary] last night and while he would not say that it had been positively determined by the president that the crop would begin on any fixed date, he did state that the President would positively not change his decree, but that if the hacendados unanimously decided that they did not want to start grinding until the 15 [January] he would not oppose or put any obstacles on the way of their so doing."[23] Smith informed New York that enforcing the restriction was difficult because "if one dissenting *hacendado* in the east starts cutting cane on January 1 that will compel his neighbors to do the same thing in order to preserve the *colono* organization." Smith was referring to the attempt by *colonos* to maintain a united front in the face of the crop restriction. The nature and character of *colono* production varied widely from region to region. While some growers were wealthy, others were constantly on the verge of bankruptcy; still others were dependent on one milling company to purchase their cane, while their neighbors might have more balanced arrangements with several millers. These variations mattered a great deal under normal conditions, but when the restrictions were imposed on growers, they could mean the difference between economic survival or being forced off the land. But if the situation was bad for *colonos,* the situation for workers was disastrous. Smith concluded his letter by observing that "there is an intense popular opposition on the part of the local unions and the field workmen to a delay in the beginning of the crop and this opposition is bound to receive careful consideration by President Machado, because actual hunger among the working classes is involved in the problem."[24]

And "actual hunger" there was. The cut in sugar production had a devastating impact on rural and urban Cubans alike. Nearly one-quarter of the Cuban population found themselves without work.[25] Factories and businesses closed. There was a 50 percent reduction in state pensions, and 15 percent of state employees lost their jobs. On average, the wages of urban employees fell by 50 percent.[26] In the countryside the wages of rural workers dropped as much as 75 percent, with some wages reaching as low as ten cents per day during the harvest and two cents per day during the dead season.[27] Many workers were paid in *vales,* or chits, which, in lieu of wages, they could cash at the plantation store.[28] Thousands of workers survived on yuca, malanga, potatoes, and corn; meat, fruit, and vegetables were far too expensive for most rural workers.[29] As a consequence of this generalized crisis, urban-rural migration went both ways: desperate and unemployed workers from the cities and towns returned to the country, hoping at least to grow enough food to survive; at the same time sugar plantation workers and coffee *finca* laborers moved to the city in the hope of finding work.[30]

The popular reaction to this economic crisis was at first both dramatic and ill defined. Throughout 1930 and 1931, both British and U.S. diplomats tried to interpret the events as best they could. One aspect of the crisis that both diplomatic missions noted was the truly national character of the crisis. Machado, they reasoned, was still worthy of their support, but it was becoming clear to observers of the Cuban scene that the country was facing a new and more volatile political situation than ever before. In the spring of 1930 one British diplomat declared that "there has been a great change in the political situation" and that "Cuba, as I see it today, is a very different place from what I have known it to be for the past seven years." Unrest was general throughout the country, and the cause was clearly economic. "In many parts of the country people are on the verge of starvation." Work was hard to find, money was scarce, trade was bad, and opposition to the government was growing.[31] In December 1931, Sir John Broderick, the British ambassador, wrote that "there is hardly a single British or American business concern in Cuba which would desire to see Machado superseded. Cuban business firms, almost without exception, are at the end of their resources. If any private Cuban fortunes remain still unexausted [*sic*] after the heavy losses of recent times, they are in the hands of the supporters of the present regime."[32] In a similar tone the U.S. assistant secretary of state observed that "the situation is very difficult. . . . The people in general are opposed to Machado but will not take any active measures against him. The upper classes are not only opposed to Machado, but they are very bitter against him and all the active opposition comes from the better elements of the Republic. This makes the situation very serious. The root of the whole matter is economic. Cuba has gone from great riches to poverty. . . . A great many men who had been very wealthy before are now very poor."[33]

What concerned the Americans and the British, therefore, was not simply the grave condition of the sugar economy and Machado's growing political isolation. They were increasingly alarmed by what the British ambassador referred to as the "nonpolitical elements" entering the political arena. By "nonpolitical elements" the ambassador meant students, professors, urban and rural workers, lower-rank soldiers, and professionals, groups which had traditionally been outside the political process.[34] As was noted in the previous chapter, in the late 1920s these "nonpolitical elements" were isolated within the small world of the university or were easily controlled through the patronage networks of *caudillos* and *caciques* loyal to the Plattist state. Traditional political mechanisms of social control, however, had never faced a crisis of this magnitude.

The diplomatic correspondence often gives the impression that if the problem was simply Machado's intransigence, then a solution acceptable to American, British, and Cuban elite interests could be found.[35] Throughout 1931 American ambassador Guggenheim did not view the mounting rural protests as "political," though he did perceive that there was a "certain amount of communist activity" and that discontent about the economic situation was becoming increasingly politicized. The ambassador expressed concern about the widespread cane field burnings and that clashes between workers and bosses occurred in every province. Guggenheim had invested a lot of energy supporting Machado, but in January 1931 he had to admit "that nearly everyone was opposed to the government except those being paid by it," and in Havana there was "serious general political unrest." The U.S. ambassador pondered how Machado could regain the support of the elite without being embarrassed or losing authority.[36] The Americans and British were stuck with Machado. "Any sign of weakness on Machado's part," wrote the U.S. assistant secretary of state, "would make the situation much worse not only by encouraging the opposition but by actually increasing its numbers."[37] As it happened, the continuing economic and political unrest did weaken Machado, and the opposition was strengthened as a result.

The Middle-Class Opposition, 1930–1932

The political and economic crises of 1927–30 generated a confrontation between Machado, who came to symbolize the evils of the Plattist state, and the rest of the population. We saw in the previous chapter how in the 1920s a fragmented and small group of radicals began to construct equally fragmented images of the Cuban people as an imagined community. These images of the people and the nation, however, were not yet popular or national. Rather, the multiple discourses of Cuban middle-class nationalists represented the equally diverse realities of middle-class life. Caught between the suffocating domination of oligarchic paternalism on the one side and the *clases populares* on the other, the small and vulnerable middle classes felt very insecure within the shifting fortunes of export capitalism. For many lower-middle-class Cubans, the threat of "descending" into the ranks of the popular classes was very real, especially after 1929. Lower-level state and private sector employees, clerks and office workers, shopkeepers and traders, modest landlords, teachers and professors, journalists, printers, junior military officers, and small-scale landowners and tenant farmers comprised a growing but socially amorphous group who typically aspired to be economically secure, *culto* ("cultured"), and *gente decente.* Consequently the middle classes looked to both the state and to "culture" as the source of their security and identity. The state, and specifically the modern state, was increasingly seen as a buffer against the volatile forces of unrestrained capitalism. At the same time, they valued education, technical and artistic ability, and reading and writing as signs of being "civilized," as opposed to the "uncultured" *clases populares* and the clientistic and corrupt practices of the oligarchy. This reification of the modern state and of "culture" tended to make the middle classes see themselves as the best representatives of national culture and modern economic development.[38]

The most important group in the late 1920s which articulated middle-class concerns was the Directorio Estudiantil Universitario, which was created in 1927. Justo Carrillo, a leader of the DEU, has portrayed the insurgent sentiment during the late *machadato* as intense but ideologically limited. The Directorio was a small group of articulate middle-class students. As we will see in the next chapter, the DEU as an organization would have a limited impact on the mass mobilizations of the early 1930s. But the Directorio did serve as a focal point of debate about Cuba's political economy and how to remedy the nation's problems. Some of Cuba's most important politicians of the 1940s and 1950s had their political baptism in the DEU. Antonio Guiteras, Raúl Roa García, Aureliano Sánchez Arango, Eduardo Chibás, Carlos Prío Socarrás, Rubén León García, and Tony Varona received their formative political experiences in the DEU. Guiteras, Roa, and Sánchez Arango eventually became leaders of the radical left, while the others were to found the reformist and populist Partido Revolucionario Cubano (Auténtico) (PRC-A) in 1934. Carlos Prío Socarrás would become president of Cuba from 1948 to 1952. A popular university professor, Ramón Grau San Martín, played an important role in bringing these students together to discuss and plan actions against Machado's regime. With the exception of Roa and Chibás, these figures were associated with the youth section of the Unión Nacionalista, until at least 1930. Most of the DEU leaders studied law, medicine, pharmacy, or literature at the University of Havana. They all came from middle-class families and all were born between 1900 and 1912.[39] By the late 1920s, these young men were ready to enter the university. Unlike most Cubans, they had the advantage of an education, but, like most people, their prospects for employment were bleak.

Of course the political response of the middle classes to the crisis of oligarchic capitalism was as varied as their social composition. As we saw above, while some sought alliances with disaffected members of the oligarchy, others drew the conclusion that a more radical break with the past was necessary. Students came to play an important role in social protest because it was at the university and other schools where middle-class and upper-class students would meet and discuss the issues of the day. Young men like Eduardo Chibás, for example, might have come from very affluent families, but most of their fellow students had more modest backgrounds. For many of these well-off young people, their conviction that a "new Cuba" was something worth fighting for meant that they were willing to sacrifice a comfortable career in business for the uncertainty of political struggle.[40] Some students and other radicals even went so far as to consider the *classes populares*—"the people"—as possible allies or at least as a social force that needed to be mobilized against the dominant classes. But making a radical break with the past is one thing and providing a viable alternative for the future is quite another.

Carrillo thought that the DEU lacked a "rigorous ideological analysis and true determination of the concrete historic position." He went on to say that

national desires are deep and extensively felt, the vibrations filter through the most diverse and unexpected means of expression. We were aware of it while riding the bus, in the café, in one's usual social group, while waiting in the doctor's or dentist's office, while reading a magazine or a newspaper, while waiting at the barbershop, everywhere the same expressions and clamor were heard. In those times, the distinctions of leader, director, charismatic messenger, and man of the masses were lost. Everyone wanted the same thing, and the very atmosphere carried the message: "Machado's got to be toppled! By whatever means. *No matter who comes afterwards!*"[41]

Another participant in the struggles of the late 1920s and early 1930s, Enrique Fernández, characterized the anti-Machado movement as "a great emotional and instinctive force. The Cuban revolution did not have any previous doctrinal preparation. [The revolution] surged into the streets, with instinct and sentiment. Its first impulse was a negation. It did not propose anything; it condemned the present; it refused to make any compromise with all visible reality."[42] Enrique de la Osa, Cuba's leading Aprista thinker and one of the country's prominent journalists, painted a similar picture: "The central objective that drove us was to bring down the regime. . . . Machado is the hangman of the Cuban people. . . . The environment is frankly and openly war-like. People are showing solidarity with revolutionary terrorism—with assassinations, with bombings, and with kidnapping; people are joining the workers' strikes and the street marches, throwing themselves at the state of siege with one great voice: 'Down with Machado!' "[43]

Jorge Mañach, a vigorous opponent of Machado and one of Cuba's leading intellectuals of the twentieth century, noted that after a prolonged period of repression, "public opinion struggled for expression in the University, in the press, and even in Congress." He went on to say:

> Beginning with complaints of merely academic character, the students of the University of Havana ended with a declaration of war against Machado himself and against the whole political system which he represented. . . . The opposition to Machado promptly took on unanimity— muffled but indisputable. For the first time, all classes in the country were united in resistance. [D]espotism and the economic crisis were the two conditions which led the Cuban people to become conscious of the Republic's fundamental evils, to consider the inadequacy of their political institutions, and to recognize the economic root of their problems and the factors both internal and external limiting their civic vitality, and to dispose themselves finally to assert their will against all these obstacles.[44]

Finally, it is worth quoting the words of another prominent enemy of the Machado regime, Fernando Ortiz:

> When the fight was going on against the *machadonia*, the supporters of that regime said that the revolution had no program. But this was not the problem with the opposition against the tyranny: the opposition had too many programs. It is precisely because to understand the great majority of the inhabitants of Cuba that it could not formulate a single and broad program of all the oppositionists, from the most reactionary elements who only wanted the *machadato* without Machado,

to the most advanced who hoped for the communist dawn that would bring a complete end to those dark times. Various revolutions have been interwoven with the mixture of rebellious sentiments: political, ethical, social, etc. Yet they still ask for one program. And there was a single program—a minimum program, where it was possible to bring together all the opposition forces.[45]

To be a "radical" was to have courage and audacity in the face of state repression. It was, above all, the *immorality and arbitrariness* of the oligarchic state that shocked and mobilized people. Historically, the *clases populares* could be managed because they were too socially amorphous to sustain mass mobilization for any length of time. After 1929 the economic crisis and Machado's repressive regime united Cubans as never before. A manichean division between "the people" and Machado developed. Yet unlike the rather abstract discussions about "the people" in the mid-1920s, the *clases populares* were not just an object of debate; now, more than in any time since the war of 1895–98, they were becoming the agents of social change. Students, communists, trade unionists, and independent radicals were faced with a situation where not only did they have to fight against Machado, but they were also thrown into the cauldron of mass politics with little or no preparation or prior experience.

As usual, the atmosphere at the university was especially tense. The military had occupied the university and students were being expelled for anti-government activity. There were frequent violent clashes between the students and the police. In February the students issued two manifestos which presented their views on the growing national crisis. In the first manifesto they demanded the reinstatement of expelled students and called for university autonomy from the state. Their document linked these issues to earlier student protests of 1922–23 and 1927. Solidarity with other student struggles in Mexico and in Spain was proclaimed. Cuban students saw themselves as part of a worldwide movement for social change. They were Cuba's new generation, and they were filled with a new and higher sense of morality than the earlier generation, which, they argued, had sold Cuba to foreigners since 1898.[46]

The second student manifesto contained more explicit criticisms of the political situation. Cuba, the manifesto stated, was in a shameful condition. The Machado regime was presenting a façade to the world: while the president continued to finance public works and sponsor lavish international congresses, Cuba was in a state of national decay. Students had little hope for employment. Peasants were losing their land, and the importation of Haitian and Jamaican workers by foreign-owned sugar companies—described as "the new slave trade"—was undermining any sense of a national economy.[47]

On April 19, 1930, the Unión Nacionalista, frustrated by its inability to weaken Machado and by the failure of the United States to back them, called a demonstration to condemn the unconstitutional government and the waste of government funds on public works. Some 200,000 people attended the rally. Students, like many others, used the occasion to vent their hostility toward Machado. While the event itself was peaceful, the social tension in the capital was palatable.[48] The leadership of the UN was caught in a bind. On the one hand, the pressure to oust Machado by any means necessary was mounting; on the other hand, the organization was still hoping that the Americans, not the Cuban people, would push Machado out. In addition, anti-American feeling was growing precisely because of continued U.S. support for Machado, so the persistent efforts of the UN to obtain American backing were criticized by the younger generation. Future DEU and PRC-A leaders Carlos Prío Socarrás, Rubén León, and Tony Varona were members of the UN youth wing at the university, and though they did not formally break with the UN, (membership in the UN was not a formal matter, at any rate) their political energies went into the DEU from that time on.[49]

With the economic crisis in full force and Machado's repression increasing, on September 30 the students organized a protest of their own. Only 80 to 100 students attended the rally, but the results of the march proved dramatic. A clash occurred between the police and the young marchers, and one of the student leaders, Rafael Trejo González, was shot and killed.[50] From then on, political tension escalated. Students began to arm themselves both for self-defense and to attack the police and Machado's supporters. They carried pistols or homemade fire bombs; they attacked known *machadista* officials in the street and bombed the homes of army and police officers.[51] Students demanded punishment for the people responsible for Trejo's death; the resignation of the secretary of education, Dr. Averhoff; the resignation of the rector of the University of Havana; an end to the military occupation of all educational centers; the right to organize a national federation of students; the right of the students to participate in the governing bodies of all educational institutions; reinstatement of the students expelled in the protests of 1927; and absolute autonomy for the university.

On November 16 thirteen newspapers and magazines signed a "Manifesto of the National Press," which condemned repression generally and government attacks on the press in particular. The manifesto noted that other sectors of the population had come out in support of the students: professional associations, opposition politicians hitherto hostile to public protests, and the press, which all had condemned Machado's repression. Freedom of assembly and the right to organize were denied, and the right of the press to report on political events was severely restricted.[52]

The student manifestos from 1927–32 convey a sense of profound indignation and shame about the economic and moral condition of the country. On September 30, 1930, the same day as the fateful student march, the DEU issued another statement proclaimed that "Cuba is living through the most tragic moments of its not so brilliant republican history. . . . The *barbarocracia* prevailing since 1925, has, in effect, drained and impoverished the country to an impossible degree, to the point of the margin of civilization. . . . At this critical moment in our history, silence is complicity. 'To calmly observe a crime is to commit it.' Today . . . we are prepared to redefine the word 'sacrifice.' . . . Our central objective is to assist with all our force the fall of the regime. Machado is our objective. Machado has made a mockery, day after day, of Martí's idea that the first law of the republic should be respect for human dignity."[53] By October, demands of an academic nature, such as university autonomy, modern education, and the reinstatement of expelled students, gave way to explicit and openly political demands. The students at the University of Havana now refused to attend classes. On October 27 the *Diario de la Marina*, the most conservative newspaper of the Cuban elite, published a DEU statement which proclaimed that it was not the students who had invaded the political arena; rather, the national crisis had obliged students to take a political stand in the name of the entire nation.[54] State violence, the DEU argued, compelled students to take the lead in fighting for national liberties and rights. The students had clearly raised the political stakes. On July 1, 1931, Machado closed the university, the high schools, and the normal schools throughout the country. The Supreme Court declared this action unconstitutional, but the schools remained closed. One year later, in July 1932, the students refused to return to their classes until Machado stepped down.[55]

Clearly, events were pushing the DEU in an unforeseen direction. Whether they liked it or not, the young student leaders were assuming the role of leaders in a national struggle against the Plattist state. While the leadership of the UN waited for the Americans to undermine Machado, the students felt that the Cuban people should oust the dictator. On October 29, 1930, the DEU released a "Manifesto Programme." The program demanded university reform in order to create new and responsible citizens for a modern society. This new education, in turn, would effect a "deep social transformation that the present conditions in Cuba demand." The national struggle for reform, the document stated, was led by Cuban students, who, like other students elsewhere in Latin America, are now obliged to participate in political struggles. "From today onward," the document stated, "we will create a new politics, that, to merit this label, will be very far from the low-down-wheeler-dealers of our current electoral system." The document included the now common demands for the right to free speech and expression, freedom of movement, and the right to assemble and organize.It also demanded that police officers who broke the law be brought to justice and that corrupt and incompetent professors be dismissed.[56]

As events forced students to use increasingly more radical tactics and rhetoric in the fight against Machado, new political contradictions surfaced. In 1930 students knew what and who they were against—the immoral and corrupt *machadato;* but, what was the alternative? As indicated in the quotations above, the intensity of the struggle encouraged activists to concentrate on the immediate objective of toppling Machado, with little or no thought as to what might come after. But as the diffuse radical groups increasingly felt the political responsibility to lead "the nation" and "the people," they were forced to articulate what their vision of a post-Machado government might look like.

For the young men and women of the DEU, their ideological models came both from within Cuba and from abroad, especially from the United States. In a recent memoir, DEU leader Justo Carrillo listed some of the influential sources of DEU politics. Hispanic positivism and American liberalism were the main intellectual influences on DEU leaders. Carrillo made particular mention of José Miró Argenter's *Crónica de la guerra,* a multivolume memoir of Cuba's war for independence, which included new information on national heroes such as Antonio Maceo and Máximo Gómez. Students were avid readers of the main magazines of the period, especially *Social, Carteles, Revista de Avance,* and *Cuba Contemporánea.* Other works mentioned by Carrillo were José Ingeniernos's *El hombre mediocre,* Ramiro Guerra y Sánchez, *Sugar and Society in the Caribbean,* the American writer Leyland Jenks's *Our Cuban Colony,* Margret Alexander March on *Our Bankers in Bolivia,* Melvin Knight's *Yankees in Santo Domingo,* and the Spanish socialist Luis Araquistaín's *La agonía antillana.* All of these writers emphasized the great social injustices brought to Cuba and Latin America by colonialism, and they provided powerful evidence against the evils of unbridled oligarchic capitalism in the Americas. Then, of course, there were the writings of Cuba's national hero, José Martí. Yet even Martí's works were not as common as they would become a decade later: before 1930 Martí's voluminous writings were still being collected by scholars, and it was the *myth* of Martí and his epic struggle against the Spanish colonialists that inspired people more than their actual knowledge of his *ideario*.[57] In other words, the political ideas of DEU leaders could be broadly described as "liberal" in the sense that they combined a deeply nationalistic sentiment with such notions as the belief in civil liberties, an independent judiciary, individual rights and civic responsibilities, the right to private property, political pluralism, the sovereignty of the people, and a modern state that represented the entire nation and not just a small oligarchy with their foreign collaborators.

Yet advocating such ideas within the context of an increasingly repressive oligarchic system certainly was radical. Moreover, the political and economic crisis was such that the Cuban oligarchy could not respond to rebellions as it had with the Veterans' and Patriots' rebellion in 1923–24. As the Plattist order increasingly came under siege, the political atmosphere changed: Cubans sensed that the country was on the brink of social revolution, though what kind of revolution was impossible to say. A combination of three things occurred to transform the political crisis of the oligarchic state into a revolutionary situation. First, in the summer of 1931, the moderate opposition leaders of the Unión Nacionalista lost political credibility with the anti-Machado forces. Confrontation increasingly replaced negotiation and the UN proved unable to adapt to this change. Second, the self-proclaimed "vanguards" of the radical left, represented by the Communist Party and a dissident group of DEU members calling themselves the Ala Izquierda Estudiantil (Student Left Wing), became, for the first time, significant forces in the opposition movement. Third, the social and class struggles in the countryside were growing in intensity, as were the attempts by militants to give political shape to these struggles.

The decline of the Unión Nacionalista began in earnest in the spring of 1931. Throughout the winter and spring of that year, Ambassador Guggenheim tried to convince Machado to moderate his repressive measures and compromise with the UN leaders. The U.S. ambassador encouraged Machado to withdraw his proposal to extend the presidential term and to permit peaceful protest and press freedom. With this in mind, Guggenheim maintained contact with the UN leadership, with the hope of brokering a compromise. Machado had in fact compromised on some issues, such as freeing political prisoners and reducing the congressional term from eight to four years.[58] In April Guggenheim proposed to the opposition that Machado should stay in office until 1934, and that the president "should take control of the situation" and compromise with the opposition. "Reforms should be carried out," wrote Guggenheim, "in the most liberal manner possible so that public opinion would be satisfied."[59]

In early 1931, UN leaders could not decide whether to compromise with Machado or threaten an armed uprising. Their hesitation over this matter only served to strengthen Machado's position. With Machado seemingly compromising on some issues, and the UN waiting for some approving sign from the Americans, Machado held the political initiative. Some UN leaders were giving up and rejoining Machado; others, however, were more belligerent and demanded an armed uprising; still others worried that if they were successful in provoking American intervention, the United States would intervene on Machado's side, not theirs.[60] On May 27 the British embassy noted that "the Government has stolen the opposition's thunder. . . . [The opposition] has dwindled to the stature of students with a grievance. . . . Now that they are invited constructively to cooperate in improving the machinery of government, they are at a loss and disunited. Each leader maneuvers for position. The fruits of office seem now almost within their grasp. Revolutionary ardor now gives way to statesman-like caution."[61] By the summer the situation had once again changed. With Machado firmly in control, and with continued support of the Americans, the opposition was stymied. They could, in effect, admit defeat and accept Machado's continued rule, or they could carry out the threats to organize an armed insurrection. They chose the latter.

The UN insurrection, known as the Rebellion of Río Verde, was significant because it was the last major rebellion led by the old *caudillos* of the 1895 generation. The Río Verde rebellion was carried out in the tradition of the Veterans' and Patriots' Movement: it was intended to provoke the United States to intervene politically and remove Machado from power. It was also similar to the Veterans' episode in that there was a near complete lack of communication among the organizers and an equally evident lack of resolve on the part of its leaders to carry through with the threatened armed insurrection. Menocal and Mendieta failed to coordinate their respective actions and plans. No one in the army joined the rebellion, and the landing of the naval forces was haphazard and easily defeated by Machado's troops. Some forty volunteers landed at the town of Gibara in northern Oriente province. Among the participants in this group were Emilio Laurent, Aurelio Hevia, and Francisco Peraza from the generation of 1895. Younger members of the expedition included Carlos Hevia, Sergio Carbó, Gustavo Aldereguía, and Julio Guanard. The younger participants in the Gibara landing were to play important roles in Cuban politics in the years to come. There were other risings at Fomento, Artemisa, and La Gallinita and in the mountain range of Guaniguanico. The rising at La Gallinita, near Santiago de Cuba, was led by a twenty-five-year-old DEU member from Oriente province by the name of Antonio (Tony) Guiteras. Guiteras, like Martínez Villena after the Veterans' defeat, was to draw important lessons from the Río Verde events. In Havana City there were street riots between rebel supporters and the army and police. All of these local risings suffered the same fate: they were easily defeated after brave, but untrained, fighting against regular troops. In contrast, both Menocal and Mendieta, after being captured in the province of Pinar del Río, were set free to pursue their political careers in peace. The Río Verde rebellion ended on August 14, four days after it started.[62]

Río Verde did not fail because of lack of popular support. Anger continued to rise against Machado across all sectors of the population, and anti-American feeling was on the rise. Rather, it was the lack of resolve by the leadership of the UN *caudillos* that caused the defeat. Even after the capture of Mendieta and Menocal, isolated uprisings continued throughout Cuba, in part because some rebels did not know that most of their leaders had given up or because they refused to surrender. Still another factor was that UN leaders never had complete control over their "followers."[63] The Unión Nacionalista was not a political party; it was a personalistic network of *caudillos* and *caciques* who mobilized their followers according to their own priorities. What they agreed on was one thing—that Machado must go—and very little else. On the surface, then, the UN and the events at Río Verde seemed to be a repetition of the Veterans' rebellion. But the crisis gripping Cuba was far deeper than the 1920–24 period. Consequently, no group of politicians in Cuba could easily maintain discipline over their supporters. Such was the case with the independent-minded Tony Guiteras. Guiteras had been a member of the DEU since its founding in 1927 and had collaborated with UN conspirators in Oriente province. But Guiteras utilized his own personal networks within the UN to carry out "armed propaganda" against the *machadato*. After the fiasco at Río Verde, Guiteras and many other insurrectionists continued to prepare for future armed confrontations. "You have finished the struggle," Guiteras told a gathering of UN leaders in Oriente, "while I am just starting."[64]

Communists, Unions, and Mass Mobilization

The young Guiteras was not the only one "just beginning" to fight. The Communist Party, the National Confederation of Cuban Workers (CNOC), and the recently founded Ala Izquierda Estudiantil, or Student Left Wing, struggled to both keep pace with and lead the popular struggles. Yet these new organizations had little direct experience with the rural population. An internal CNOC document acknowledged that unions in the early 1930s were almost entirely urban based, and that even there the level of organization was extremely weak at the factory level. Because of Machado's repression, the largest unions—port, construction, and transport workers—were much smaller than they had been in the mid-1920s.[65] In addition, CNOC organizers had to contend with the hostility of unions outside of their orbit, which made the political objective of "working class unity" even more illusive. For example, in the spring of 1931, at a conference called to build unity among eighteen unions, a delegate from the non-CNOC National Federation of Tobacco Workers complained about the "aggressive tactics" of CNOC union raiding. The CNOC's delegates, meanwhile, attacked the tobacco workers' union for being "social reformist" and "social fascist." After eight hours of debate, the conference failed to reach an agreement on organizational unity. The meeting issued a final statement, signed not in the name of the CNOC but by "unions in general," proclaiming the need to continue to struggle for working-class unity.[66]

It was, however, in the countryside where the most dramatic class battles were taking place. Consequently, the Communist Party of Cuba, under the guidance of the U.S. Communist Party and the New York–based Caribbean Bureau of the Comintern, was directed to organize and unite the Cuban proletariat. The CNOC had some success in making contact among sugar workers in the provinces of Santa Clara, Camagüey, and Oriente.[67] But most of these early contacts among sugar workers, especially cane cutters, were, at best, tenuous, and CNOC organizers had greater success among skilled workers in the *ingenios* (mills).[68] The more numerous cane cutters and field workers were far more difficult to unionize, as we will see shortly.

Between 1930 and 1933, strikes affected many of the sugar mills in Cuba. There were numerous mill occupations, hunger marches, and land occupations throughout the island. Some of the most dramatic actions took place at the important sugar mills of Mabay, Niquero, Media Luna, Romelia, and Esperanza in Oriente province, the Jatibonico mill in Camagüey, the Nazábal, Purio, Hormiguero, Constancia, Santa Isabel, and Carmita mills in Las Villas, the Soledad and Cuba mills in Matanzas; and, the La Habana and Merceditas mills in Havana province. In total more than twenty-five mills were seriously affected by strikes among mill workers, and there were more than one hundred strikes by cane cutters. More than twenty thousand workers participated in these actions.[69] Workers demanded the eight-hour day, payment in cash wages, immediate back-pay, better water and sanitation in the *bateys*, and an end to the repression and violence of the rural guard against workers and union organizers. Some of the strikers demanded an end to the Chadbourne Plan because they felt the massive unemployment in the sugar sector was caused by the crop restrictions.[70] Other demands included a reduction in the costs of goods at the company stores, overtime pay after eight hours of labor for skilled mill hands and cutters alike, regularly scheduled shifts instead of haphazard work rotations, and recognition of the workers' right to organize. The strikers also protested the fact that armed guards often supervised the cane cutters.[71]

The CNOC's union organizers were active in these struggles. Throughout 1931–32, there were numerous clandestine meetings of sugar workers. In many of the meetings they discussed the idea of forming a single union. Communists and noncommunists alike participated in these gatherings.[72] By December 1932, this activity culminated in the formation of the National Union of Sugar Workers (SNOIA). The founding convention took place in Santa Clara, with representatives from thirty-two mills in six provinces.[73] For the first time in Cuban history, unions gained a tenuous foothold in the countryside, and though there would be setbacks in the years to come, from then on rural workers would play an important role in Cuban politics.

By June 1933, the SNOIA leadership was in a better position to make a more objective evaluation of the 1931–32 strikes. The CNOC's analysis of the period concluded that from a political and strategic perspective, the events in the sugar sector were an important step in the revolutionary struggle. "[The strikes] caused repercussions in other sectors of the proletariat, which brought the working class forward in the struggle for hegemony in the development of the agrarian anti-imperialist revolution."[74] But the CNOC/SNOIA documents make it clear that they were not blind to the limitations of the 1931–32 events. Union organization and strike activity, SNOIA admitted, was cyclical, responding to the seasonal nature of sugar production. The founding convention itself was held in December, at the end of the "dead season" when it was easier to bring people together. More important, much of the rank-and-file organizing was limited to the harvest season (January until summer), which was understandable given the large concentration of laborers in the fields and mills. Yet after the harvest, workers returned to their home villages or to the cities and towns. Not only was the union quickly forgotten, but the union often forgot the workers. Harsh living conditions and near starvation forced workers to organize hunger marches and self-help community groups without union assistance. The SNOIA document recognized that community organizing in the broader sense was as important as union organizing at the workplace, and SNOIA organizers were not paying sufficient attention to these popular initiatives.[75]

More explicit political problems were noted by the SNOIA documents. The mill workers' strikes of 1931–32 were largely spontaneous in nature. Hastily formed strike committees called on workers to stop work, with little or no long-term planning about how to prioritize tactics and strategy. More often than not, the demands were local in character, and strikes took place in isolation from each other. The strikes at the mills in Oriente province occurred independently of SNOIA and/or CP organization. Yet the largest mills in eastern Cuba—Jaronú, Boston, Preston, Vertientes, and Cunaguá—were unaffected by the strike actions.[76] Mill workers provided the backbone of the strikes, while support among the field hands was weak. Typically, there was little contact between mill hands and cutters, and, when there was, the lack of coordination and shared concerns undermined unity of action. A further complicating factor was the reality that out of the approximately half a million field hands in the sugar industry at the time, as many of 100,000 of these were Haitians and Jamaicans. These non-Cuban workers were brought to Cuba during the *zafra* and shipped back to their countries of origin when the cutting and hauling was completed. Usually foreign workers did not participate in community social activities, let alone in the larger political struggles.[77] Since the Haitian workers spoke creole and French and the Jamaican workers spoke English, union organizers confronted a language problem when trying to mobilize workers. Desperate migrant workers were often used by the sugar companies to break strikes, which encouraged racism and violence against foreign labor. Wages and working conditions varied from mill to mill. So, too, did sanitary conditions, housing, recreation facilities, and access to electricity and clean water. Since conditions were not uniform, and since local mill managers and regional *caudillos* collaborated in maintaining order, it should not be surprising that union organizing was difficult.

Nor should it be forgotten that the CP and CNOC were founded in 1925 and SNOIA was created in 1932. These young organizations recruited most of their members in late 1932 and 1933 and were thus not in a strong position to lead such complex and intense class struggles. Furthermore, workers in other parts of the economy showed little or no solidarity with the sugar workers from other sectors of the working class. The expected sympathy strikes from the railway workers in the east did not materialize. The Havana unions showed little interest in the plight of rural laborers. Even CNOC unions in the capital were not inclined to support the sugar workers. A CNOC document noted that "the efforts made by CNOC to develop and lead the struggles were weak, and although manifestos were issued with concrete demands, the political work carried out was sectarian in nature, not leaving the narrow circles of Havana. . . . A general awareness of the struggles of the sugar workers hardly exists, contributing in great measure to the limitation of the solidarity movements in the rest of Cuba."[78] There was a constant tension between the propaganda of these groups, which proclaimed their vanguard roles in the revolutionary struggles, and their actual understanding of and control over events.

The political vision of the Marxist left in Cuba from 1929 to 1936 was directed by the politics of the Comintern's "Third Period." Between 1929 and 1935, the political orientation of the Comintern was characterized by a rigid class-against-class interpretation of world events. Alliances with reformist and national-populist elements were rejected in favor a purely worker-based revolution. The Comintern's analysis of Latin American reality was that the continent required "bourgeois democratic revolutions" directed against the "neofeudalist" oligarchies of the region. There was little room in the Comintern's analysis for the specific national realities of individual countries. The Latin American communist parties faithfully followed Moscow's line, and the Cuban CP was no exception. The consequences of this political line were to have a decisive impact on the character of Cuban working-class politics in the years to come.

Given the intensity of the crisis in Latin America between 1929 and 1933, it was inevitable that some people attempted to formulate Marxist strategies based on specific national realities and not primarily on the precepts of the Comintern's "orthodox" Marxism. We saw in the previous chapter that José Carlos Mariátegui in Peru and Julio Antonio Mella in Cuba were pioneers in these efforts. In the early 1930s, the Ala Izquierda Estudiantil located themselves within this tradition and they, too, developed a unique Marxist perspective on Cuban reality in the early 1930s.

As with most of the non-Stalinist groups in Latin America during this period, the Ala Izquierda Estudiantil existed for only a short period, from 1931 to 1935. As a consequence of its limited size, the organizational impact of the Ala Izquierda Estudiantil was negligible. But the leftist students made some valuable contributions to the political debates raging about the complexity of the social and political struggles taking place.[79]

The Ala was founded by a group of DEU dissidents who came to regard the *Manifiesto-Programa* of the DEU as too reformist and not sufficiently anti-imperialist. In essence, the Ala viewed the DEU as little different from the Unión Nacionalista: according to the Ala, the DEU was not seeing the root of the problem in Cuba because, while they were certainly anti-Machado, they also needed to be anti-imperialist and anti-capitalist.[80] For the students of the Ala, capitalism and imperialism were at the root of Cuba's problems. Like the CP, the Ala believed that students should make a strategic alliance with workers and peasants. Petite-bourgeois students could not be the leaders of a genuine revolutionary movement. The Ala made a point of attacking the *caudillismo* of the UN, as well as the apparent willingness of the DEU to subordinate itself to UN leadership. According to the Ala, the central weakness of the DEU/UN position was their failure to acknowledge the existence of independent working-class organizations and the need to form a United Front of all groups opposed to the Cuban capitalist class and the United States.[81]

Nothing in the Ala's own *Manifiesto-Programa* distinguished its position from that of the Communist Party. While the Marxist students were not formally affiliated to the CP, the political influence of the party was clear. Some Ala activists were members of the CP, while others joined the party later. Others, however, never joined the CP. Some went on to fight with the International Brigades during the Spanish Civil War.[82] At the same time, the Ala carried on a constant debate with the Communist Party over questions of Marxist doctrine and theory related to Cuban conditions. A founding member of the Ala, Ladislao González Carbajal, explained that "many compañeros wanted to clarify what was the exact relationship between the Ala and the CP. There were numerous opinions and declarations and much time was wasted, but in the end it was decided that the Ala would maintain its ties with the CP from the point of view of the anti-imperialist struggle, but that the CP's programme and doctrine was more far reaching. We also agreed that the student members of the CP could join the Ala, which did not imply that they could carry out their political line within the Ala."[83] Three of Cuba's most prominent non-Communist leftists came out of the Ala: Raúl Roa García, Pablo de la Torriente Brau, and Aureliano Sánchez Arango were articulate and independent-minded men whose writings and teaching influenced students and other young people in the 1940s and 1950s. Pablo de la Torriente Brau was a prolific writer and organizer before he was killed fighting Franco in the Spanish Civil War. Raúl Roa García was a popular university professor whose teachings played a decisive role in forming the political consciousness of young radicals in the late 1940s and 1950s. And Sánchez Arango, though he was to abandon the ranks of the radical left, advised and counseled political activists in the struggle against Batista between 1952 and 1959.

Yet the Ala was not a CP front group, and it did carry on polemics with the party. At the heart of these discussions was what the leftist students regarded as the CP's subservience to Moscow and the need to develop a Cuban Marxism applicable to Cuban conditions. The independent position of the Ala Izquierda Estudiantil was set out in a long document addressed to the Central Committee of the CP, dated October 5, 1932.[84] The Ala position paper attacked the Cuban CP because its analysis of Cuban social and economic reality was based on foreign models of class analysis. The CP insisted that the industrial working class must lead the revolutionary struggle, whereas the Ala document pointed out that this social class hardly existed in Cuba. At the same time, the CP was accused of underestimating the revolutionary potential of the Cuban peasantry and petite bourgeoisie. In addition, the Cuban Communist Party's analysis had nothing to say about the complex and highly variable condition of *colonos* and the Afro-Cuban organizations. The Ala document pointed out that the CP simplified the internal divisions among the Cuban ruling classes. By underestimating the internal contradictions of Cuban capitalist development, the CP failed to grasp the complexity of the nationalist dimension of the social and political struggle taking place in Cuba.

To illustrate their point, the authors of the Ala statement referred to the nationalist and corporatist organization, the ABC Revolutionary Society, which was founded in 1931.[85] The ABC was created by disgruntled followers of the UN after the Río Verde events. Many middle-class Cubans hoped that the new organization would represent their aspirations for both modern economic development and political stability. Yet the failure of the traditional politicians to bring down Machado in 1931 drove many otherwise moderate people to support terrorist actions to bring down the dictator. The new organization quickly developed a mass following, especially among young professionals and students. Its leaders were prominent Cuban intellectuals, and its ideology was a mélange of populist nationalism, protofascist corporatism, and liberal democratic economic principles. The ABC, at least in its rhetoric, was firmly opposed to foreign control of the Cuban economy, and its program promoted the vision of a Cuban nationalist path to capitalist development. According to the Ala, the prominent role of the ABC in the post–Río Verde struggles against Machado needed to be taken very seriously: the ABC proved that the *clases económicas* in Cuba were not all the puppets of imperialism, and their nationalism represented a serious challenge to the radical left.[86]

The Marxist students aggressively pointed out to the CP Central Committee that as a result of the party's simplistic analysis of Cuban reality, the influence of the party and of radical elements generally was minimal. The trade unions had only a minor impact on the dispersed and fragmented working classes. The party's control of the larger CNOC unions was weak, and the Ala went so far as to conclude that the CNOC was not a mass organization. Membership existed largely on paper, especially in those unions directly under CP control. While this situation did not prevent workers from carrying out militant class-based actions, the party's control and influence over these activities was superficial at best. Afro-Cubans were among the most exploited and militant workers, but the Communist Party ignored the unique problems facing black workers.[87]

Without further evidence it would be tempting to dismiss these criticisms of the CP as exaggerations made by a small sect in the heat of a brief polemical exchange. But as we have seen, similar criticisms of the Communist Party were made from within the CP and CNOC themselves. By late 1932, the strike wave was over. With the dead season nearing an end, workers readied themselves for the upcoming grinding season. Meanwhile, Machado seemed to have the opposition under control. The student groups were vocal and militant but too small to have much of an effect. The Unión Nacionalista was waiting for the United States to act against Machado, and CNOC and SNOIA were fighting hard to establish a foothold among the *clases populares*. On December 20, 1932, the British ambassador described the situation in Cuba as "superficially tranquil." After noting the seasonal nature of protest in Cuba, he went on to observed that "coming suddenly after a long period of intense disturbances marked by murders and terrorism, one is inclined to doubt the reality of the improvement in Havana or to regard it as simply a lull in the bitter political feuds that have only grown more deeply rooted with the passage of time and that cannot be entirely appeased until the Machado Government has been supplanted. . . . Real political peace in Cuba is a long way off."[88]

Between January and April 1933, both the British and American embassies had little of substance to send back to their respective capitals. As we will see in the next chapter, however, as of April 1933, the staffs of both embassies would be very busy indeed. The opposition was preparing to challenge Machado with renewed energy. Meanwhile, with the dead season coming to an end, the unions and the Communist Party were preparing for the inevitable battle with the sugar companies and with Machado.

CHAPTER FOUR

Between Mediation and Revolution

The Collapse of the Plattist State, 1932–1933

When Ambassador Harry F. Guggenheim's replacement, Sumner Welles, arrived in Havana in May 1933, it was clear to all concerned there was a profound crisis in Cuba. For eight years Cuba had been ruled by Gerardo Machado y Morales. Until 1930, Machado's rule was not seriously threatened. After 1929, however, the economic crisis sparked by the world depression threw the established political and economic order into chaos. All factions of the Cuban elite were increasingly besieged by social forces that were outside traditional political circles. Prior to 1933, the occasional student march or workers' strike was ignored or suppressed by the police or the rural guard. By early 1933 the intensity of popular protest reached unprecedented levels. Machado was increasingly isolated from other sectors of the political elite, and economic crisis and labor unrest undermined social order.

Ambassador Welles and the U.S. State Department worried that if Machado did not compromise with the elite opposition, there would be chronic political uncertainty, and, even worse, a social revolution. For the elite opposition to Machado, Welles's arrival encouraged their hope that the *machadato* would end, while still preserving the established political system. In a pattern typical of past U.S. diplomatic interventions, Welles was charged with negotiating a realignment of elite forces that would restore political and economic order. Whether or not Machado retained power was conditional on the Cuban president's acceptance of the mediation process. Cuban politics had worked this way since the imposition of the Platt Amendment on the Cuban Constitution of 1901.

But there were two things that made this particular crisis different. First, Machado unexpectedly resisted the U.S. ambassador's attempts at mediation. Machado had agreed to the mediation process because he thought it was intended to keep him in power. When Welles informed Machado that he would have to shorten his stay in office by one year, Machado responded by threatening to reject the mediation altogether. In direct defiance of Welles, Machado intended to stay in office for the full term. Machado even threatened a military confrontation if the United States attempted to oust him by force.[1] With Welles and Machado locked into a battle of wills over the issue of the purpose of the mediation process, political uncertainty gripped the island.

The second problem proved to be far more serious than Machado's resistance to the mediation. In the early 1930s social protest from the *clases populares* became so widespread that the established mechanisms of social and political control no longer functioned. By 1933, many people from both the ruling elite and the radical opposition realized that to simply repress or ignore the *clases populares* was no guarantee of social peace and economic security. The popular classes were generating their own political and social responses to changing circumstances. This not only undermined the mechanisms of social control of oligarchic capitalism, but it also profoundly challenged the political capacities of those who claimed to represent the *clases populares*.

Between Mediation and Revolution

By the spring of 1933, Cubans were living through a political and economic crisis where numerous bombings, kidnappings, mysterious seizures of weapons and munitions, and urban and rural protest were daily occurrences. Clashes between the police and students often ended in violence. Between March 3 and May 7, the police shot and killed thirty-two students, while thirteen policemen lost their lives in the same period.[2] Women's organizations took to the street, protesting the high cost of living and political repression, as well as demanding the right to vote.[3] Machado replied to the growing social unrest by imprisoning oppositionists and ordering the police to attack demonstrations. Many antigovernment activists were "shot while trying to escape."[4]

Cuban exiles living in the United States, the Dominican Republic, Honduras, Mexico, and Spain returned to Cuba expecting to play a role in bringing down the dictatorship. In Miami alone there were about a thousand political refugees. The exiles were divided into five main groups: the Conservatives, led by former president Mario Menocal; the Liberals under Miguel Gómez; the Unión Nacionalista, led by Carlos Mendieta; the DEU group with José Irisarri, Sarah del Llano, and Clara Luz Durán; and the recently founded ABC Society, represented by Dr. Oscar de la Torre and Dr. Carlos Saladrigas. In April these five factions formed a united *Junta* (committee) under the leadership of Oscar de la Torre, a noted scientist and a professor at the University of Havana. Between May and June two thousand exiles returned to Cuba from the United States.[5] Exile committees in New York and Miami raised funds and organized public meetings in support of the people's struggle. Cuban exiles in Washington and other centers spent considerable effort lobbying Congress and businesses involved in Cuba to withdraw their support for Machado.[6] Welles's mediation added fuel to the expectation that change was coming and the specter of popular rebellion permeated the political atmosphere.[7]

It was within this environment of social confrontation, tense expectation, and rumor that the opposition groups mobilized to confront Machado and the Plattist state once again. This was the situation Ambassador Sumner Welles faced when he arrived in May 1933. The unfolding of Welles's mediation is recounted elsewhere.[8] Welles went to Cuba to restore order and prevent revolution. To accomplish this, Welles opened negotiations with the moderate opposition. By July 1 the ABC Organization, the Organización Celular Reforma Revolucionaria (OCRR), university professors, institute professors, secondary school teachers, the Unión Nacionalista, and the Association of Veterans had agreed to participate in the mediation.[9]

Throughout the spring of 1933, Machado, Welles, the elite opposition, and the radical popular sectors were locked into a four-way fight over the future direction of Cuban politics. Would Machado outlast the mediation? Or would Welles remove him? Should the opposition trust Welles? Or should the mediation be rejected out of hand? Would the Plattist state be retained in a post-Machado Cuba? These questions were all the more pressing in light of the larger question: Was Cuba on the brink of social revolution?

It is important to keep in mind, however, that, for the moderate opposition, the principal enemy was the Cuban political elite and Machado, not the United States. The post-1898 generation of middle-class Cubans was not so much anti-American as it was anti-intervention. Welles, like General Crowder before him, symbolized interventionism. There was an important difference between admiring and even emulating American trends and institutions, and having the United States *impose* them on Cuba. The middle-class youth who came of age in the 1920s and 1930s were caught between the powerful myths of Cuba's wars for independence and the equally powerful presence of U.S. economic, political, and cultural modernity. The

reformist nationalism of the Cuban middle classes reflected these competing pressures. Franklin D. Roosevelt's newly proclaimed "Good Neighbor
Policy" and New Deal liberalism strengthened the moderate nationalist perspective: Pan-Americanism without U.S. military intervention seemed to
promise both genuine independence for Cuba and modern political and economic development. Alberto Lamar-Schweyer, Machado's press secretary at
the time, observed that "the eyes of the opposition were fixed on Mr. Roosevelt, whose coming into power was given out by the Havana newspapers
as the commencement of a new era for Cuba." [10] Moderate Cuban nationalists hoped that the "Good Neighbor Policy" would provide more space for
Cuban economic development. From their perspective, anti-Americanism
was impractical: even if such sentiment was widespread, which it was not,
a frontal attack on the United States could only end in defeat. Yet the Platt
Amendment denied Cubans the sovereign right to negotiate the terms of
Cuban development, and this, too, was intolerable. Middle- and upper-class
nationalists wanted capitalist modernity—especially American modernity—
but on *Cuban terms* and without the humiliation of U.S. intervention. [11]

Among the moderate middle-class nationalist groups, the ABC organization emerged as the leading group among the anti-Machado forces. The ABC
was founded in late 1931, largely in response to the failure of Río Verde and
the decline of the Unión Nacionalista. The organization's name came from
its secretive structure: the leading cell of the movement was "A," the second
level cell "B," and so on. [12] Each cell had about ten members. Cells acted independently of each other, so even if Machado's police succeeded in destroying one cell, the others were not threatened by this setback. This method
of organizing permitted the ABC to take advantage of the intense and spontaneous popular reaction against Machado. One of the peculiar features of
the ABC was that while its organizational structure was highly secretive, the
ABC managed to tap into the popular sentiment against the *machadato*. It
was in this sense that the ABC became the first mass movement in twentieth-
century Cuba.

The supporters of the ABC were mostly young and from the middle
classes. [13] The ABC's program opposed the politics of class struggle. Instead,
they tried to build a multiclass and mass insurrectionary movement favor-
ing a "new Cuba" based on national capitalist development. Their program
was corporatist and protofascist. Corporatist movements were a response to
the development of a mass workforce and the creation of new urban social
classes; corporatists wanted to work out ways to control and manage the
process of rapid social class formation while guaranteeing capitalist develop-

ment. Thus the ABC recognized the need for the incorporation of the middle classes and small business people into the process of state formation and that the working class needed to be controlled through corporatist political structures. They wanted a "new man for a new Cuba" with liberty, social justice, and control of Cuba's national resources. They supported the right of workers to organize unions and the demand for an eight-hour workday. Women should have the vote. The ABC declared their opposition to monopolies, the *latifundios* of the large sugar companies, and control of the national wealth by foreign banks. They were in favor of legislation to encourage small rural proprietors and to gradually eliminate *latifundios* through a progressive land tax. The ABC supported rural cooperative societies, which would be aided by an Agricultural Bank. Cuba did not have a national bank, so the ABC's program called for formation of such an institution, which could provide credit to small and medium-sized producers and businesses.[14] Jorge Mañach, one of Cuba's leading intellectuals and an author of the ABC program, wrote that "Cuba . . . needs to achieve without delay a fundamental solution to its economic problem, assuring to the Cuban his proper and inalienable relationship to the riches of his country. This presupposes a policy of economic restoration which necessarily would put a check, legally and effectively, to foreign interests exercising an excessive domination which limits or conditions the Cuban means of support. Only a magnanimous acquiescence to such a policy on the part of the United States will leave clear all doubt, both in Cuba and in Latin America as a whole, the friendship of the great Republic of the north for this young republic of the Caribbean."[15]

The ABC's view of the new Cuba was elitist. They believed that the Cuban people were not ready for liberal democracy and that state intervention, directed by an intellectual elite, was required to prepare Cubans to assume their civic responsibilities. At the same time, the ABC Manifesto stated that the organization was opposed to both fascism and communism because both ideologies contradicted the principles of political liberty.[16] The leaders of the ABC, Dr. Joaquín Saénz, Dr. Juan Andrés Lliteras, Dr. Jorge Mañach, and Dr. Francisco Ichaso, while respected intellectuals, were remote from popular concerns and mass politics.[17]

The ABC was more of a movement than a political party. Its influence had much less to do with the group's program than with its tactics.[18] The ABC employed the tactics of bombings and assassinations: they wanted to maintain an environment of insurrectionary violence which, they believed, would eventually bring down the dictatorship. When Machado was ousted from office in August 1933, for example, the correspondent for the *Daily Worker*, the newspaper of the Communist Party of the United States, reported that "the city is wild. Tens of thousands of workers and city poor in general have come into the streets under the banners of the ABC. They launched themselves against the president's palace and the homes of the government leaders. But the masses were alone in this. The leaders of the ABC called off a scheduled demonstration so as not to mix with the 'popular trash.' "[19] The British ambassador, when referring to the ABC, expressed his "surprise to hear university professors and lawyers and doctors of education and intelligence attempt to justify the nightly bombings in the capital and its surroundings, on the grounds that they serve to keep alive amongst the people a spirit of uneasiness and of revolt until comprehensive plans have been prepared for a series of systematic direct attacks on the machinery of the Government."[20] Police officers and *machadista* soldiers were frequent victims of ABC attacks. Two prominent examples were the president of the Senate and the chief of the Secret Police, but many lower-rank figures were killed by ABC squads.[21] These tactics brought the ABC a degree of prestige and respect in opposition circles that far exceeded its size. In early 1933 ABC membership was around two thousand, but given the group's secretive structure this figure should be treated with caution.[22] Ruby Hart Philips, the wife of the *New York Times* correspondent in Cuba, J. D. Philips, wrote that after Machado's ouster, "three million people have suddenly become ABC members. Their green flag seems about to replace the Cuban flag."[23] With politically motivated violence occurring almost daily, Cuba appeared to be on the brink of civil war. In the public's eye the ABC appeared to lead the insurrection against Machado, but to what degree they actually did so is not clear. What was clear was that the ABC tapped into the insurgent energy of a population in revolt. They were not the only ones to do so.

The social base of the DEU was essentially the same as that of the ABC. With a middle-class and largely young following, both groups had the same concerns for the political and economic inclusion of middle-class Cubans into a "new Cuba." For a brief period the two organizations shared leadership cadre, with several DEU representatives joining the *Célula Directriz* (Cell "A") of the ABC.[24] Politically, however, DEU members tended to be more sympathetic to liberal democratic ideas. Like the ABC, the DEU were driven by events to support a mass insurrection against the *machadato*. Unlike the ABC, however, the DEU's program, which was written in Miami in July 1933, contained greater detail on issues such as future electoral, judicial, and legislative reform, something the ABC program did not do to the same degree. The DEU called for the banning of the old political parties of the Plattist state, a new constitution without the Platt Amendment, and the election of a Constituent Assembly.

The DEU wanted a provisional government to replace Machado and, through negotiations with the United States, establish a truly independent Cuba.[25] For the DEU, U.S. economic imperialism was a threat, but they hoped that Cubans could create a nationalist space without U.S. political intervention and economic domination. The DEU shared Mañach's hope that U.S. policy toward Cuba would exhibit "magnanimous acquiescence." According to the DEU, "the Provisional Government could not only restore, for the United States and for our own good, the purchasing power of our markets, but that the U.S. consumer market in the United States will be open for Cuba."[26]

This argument, however, was difficult to sustain when it was clearly the United States that kept Machado in power and it was U.S. capitalists who restricted the opportunities for Cuban capital. The students of the DEU were aware of this problem. "The Provisional Government will denounce the existing Commercial Treaty with the United States, proposing in its place agreements, based on principles of equality, which will intensify economic relations with Canada and other American countries, and will stimulate closer moral and cultural identification with the countries of Ibero-America."[27] It was precisely this moderate approach to "U.S. imperialism" that caused the Ala Izquierda Estudiantil to split from the DEU in 1931.

It was because of these pressing issues of national political and economic development that the DEU began to see itself as something more than a student organization. By 1933, the DEU and the ABC were competing for the political leadership of the middle-class opposition to Machado. Justo Carrillo explains how this competition came about: "Logically, the ABC filled an historic vacuum created, precisely, by the absence of an expansionist program from the DEU. The Directorio committed this grave error near the end of 1930, when all segments of Cuban society were behind their rallying cry of total and definitive change of regime. They did not know how to exploit this advantage to organize a militant apparatus with the backing capable of carrying out the revolution; instead, the Directorio chose to remain hemmed in to a strictly academic sphere."[28] The DEU attempted to rectify this situation in July 1933. For the first time in any DEU manifesto, the student group hinted that it might play a more permanent role in Cuba politics. "The student movement did not come into existence only to fight and overthrow Machado, but to bring about a total purification of the system, adjusting the political machinery to its true function within an authentic democracy. . . .

A people that does not feel itself to be free is an irresponsible people; and an irresponsible people does not have the capacity to play any historical role, and such a people will definitively fall under the orbit of more powerful peoples."[29] The DEU represented the highest national ideals and they saw themselves as the conscious historic agent capable of representing and leading the Cuban people to national maturity.

This self-awareness on the part of the DEU as potential national leaders stemmed from the widely held view among radicals, in Cuba and in Latin America generally, that an intellectual elite must take on the task of nation building.[30] The university reform movements of the 1920s encouraged the idea that the youth of the continent embodied progress and modernity. The ideas of the Argentine positivist philosopher José Ingenieros were of particular importance: Ingenieros argued that youth needed to establish an "aristocracy of merit" against the dead hand of the colonial past and the "ignorance" of the popular cultures of Latin America. The DEU could mobilize respectable numbers of students for marches and rallies, but it is striking that in early 1933 the total number of actual members reached only thirty-six.[31] Prominent among this group were Rubén León, Justo Antonio Rubio Padilla, Carlos Prío Socarrás, José Miguel Irisarri, Justo Carrillo Hernández, Ramiro Valdés Daussá, and Sarah del Llano.

Before Welles's arrival, opposition to Machado was a matter of taking sides in a straightforward confrontation between the dictatorship and the people. As of June 1933, however, the political situation became mired in the more complex problems of providing alternatives to U.S. hegemony and to Machado's regime. Welles's mediation initiative presented the Cuban opposition with a choice: either step back from the unknown of total independence and accept U.S. hegemony, or risk a revolutionary confrontation with both Machado and the United States. Alberto Lamar-Schweyer wrote that in general the opposition looked to the new Roosevelt administration as "the commencement of a new era for Cuba," and, he added with characteristic exaggeration, "outside of the students, nobody dared to deny that the solution to our crisis would come from Washington."[32] Welles, after all, made no mention of abolishing the Platt Amendment or redefining Cuban–United States relations.

It was within this context that the DEU, unlike the ABC, hesitated when faced with Welles's mediation. Justo Carrillo, after noting that in early 1933 the DEU was functioning under difficult circumstances, with many members in prison and others in exile in Miami and New York, explained how the DEU came to reject the mediation process. The DEU hesitated when faced

with joining the mediation because of the organization's "lack of ideological maturity." As a result, the DEU was responsible for "delaying and obstructing the regime's fall. Worse still, the Directorio did not perceive that
the presumed acceleration of the process would not necessarily facilitate
our ultimate revolutionary objectives, especially if it came as the result of
a change of ill fated, though temporary, alliances and the acceptance of the
foreign mediation principle. The Directorio did not perceive that this was
rather a time to stand alone, if necessary, and fight for decisive victory over
the Old Cuba."[33] Ruby Hart Philips described the early mediation discussions between the DEU-ABC "boys" and Welles in the following terms: "I told
him [Welles] that they [DEU-ABC] were well educated . . . quite charming
boys, outside of their tendency to throw bombs. . . . They agreed to cur-
tail terroristic activities, although in their meeting held after the interview
[with Welles], the boys told me they had a most difficult time persuading
the others."[34] According to Carrillo, the "popular clamor" against U.S. diplomatic intervention forced the DEU to reconsider their support for the mediation. Carrillo does not say who was behind this "popular clamor," but there
can be no doubt that the student body as a whole was against U.S. intervention. An undated DEU manifesto, clearly written before the open rejection
of the mediation, stated that "we do not know the concrete objective of the
Special Envoy [Welles] of the United States. He speaks to us about friendly
mediation in the name of humanity. He tells us that he will not intervene on
the basis of the Platt Amendment. However, the history of Yankee meddling
in our America justifies our reserve. The Platt Amendment causes many of
our great problems, the enumeration of which is obvious, and it constitutes a
round denial of the noble and high content of the Joint Resolution of 1898."[35]
After a series of feverish telephone exchanges between the DEU activists in
Havana and in Miami, the DEU came out against the mediation.[36]

On July 16, 1933, the DEU issued a manifesto stating that "the mediation
makes light of the Cuban people's right to self-determination and it tends to
inculcate in the population, once again, the view that our internal difficul-
ties can only be solved through foreign collaboration." The DEU viewed the
mediation as another form of intervention and that it was not simply the
removal of Machado which motivated them, "but a complete purification of
the whole system."[37] Another DEU document, written after the decision to
reject the mediation, pointed out that within the context of the world depression, U.S. economic interests were attempting to recapture lost ground
in the Cuban market. Unfortunately, the manifesto stated, this could result
in the complete destruction of the Cuban economy. Welles wanted to "re-

store the purchasing power of the Cuban market as a consumer of American goods." Indeed, between 1923 and 1933, Cuban imports from the United States fell from $191 million to $22 million, while the U.S. share of imports to Cuba declined from 74.3 percent during World War I to 57.4 percent in 1931.[38] Cuban light industry had partially replaced U.S. imports, along with cheaper British, German, and Japanese goods. The Customs Tariff Law of 1927 had afforded Cuban light industry with modest protection, and Cubans were more self-sufficient.[39] The DEU was thus very concerned about a shattered Cuban economy falling even more under the domination of U.S. "economic imperialism." But the DEU statement declared that "politically, the present government of the United States is not imperialist and it declares its profound respect for the sovereignty and self-determination of all peoples."[40] The students made a distinction between "economic imperialism" and the "good political intentions" of the Roosevelt administration. The DEU was waiting to see whether Welles would represent Roosevelt or the "economic imperialists" of Wall Street. But the DEU's hope that Roosevelt and Welles viewed Cuban affairs differently proved futile: both the U.S. president and the ambassador wanted tighter control over Cuban affairs, yet before this could be done, political stability was required.[41]

The ABC, on the other hand, quickly came out in support of the mediation. Their reason for doing so was simple: the leaders of ABC were afraid of social revolution. By accepting Welles's mediation, the ABC could gain access to state power without class struggle and social upheaval, or so they hoped.[42] In supporting the Welles initiative, the ABC effectively abandoned the ranks of the opposition: to negotiate with Welles was to accept the legitimacy of Machado's rule, and this was something the majority of the opposition had refused to do since the constitutional reforms of 1926–27. On June 15, the ABC handed Welles a memorandum promising that from that date on, the ABC "enters into a formal obligation to refrain from all forms of agitation against the constituted authorities in Cuba."[43] This decision by the ABC was to prove fatal for the organization. Participating in the mediation was to be the ABC's version of "Río Verde"; just as the *caudillos* of the UN lost credibility in 1931, so too did the ABC in June 1933.[44] The ABC, according to journalist Carlton Beals, "had definitely ceased to represent the new Cuba. In certain ways it had been, and to some extent still is, a picturesque Cuban counterpart of American technocracy, a preliminary syndicalization of middle class professional failures, caught between the cogs of American big business, the Machado bureaucracy and the proletariat . . . by the time the ABC had decided to become Welles' chosen step child, it was already a hybrid organization."[45]

The decision by the ABC to enter the mediation discussions strained relations with the DEU to the breaking point. On August 3, the DEU ordered the withdrawal of its two representatives from the *Célula Directriz* of the ABC.[46] Yet the DEU still did not completely break with the ABC. Justo Carrillo explained the political confusion as a natural consequence of the environment in Havana. "The solidarity in Havana couldn't help but be influential; the leaders of a new, powerful reformist movement, in which the DEU and the ABC were the vanguard, would naturally move ideologically closer. . . . The optimism evaporated when in due time it became apparent that neither was Roosevelt the hope of the Americas nor was the ABC the hope of Cuba."[47] Carrillo's judgment reflected the official position of the DEU:

> Public opinion is now aware of the treasonous behavior of certain sectors who have seemingly grown—with great personal prestige for some —with the popular exaltation caused by resistance to the Tyranny. This treason has three aspects to it: treason to the REVOLUTION because they have carried out acts which are now essentially invalid by recognizing—more or less explicitly—the legality of a government that has instituted crime and theft as public policy. Treason against CUBA because they declare unabashedly the incapacity of our people to control their own destiny. Treason against Ibero-america because they have encouraged Yanqui intervention and supported the efforts in Our America of interests, who, in the last century and a half, have shown hostility to the development of our peoples.[48]

Within the ABC itself, the decision to participate in the mediation provoked an internal crisis. In June a faction calling itself the ABC Radical broke away from the ABC. Its first communiqué declared that "to accept the mediation was to betray the revolution" and that change should come to Cuba through popular revolution and not because of Welles's intervention. The ABC Radical repudiated all U.S. interference in Cuban affairs. Like the DEU, the ABC Radical wanted a provisional government to replace Machado, the dissolution of the Congress and the judiciary, a new electoral census, and the prosecution of those responsible for crimes during the *machadato*.[49] Overall, the ABC Radical was to play a minor role in Cuban politics and the group dissolved in 1934. But the formation of the ABC Radical was another indication of the ideological confusion within the opposition in the face of widespread mass mobilization. The founder of the ABC Radical, Dr. Oscar de la Torre, wrote that there had never been ideological unity within the ABC and it was Welles's mediation that brought the internal divisions to the surface.[50]

The moderate opposition, then, was clearly trapped between revolution and mediation. Until the middle of August 1933, there was every reason to think that Welles, and not the antimediation opposition, would bring down Machado. What complicated matters, however, was the insurrectionary activity of social groups outside the influence of the middle-class opposition. Without mass pressure from the *clases populares,* moderate nationalists would have been where they were in 1925–29 — unable to challenge Machado or to change social and economic conditions. At the same time, the popular classes were developing their own forms of collective action and politics without the guidance of the DEU/ABC members. The claims by these organizations to be leading "the people" assumed that the subaltern strata of Cuban society were incapable of developing their own responses to economic and political crisis and change. The inherently elitist ideology of both the DEU and ABC mitigated against any meaningful political contact between the two social groups. This belief that the *clases populares* required external direction was hardly surprising given the ideological mélange of neopositivism, socialism, populism, liberalism, and fascism so commonly found in the magazines and books of the day. Middle-class radicals were caught between, on the one hand, their limited capacity and willingness to organize the popular sectors, and, on the other hand, the insurrectionary efficacy of popular nationalism fueled by mass mobilization "from below." Nationalist and radical political rhetoric was outpaced by the explosive energy of popular rebellion.

The *clases populares* fought to gain control over their lives according to the local, regional, ethnic, and class conditions they confronted. Demands for "national liberation" were certainly relevant to workers and peasants, but such demands were infused with the immediate social, economic, moral, and ethnic concerns of poor and working-class Cubans. This tension within nationalist politics generated contradictory visions of what a future state could or should do for Cubans. Indeed, given that most of Cuba's leading nationalists were usually urban and from middle- or upper-class backgrounds, and that they paid little or no attention to the practical concerns of poor Cubans, there was no compelling reason why the popular classes should follow their lead. This was the basic contradiction within nationalist discourse and practice: as nationalist activists became aware that the source of their power against Machado came "from below," so, too, did the poor and marginalized learn that they could gain more control over their lives through mobilization and struggle. But prior to the summer and fall of 1933, there was no organic connection between the two social sectors. Nationalist and antioligarchic agitation was not responsible for mass mobilization or for bringing the *clases populares* into self-conscious political struggle.

As we will see, this contradiction was not unique to the middle-class opposition. Those groups who directly engaged with the urban and rural poor, such as the Communist Party, the Ala Izquierda Estudiantil, the National Confederation of Cuban Workers (CNOC), and the National Union of Sugar Industry Workers (SNOIA), also assumed that the workers and peasants of Cuba required political education from a revolutionary vanguard in order to acquire true class consciousness. Yet the working classes and the poor were not waiting for change to arrive from external influences or radicals in a distant Havana.

The Collapse of the Machadato: July–September 1933

If the DEU and the ABC were willing to entertain the idea of a U.S.-sponsored solution to the Cuban crisis, there were other organizations that rejected Welles's mediation from the start. The Communist Party, the Ala, the CNOC, and the SNOIA promptly rejected any form of U.S. intervention in Cuban politics. The mediation between ambassador Welles, the elite opposition, and Machado meant nothing to the workers and their organizations.[51] Their programs varied on how to bring about change and who to include as allies or enemies, but they all accepted the principle that "the revolution" was the source of Cuban sovereignty and not an American-brokered compromise between the Cuban political elite.

For the radical left, the task was to prepare the workers and peasants for a decisive confrontation with Machado and U.S. domination. The Marxist left wanted an "agrarian anti-imperialist revolution" against the Cuban capitalist class and U.S. imperialism. The idea of an "agrarian anti-imperialist revolution" refers to the official position of the Communist International toward the political tasks of Marxist revolutionaries in the developing countries. In broad terms, orthodox Marxists believed that the nonindustrialized nations should first pass through a stage of "bourgeois democratic" and "agrarian revolution" before advancing to the "socialist stage." In the agrarian phase, the rural proletariat would be granted land and the urban poor would have the right to return to the land. Large *latifundios* would be broken up to make the land available to these workers. Peasants who did not have secure title to the land they occupied would receive such a title from the state. This first stage of the anti-imperialist revolution would lay the foundation for the socialist stage, which would be characterized, in theory, by peasants becoming part of larger agrarian cooperatives (collective farms), which in turn would provide the basis for a socialist process of industrialization.

This political vision was framed within the Comintern's "Third Period." The Third Period position argued that world capitalism was entering its final crisis. As a result, any compromise with capitalism and imperialism was not only reformist, but also by implication counterrevolutionary and reactionary. All forms of reformism and nationalism were viewed as threats to working-class unity and to final victory. Accordingly, Communists fought against reformism within the trade union movement. After 1930, the Cuban party underwent a "proletarianization" of both its political line and its leadership: the CP leadership became increasing "workerist," trade union oriented, and subservient to Moscow's political line. From 1929 on, Communist union activists fought bitterly against anarchists and moderates within the CNOC, eventually gaining influence within some union leaderships. As of 1933 Blas Roca, César Vilar, and Joaquín Ordoqui became prominent party leaders. All three men were to lead the party into the 1940s and 1950s.[52]

The international situation seemed to encourage the Comintern's perspective. Fascism was on the rise in Germany and Italy. Armed struggle erupted in Nicaragua in 1927, and there was mass insurrection in El Salvador in 1932. The Mexican revolution veered to the left under the populist and nationalist Lázaro Cárdenas after 1934. The anticolonial struggles in China, India, and Ethiopia were eagerly followed by leftists. The world economy was in crisis, and class struggles were at a high point nearly everywhere. The Great Depression hurled communities of hitherto isolated peasants and workers into a world economic crisis: the collapse of prices and markets for colonial primary products exposed the vulnerability of all colonized social classes to an international capitalist economy managed largely in New York, Washington, London, and Paris.[53] For communists in the early 1930s, the world did indeed seem ready for revolution, and the political and economic crisis in Cuba very much fit the pattern.[54]

Cuban leftist organizations grew considerably between 1930 and 1933. The Ala Izquierda Estudiantil was a very small group in 1932; by 1933 the Ala had some five hundred members. Most members were based in Havana, but Ala branches formed in Santiago de Cuba, Manzanillo, Bayamo, Holguín, Camagüey, Cienfuegos, and Santa Clara. Most of these regional groups were founded in early 1933.[55] In a similar way, the Communist Party, the CNOC, and the SNOIA gained both experience and new members in the struggles of 1930–32. The CNOC made important inroads into the transport, port, and tobacco industries.[56] Textile-worker and some manufacturing unions joined the Confederation. In 1933 CNOC formal membership—including the 100,000 SNOIA members—was approximately 300,000.[57] Communist Party membership hovered around 3,000, and there were party cells in every major city and town. [58] In the province of Santa Clara, party membership increased six times between November 1932 and June 1933.[59] In Las Villas the party grew seven-fold between November 1932 and March 1933.[60]

Outside the capital, insurgent activity and social struggle continued throughout the spring of 1933. However, it is far from clear to what degree the Communist Party and other radical groups played a leading role in these activities. In the eastern provinces of Oriente, Camagüey and Santa Clara, train, road, and telegraph communications were attacked by unknown assailants. Train lines were bombed in the Matanzas area. In Sancti Spíritus, province of Santa Clara, troops were sent to quell worker unrest at the Jatibonico sugar mill. The repression at the mill was such that the American manager complained to Havana authorities about the violence inflicted upon the workers. Mill administrators and the rural guard often perpetrated violence upon the sugar workers. At the Punta Alegre mill, forty-eight Haitian workers were forced to work at gunpoint, and another twenty-three foreign workers were expelled from the mill.[61] On February 15, 1933, the manager of the Cuban Cane Company mill Manatí in Camagüey informed the Latin American Trading Company in Havana that the mill laborers threatened to strike for better wages, but company investors should "not be alarmed as the army is taking steps to avoid any paralysing [sic]."[62] In early 1933, peasant uprisings took place in Oriente, Camagüey, and Santa Clara. In each case the peasants demanded land and an end to the violence of the rural guard. All these actions were crushed with ruthless violence by the army and the rural guard. With the sugar harvest fast approaching, the cycle of government repression and of worker resistance intensified. By April, the government's ability to control the situation in the countryside was limited. The British embassy, referring to the mounting rural protest as a "campaign," reported to the Foreign Office that "[it] is almost impossible for the Government to deal satisfactorily with this kind of campaign. If the entire armed forces of the republic (some 12,000 men) were placed in railway protection duty, they probably could not cover all the railway properties. In any case, at this time of year most of the army and rural guards are engaged in the protection of cane fields and sugar mills; and despite this protection, cane fires are nightly occurrences."[63]

The fact that rural protest intensified as summer approached is not surprising. The nature of sugar production generated cyclical social and political struggles. At the beginning of each year workers returned to the mills, ready to begin the harvest and find the best working conditions possible. At the same time, the sugar companies tried to keep costs down by obtaining the cheapest labor possible. This struggle became more intense when the crop restrictions were imposed in the late 1920s. The sugar harvest of 1932–33 was 50 percent less than the harvest of 1922–23; the harvest lasted only sixty-six days; and wages for sugar workers fell to the levels of 1909–10.[64] Delaying the date of the harvest meant that workers went hungry longer. Small-scale *colonos* attempted to keep wages and labor costs to a minimum because they were squeezed between their debts to the milling companies and the costs of the wage bill and other labor costs. This situation resulted in numerous localized conflicts among workers, *colonos*, and mill owners. Ambassador Welles wrote that "the average laborer on the plantation has been paid less than the minimum amount required to feed himself and his family and the conditions of distress and actual destitution cannot be exaggerated. The field is consequently particularly ripe for agitation by labor leaders and for the formation of labor unions under the control of such leaders."[65] Another diplomat wrote, "Nine out of ten men are starving and they may easily be goaded again to take possession of the mills."[66]

Rumors abounded about huge quantities of arms pouring into the country in preparation for antigovernment rebellions.[67] On April 29, 1933, approximately one hundred rebels attacked the military barracks at San Luis, between Santiago de Cuba and Bayamo. The leader of the attack was twenty-seven-year-old Antonio Guiteras, a former DEU member from Oriente province. Guiteras had come to believe that armed struggle was necessary to bring Machado down.[68] For several weeks Guiteras and his followers successfully kept the army off balance by using guerrilla tactics. The attack on San Luis failed in its objective to spark a mass insurrection against the Machado government, but there was widespread concern that the San Luis episode was a sign of things to come.[69] The young revolutionary was later to become Minister of the Interior, War, and the Navy in the Grau administration and its most radical spokesman. Following the San Luis attack, Guiteras's reputation as a brave and decisive leader grew: the radical journalist Carlton Beals referred to Guiteras as the John Brown and Augusto Sandino of Cuba.[70] Other armed confrontations in the countryside took place, but many of these attacks were carried out by local *caudillos* and bandits whose objectives were far less political than were those of the young radical nationalist leader.[71]

By July 1933, the tensions over the labor situation added to those generated by the mediation negotiations. On July 25, Havana and other urban centers were in the grips of a growing general strike. Starting with Havana bus drivers, the strike quickly gathered the support of taxi and truck drivers, railway men, dock workers, postmen, milkmen, bakery workers and bakers, printers and newspapermen, icemen, waiters, barbers, and small-scale vendors in street markets. Commerce and transport was brought to a halt in Havana and other major cities. The motivations behind the strikes were as varied as the strikers themselves: transport workers protested the wage differences among employees doing the same work but employed at different transport companies; bakery workers and small-scale vendors struck against the wholesale "trusts" that forced sellers to charge high prices for their goods; and other sectors fought for higher wages or for the recognition of their unions.[72] In some cases CNOC unions and Communist Party members led the strikes, but more often than not they trailed behind events.[73] Throughout the months of July and August, bank clerks, domestic servants, bakers, and office workers organized their own unions without the support of the CNOC or the Communist Party. [74]

What united this diverse group of strikers was their shared antipathy toward Machado.[75] While the general strike started as a spontaneous movement fueled by economic concerns, it quickly turned into an insurrectionary movement against Machado.[76] On August 4, the *Havana Post,* the newspaper of the American colony in Cuba, reported that "the strike has assumed alarming and nationwide proportions. . . . In every city of the island transportation has ceased with indications that the movement will continue to grow." [77] In the late afternoon of the same day, a false radio report announced that Machado had resigned: thousands of people flooded the streets of Havana in celebration, only to be met with bullets and the disappointing news that Machado was still president. On August 8, Havana was the scene of more rioting. In the ensuing clashes at least 13 people were killed and more than 120 wounded. Striking bus workers burned buses and attacked strike breakers. A demonstration of veterans from the wars of independence was violently quashed by Machado's police: the subsequent popular outrage over this action brought even more people into the streets.[78] Charles Thomson, a historian working for the U.S. Foreign Policy Association, wrote that "commerce and industry joined forces with labor. Theaters closed and shops, stores and factories lay silent behind heavy iron shutters. Banks and government offices continued to function, but telegraphers and mail carriers voted to strike. The capital, with its streets almost empty, took on the aspect of a deserted city."[79] According to the British embassy, 90 percent of the urban population was behind the strikers.[80]

Neither Machado, the elite opposition, or the U.S. State Department knew what to do about this situation. Throughout July, Welles worked to remove Machado before the political and economic situation became uncontrollable. While Machado was confident that he could survive a test of wills with the ambassador, the pressure from below complicated matters considerably. Machado's response was to negotiate with the CP and CNOC: he offered legality to the unions and the party in exchange for an end to the general strike. After a heated debate within the party's Central Committee, Machado's offer was accepted. The CP paid a high political price for this decision: for years to come, many in the radical nationalist movement regarded this as a betrayal of the anti-Machado struggle. The party later acknowledged its error, but the damage was done. Moreover, the CP overestimated its influence on the strike movement: the strike continued despite their call for workers to return to work. The agreement between the party and Machado lasted only seventy-two hours: Machado and the CP had overestimated each other's influence on events and underestimated the insurgent energy of the people.

Welles and the British embassy pointed to "outside agitators" from the Communist Party and the unions as the source of the conflicts in the countryside,. Yet both embassies also reported that labor conflicts were fueled by local economic conditions and that party and union organizers arrived on the scene after the clashes began.[81] The Communist Party and CNOC themselves acknowledged that in many cases they did not lead the strikes, especially in the summer and fall of 1933. The Executive Committee of CNOC noted that the CNOC "overestimated their influence" and that in many cases the objectives of the strikes were not clear. The CNOC's organizers often arrived at the mills only to find them already occupied by Cuban, Haitian, and Jamaican workers. What surprised party and union organizers was that workers had occupied mills and raised the red flag before outside organizers arrived. Some of the workers who participated in these spontaneous occupations were influenced by Marcus Garvey's United Negro Improvement Association. The UNIA's black nationalism was clearly seen as political competition for the CP: one CNOC manifesto, after commenting on the multiracial composition of the sugar workers in the east, concluded with the slogan, "against all forms of nationalism that divide the working class."[82]

Throughout the first half of 1933, there were violent clashes in the interior provinces of Santa Clara, Camagüey, and Oriente. In the city of Santa

Clara, striking workers and their supporters stormed the city hall with machetes and clubs. Fifteen people were seriously injured and the army was called in to patrol the city. Elsewhere in Santa Clara province, peasants at Güines and at the sugar mill Gómez Mena occupied land and divided it up among themselves. The peasants at the mill were supported by the local *caudillo* Juan Blas Hernández. Blas Hernández ordered his followers to defend the peasants against the mill management and the rural guard; he also came to the defense of striking workers at the Morón mill in Camagüey in September 1933.[83] In Cienfuegos, workers took over the city council, the board of education, and the local sport club. The strike committee then confiscated the houses of Machado's local supporters and gave them to the unemployed.[84] Cienfuegos tobacco workers demanded that they receive better pay and sanitary conditions, that children under fourteen not be employed, that Afro-Cuban workers receive the same treatment as others, and that the factory owners negotiate with the union and not with individual workers.[85] At the Punta Alegre mill in Camagüey, which was the scene of the violent clashes in February, British West Indian laborers joined Haitian and Cuban workers in occupying the mill and expelling the management. Armed supporters of the government tried to retake the mill, but they were unable to do so.[86] Clashes between striking workers and strike breakers occurred in Sancti Spíritus, Marianao, Madruga, and Santiago de Cuba.[87] In February 1933, workers occupied the Nazabal sugar mill in northern Santa Clara. The laborers demanded recognition of their union and access to land for the cultivation of food during the dead season. On August 17 there was severe rioting in Santiago de Cuba, which was fueled by a bitter strike at the Bacardi distillery.[88]

Welles and his British colleagues might have wanted to blame the Communists for all this activity, and the CP itself often tried to claim that it led these struggles. Yet the evidence clearly points to a more spontaneous and complex series of events than either the diplomats or the Communists were willing to acknowledge. The influence of Garveyism in Cuba remains to be studied, but the UNIA was active in Cuba, especially among British West Indian mill laborers.[89] The Unión Obrera de Oriente, a non-CNOC Trotskyist union based in Santiago de Cuba, recognized that workers in the east faced a complex set of circumstances: regional *caciques*, many of whom were loyal to national *caudillos* such as Mario Menocal and Carlos Mendieta, exercised strong influence over many workers. The Unión Obrera criticized CNOC organizers sent to the east because they were often insensitive or unaware of the interplay of local politics and class struggle.[90] Nor should it be forgotten that the CP and CNOC were founded in 1925 and the SNOIA had been created only in 1932. As we have seen, these organizations recruited most of their members in late 1932 and 1933, and thus they were not in a strong position to lead such complex and intense class struggles.

By the end of the summer of 1933, President Machado was replaced by Carlos Manuel de Céspedes. Ambassador Welles, of course, hoped that Machado's departure would bring an end to the political crisis. Yet from the very beginning it was clear to most Cubans that the United States had "virtually imposed upon the Cubans the government of Don Manuel de Céspedes."[91] Too much had changed in Cuba to permit history to repeat itself. By 1933, all that remained of the *machadato* was Machado himself, and Céspedes was now in the same position. As a consequence, the Céspedes government, which was to last until September 5, had no mandate, no popular support, and no ability to calm the political situation. It was true that Machado's exit somewhat abated the strike situation in the capital. Some unions won legal recognition, and wage increases were granted to some laborers.[92] However, the widespread attacks on Machado's supporters and the police continued with ferocious energy. After a few days the strike wave gathered steam again. The CNOC issued a manifesto exhorting the workers to maintain the strikes even though Machado was out of power, and they called for the formation of a worker's and peasant's government.[93] The harbor and railway strike spread beyond the Havana-Matanzas region.[94] On August 20, ten thousand poor and working-class Cubans demonstrated in Havana, demanding that *machadistas* be prosecuted and that their economic demands be satisfied.[95] The port workers won their strike and returned to their jobs, but 3,000 shoe workers, 1,500 textile workers, 800 cardboard workers, and 700 hat and cap workers continued to stay away from work.[96]

The immediate problem for Welles and the Cuban elite at the end of August was clear: the removal of Machado was not the beginning of the end of the Cuban crisis; rather, it was the beginning of a new phase of the crisis of political power. Welles complained that many in the opposition were "taking the attitude that a triumphant revolution had placed the Government in power and that they are consequently entitled to dictate the policies of the Government."[97] Welles's mediation efforts were moribund, and the Cuban state was in tatters. No one seemed ready to take decisive action.

CHAPTER FIVE

What Do the People Think and Feel?

Mass Mobilization and the Revolution of 1933

The deadlock between the fractious Cuban elite and the American ambassador was broken by a group largely on the sidelines of the unfolding struggles of the past year. On September 3 and 4, at the Camp Columbia Barracks outside of Havana, a group of Non-Commissioned Officers (NCOs), sergeants, corporals, and enlisted men confronted their senior officers over issues of back pay, living conditions, and promotion possibilities. The officers refused to listen to the demands of the rebels and abruptly withdrew from Camp Columbia. As a result, the lower-rank soldiers found themselves in control of the barracks and in a de facto state of mutiny. On September 5, the students of the DEU and other opposition factions declared their support for what became known as the "sergeants' revolt." What started as a minor dispute involving a marginal group of low-rank officers turned into a passive coup against the Céspedes government. Yet if the soldiers were not out to take power, neither were the opposition groups that rallied to their cause ready to assume the offices of government.

The young and relatively inexperienced revolutionaries found themselves pushed into the halls of state power by worker and peasant mobilizations "from below." Between September 1933 to January 1934, a loose coalition of radical activists, students, middle-class intellectuals, and disgruntled lower-rank soldiers formed a Provisional Revolutionary Government. This coalition promised a "new Cuba" with social justice for all classes and a Cuba free of the Platt Amendment. The new regime claimed its legitimacy from the popular rebellion that had brought it to power. For the first time in Cuban history, the country was governed by people who did not negotiate the terms of political power with Spain (before 1898) or with the United States (after 1898).

In the immediate aftermath of the sergeants' revolt, on September 5 a short-lived "Pentarchy" of five leading nationalists formed a *junta* to direct the government. Ramón Grau San Martín, Sergio Carbó, Porfirio Franca, Guillermo Portela, and José Miguel Irisarri signed a manifesto promising a "new Cuba" with modern democratic institutions. None of these people were political leaders from the traditional elite. Grau, Franca, and Irisarrí had participated in the Veterans' and Patriots' Movement of 1924. Ramón Grau San Martín had distinguished himself by vigorously opposing Machado's extension of powers in 1927 and by supporting the DEU and the student protests of 1930–31. Grau had been jailed by Machado on several occasions in 1931 and 1932 and was exiled to the United States until he returned to Cuba in August 1933. Sergio Carbó was a journalist and a supporter of General Menocal. It was as a *menocalista* that Carbó participated in the 1931 rebellion at Río Verde. Franca, a conservative banker, was named as secretary of the treasury. Portela, like Grau, was a university professor at the University of Havana. Fulgencio Batista, one of the sergeants who participated in the Camp Columbia revolt, was promoted to the rank of colonel and appointed as chief of staff of the Cuban army. Batista was asked by the other five to be the sixth member of the *junta,* but he declined, giving the reason that his place was in the army and not in politics.[1] While these people were generally known and respected among middle-class nationalists, none had a large political following. Rather, they were prominent members of a politicized minority thrust into the cauldron of mass politics.

For the next four months, political events unfolded without U.S. approval, though the approval of the new government (or lack thereof) came to matter more and more as the days went by. What drove the politics of the Grau coalition was the social dimension of the nationalist struggle. The Plattist state had exhausted itself trying to repress the building forces of class and nationalist struggle; now, in September 1933, the revolutionaries found themselves trying to both articulate and harness the very forces they had helped unleash against the Plattist state. As early as September 7, two days before the Pentarchy dissolved, Cuba's new leaders issued a political memorandum that outlined their view of the situation. After stating that the "new Government of Cuba does not correspond to trends of a communistic nature; neither are the members composing it communists," the memorandum declared:

> The elements composing the Executive Commission [the Pentarchy] are not . . . the originators of the movement which placed them in the exercise of public power. The leaders of the movement, demonstrating exceptional disinterestedness, did not appropriate for themselves

the fruits of the victory, and taking as their aim the greatest advantages of the country, entrusted the function of government to the persons whom they considered fitted for the mandate. . . . At the present moment order is being preserved throughout the Republic. The disorders that have taken place since the 4 [September] instant have been of less importance than those which occurred under the preceding administration. And the events that have transpired in some sugar centers, are not the consequence of the political and economic character of the present regime, but a continuation of the disturbances of that kind, which were happening under the authority of the Government which terminated on the 5 [September]. . . . The idea that the Executive Commission is the result of the coup of a faction which can give it only precarious and ephemeral existence is derived from vague reports, which are often exaggerated, with respect to the true situation now prevailing in Cuba; but it loses all appearance of reality by the fact of its having been put in contact with all sectors of those who were in opposition to the dictatorship, in order to form a strong cabinet of National Concentration in which there are truly represented all the militant groups that fought for the purpose of restoring in the Republic, right, civil liberties, the laws, and the honor of the people as an homage to civilization.[2]

In order to "restore the Republic," the government decreed a dramatic series of reforms. The Platt Amendment was unilaterally abrogated, and all the political parties of the *machadato* were dissolved. The new regime granted autonomy to the university, women could vote, the eight-hour day was decreed, minimum wages were promised to cane cutters, and compulsory arbitration was promised. The government created a Ministry of Labor, and a law was passed establishing that 50 percent of all workers in agriculture, commerce, and industry must be Cuban citizens. The Grau regime set agrarian reform as a priority, and peasants were promised legal title to their lands. The popular clamor for a "new Cuba" was impossible to resist, and that was what the Grau government promised.[3]

But making promises is one thing and implementing them is quite another. The tumultuous history of the September revolution has been recounted elsewhere.[4] The leaders of the September revolution were faced with four significant problems. First, they had no organizational backing, either from their own political followers or from a state apparatus. Second, there was intransigent opposition from the United States and from the old political parties and traditional *caudillos*. Third, the initial hope of the revolutionaries that the social struggles of the *clases populares* would abate proved to be false. Fourth, and most important, the economy was in ruins. As we will see in the second part of this chapter, the Provisional Government had no adequate response to the economic crisis. In this sense, the Grau government inherited a crisis more than it held real political power.

From September on, the class struggles in the urban centers and in the countryside continued with even greater intensity than in August. These struggles were encouraged by the Communist Party and the leaderships of CNOC and SNOIA, who, following the Comintern's line, condemned the Grau administration as "social fascist" and a "bourgeois latifundista" government.[5]

Within one week the Pentarchy dissolved, and a new Provisional Revolutionary Government under Ramón Grau San Martin was formed on September 10, 1933. This first week of September was an eventful one in Cuban history. In the political chaos after the resignation of Céspedes on September 4, ambassador Welles moved out of his official residence and into the luxurious National Hotel near the Havana waterfront. Welles had already intended to leave Cuba on September 14. There had been much speculation in Cuba about how long he should continue serving as ambassador, and, given the political tensions generated over the mediation process, Welles himself thought it best that he leave Cuba.[6] His stay at the hotel was prolonged by the fall of Céspedes and the ensuing events.

On September 9, four hundred officers of the army had moved to the National Hotel. With the collapse of the *machadato* and the Céspedes government, coupled with the NCO mutiny of September 4, the ranking officers decided not to support any government without the full backing of the United States and the parties of the traditional elite. The officers were backed by supporters of the ABC and the Unión Nacionalista. Members of the army loyal to "the revolution" of September 4 in turn surrounded the National Hotel. They were commanded by the recently promoted Colonel Batista.[7] In the midst of this turmoil, several U.S. destroyers were sent to Cuba to protect American lives and property. In all, sixteen ships surrounded the island.[8] Despite the repeated statements by the U.S. Department of State and from Welles himself that the United States had no intention of armed intervention, many Cubans felt an invasion was imminent. It did not help matters when Welles stated on September 5 that "if order was maintained, and blood not spilt, the independence of Cuba could yet be saved."[9] This was a threat solidly in the Plattist tradition. In addition, the fact that Welles was staying in a hotel with several hundred *machadista* officers was, to say the least, poor public relations. His refusal to even acknowledge a change of regime added fuel to the fire. After commenting on the events of the week, Grant Watson of the British embassy wrote:

> Very significant also is the altered position of the United States Ambassador. Usually the United States Ambassador in Cuba acts as a Governor rather than as an Ambassador, and his wishes as regards the Government and appointments are accepted as decrees. The new revolutionary Government, however, has been set up without any consultation with Mr. Welles, almost in opposition to his wishes. . . . Thus we end the week in Cuba under a de facto Government which has not been recognized, under an army led by sergeants, with the United States Ambassador living in a hotel surrounded by soldiers and machine guns, and the island surrounded by United States men-of-war.[10]

Grau's cabinet ministers were Dr. Manuel Márquez Sterling (secretary of state), Dr. Joaquín del Río Balmaseda (justice), Antonio Guiteras (interior), Colonel Manuel Despaigne (treasury), Gustavo Moreno (public works), Ramiro Capablanca (presidency), Manuel Costales Latatú (education), Carlos E. Finlay (health), and Julio Aguado (defense).[11] These men represented the aspirations of the generation that had come to political age in the 1920s. All were firmly against the Platt Amendment, and all of them wanted to reduce Cuba's dependency on the United States. They were the political products of the struggles of 1923–24 and 1927–30. Grau was the choice of the DEU. Márquez Sterling was a respected diplomat and journalist close to Unión Nacionalista circles. Despaigne had been a member of General Crowder's "Honest Cabinet" ten years earlier and had also been a leader of the Veterans' and Patriots' Movement. Guiteras, who had participated in the high school student movement in the early twenties, had been a member of the eastern DEU since 1927. He was chosen for the cabinet because of his contacts and support in eastern Cuba. No other member of the cabinet had the prestige necessary to counter the *caudillos* and the influence of the ABC in Las Vilas, Camagüey, and Oriente.[12] Batista continued as the new commander in chief of the army.

Despite their individual political experiences, none of Grau's ministers were national political figures or people with much experience in mass politics. Like the Pentarchy before them, they were chosen by relatively small groups of followers with whom they had associated during the anti-Machado struggle. As we will see shortly, there were also fundamental political differences among them, though it is difficult to determine to what degree these differences existed before Grau formed his cabinet or if discrepancies developed in the course of the struggles to come. What is clear is that as the political and economic situation unfolded throughout the fall of 1933, a centrist faction formed around Grau and the DEU, a leftist group emerged alongside Guiteras, and Batista and his followers formed on the right.[13] What mattered most in September 1933, however, was that for the first time in Cuban history the country was nominally led by men who did not have the approval of the United States.

While all this was occurring, Batista, the new commander of the armed forces, was quickly becoming a concern for some within the government. Batista was taking advantage of the chaotic situation to consolidate his position within the army. He did this by ensuring that his friends and followers were appointed to key positions and that *machadista* commanders were weakened. On September 26, when referring to the numerous strikes throughout the island, the *Havana Post* said, "The army under Batista is the only organized force on the island. Everyone else is pushing in different directions."[14] Three days earlier, on September 23, Salvador Rionda of the Cuba Cane Corporation received word from his Havana office reporting that Batista had telephoned at two in the morning to say that he was sending a large contingent of soldiers to retake the Manatí mill from striking workers. In the same message Rionda was informed that the company had signed a statement of protest with all the large mill owners in Cuba complaining about the government's inability to protect lives and property at the mills.[15] When the Shell Oil workers went out on strike in October, the company appealed to the British embassy for assistance. A refinery holding two and a half million gallons of oil was left completely unguarded. The embassy called Batista, who promptly sent soldiers to guard the refinery.[16] Through the month of October the press made numerous references to Batista's growing influence, both within and outside the army. As early as October 4, Batista was issuing statements declaring that only he could bring order to the labor situation, and that he was working diligently to reorganize both the Havana police force and the army.[17] On the same day the British embassy reported that "the better behavior of the troops increased the prestige of the Chief of Staff, Sergeant Batista, who from this moment becomes the real dictator of Cuba."[18] On November 15 Watson reported that "the army under Batista has shown itself to be the strongest organization in the country, and it is working for the restoration of peace and order."[19]

As the fall of 1933 passed, it become clear that the Grau regime and the army were not of one mind as to Cuba's future direction. On the one hand,

Batista and the new group of officers needed to defend the Grau regime if only because it was their mutinous act that started the September revolution in the first place. Until Batista could be certain that the *machadista* officers could not take their revenge, he was forced to remain within the camp of the revolution. On the other hand, the sergeants-turned-officers wanted to consolidate their new positions rather than encourage social change. They were reshaping the army in their own image, but this would take time, especially in the midst of the political crisis. The more Batista and his followers consolidated their posts, the more they voiced their disapproval of Grau's social policies.

From the middle of October there was no more pretense that Batista and the army supported the Provisional Government. Batista simply ignored the administration and went about his work defending U.S.-owned plantations and breaking strikes. On November 3, in a meeting at the house of Sergio Carbó, Antonio Guiteras, acting as the minister of interior, confronted Batista with the charge of treason against the government. Batista did not feel powerful enough to move against Guiteras, however, so he retired to Camp Columbia for a few days to let things cool off.[20] By December Guiteras was trying to counter Batista's monopoly on armed force by forming workers' militias to both defend the government and resist Batista. He also had cultivated contacts in the navy.[21] Guiteras was now the "leader of the radical wing" of the Grau regime, insisting that the only way it could survive was to move to the left and build alliances with the unions and the communists.[22]

Throughout November the Cuban press began referring to Carlos Mendieta as "the next president of Cuba."[23] Meanwhile, the tensions within the Grau administration finally took their toll on the DEU. The growing threat from Batista was alarming, but they could do nothing but express their concern to Grau, who, in turn, could do nothing but talk to Batista. Partially because of these building tensions, on November 4 the DEU dissolved and in a published statement announced that individual members would support the Grau government in whatever way they saw fit.[24] With the dissolution of the DEU, the Grau government was further weakened.

With the 1934 sugar harvest fast approaching, the U.S. government and the sugar companies were anxious to work out a solution to the Cuban crisis. On October 26, Salvador Rionda, an executive director of the U.S.-owned Cuba Cane Company, sent the following assessment of the situation to his New York office: "Now I come to a subject that neither you nor myself can decide but I believe that you can suggest to some of the sugar companies in

New York the importance of the sugar companies coming to an agreement on what should be paid during the next crop in the different provinces for the cutting and hauling expenses and pressure should be brought to bear on the Government of Cuba (that will probably be changed during the next few days) to state the rate of cutting and hauling for the different Provinces in Cuba for the next crop." [25] Perhaps Rionda's mention of the government falling in a "few days" referred to an ABC–Unión Nacionalista rebellion that took place on November 8 and 9. The rebellion failed because Guiteras and his followers, the students, the ABC Radical, the Ala Izquierda Estudiantil, and even rank-and-file members of the Communist Party rallied to defend the government. Batista stayed on the sidelines on November 8 but on the next day, seeing that the rebellion was ill organized and doomed to fail, ordered the troops to finish off the rebels. [26]

Despite this tense situation, there were two things that gave the Grau coalition space. First, its enemies were no better organized, at least for the time being. [27] Second, the unleashed insurgency "from below" kept the United States, the traditional elite, and Batista off balance. With the intervention of the *clases populares,* the established notions of political timing, of tactics, and of whom to appeal to for support were thrown off center. For all the administrative and political weakness of the government, they could at least claim to be the product of nationalist insurgency and not its enemy.

In the meantime, the working classes and the poor were not waiting for change to arrive from a distant government in Havana. The ouster of Machado in no sense diminished the intensity of the class struggles. In the countryside most sugar mill occupations and strikes took place after Machado's fall. Between late August and December, there were strikes at sixteen mills in Camagüey Province, including the important Cuba Cane Company mills of Morón, Jaronú, Violeta, Stewart, Senado, Elia, and Francisco. [28] In Oriente Province, the United Fruit Company mills Preston, Boston, Vertientes, and Banes were occupied by strikers. [29] The Mabay mill at Bayamo was the scene of sharp clashes between workers and the rural guard. The same situation existed at the Nazabál, Parque Alto, and Herminguero mills in Las Villas. [30] The occupations at the Mabay mill and the mills in Las Villas became known as the "soviets" of the Cuban revolution of 1933. [31] As early as September 21, eighteen mills in Oriente were shut down by strikes. [32] At the Cuba Cane mills Manatí, Elia, Francisco, and Tuinucú, the company was "very nervous about the worker situation": workers at these mills demanded higher pay and refused to consider any compromise offered by the company. [33] While the company complained about the workers' demands, they did admit that "the vast majority of articles of basic necessity had risen in price by over 100 percent and maybe we were mistaken to impose on our expert operators a wage cap of $1.00 per day during the first five months of the dead season."[34] In another company letter on the labor situation, an official remarked that "until Cuba has a strong government any agreement with the workers is useless."[35] The company wanted the government of Cuba to issue a decree on the labor troubles, but expressed pessimism, "because we do not have confidence that such a decree would be effective because the government lacks sufficient authority to implement any decision it makes, and, even more sadly, because we cannot expect a solution with people [the workers] who know that the government needs them and that the government cannot consolidate itself without them."[36] A report from the Manatí mill stated that support was requested from a U.S. destroyer anchored nearby. The captain and a "very large sailor" came back to the mill, but their visit had no effect. The report described how armed workers had taken over the mill and noted that the company's chief of security had joined the strikers. The overseer of the workers was forced to leave because of death threats. The author of the report stated:

> The writer after having spent twenty-two years in plantations in Cuba has never seen anything like these strikes that seem to have been organized all on more or less the same plan although at some places they have been more violent than at others. Here the strikes have been very violent and at times it looked very much as if we would lose our lives. . . . The property of the Manatí Sugar Company has been in the hands of the strikers from Saturday (Sept. 16) morning until Saturday (the 23rd). We have not been allowed to work in the office, the first few days we were not allowed to circulate in the batayes on foot or in automobile, our track motors were used by the strikers without our permission . . . we could not talk by telephone to the wharf or any of the colonias, the long distance phone was left but the line was tapped so that all our conversations with Havana were heard, all the servants of the house were told not to work or that they would be beaten-up and all of us had to cook for ourselves. The strikers run the electric plant at night as they needed water but we had no intervention and they gave lights as they pleased, distributing ice as they pleased among themselves, but having the rest of us without any. A complete SOVIET REPUBLIC! The army soldiers were of little use as you probably know what has happened in Cuba with students, soldiers, sailors, and workers![37]

On October 1, at the Estrada Palma mill in Oriente, soldiers armed with machine guns clashed with workers occupying the mill; after extensive fighting the workers were ousted from the mill.[38] The assistant general manager of the Elia mill in Camagüey, a Mr. Estrada, made an emergency telephone call to the Cuba Cane office in Havana complaining that "strikers with a revolutionary attitude assaulted the administration offices." The strike committee gave Estrada two hours to fulfill their demands "or they would not be held responsible for what would happen." The local army detachment was called in by Estrada, but the mill remained under siege. Estrada then informed Havana that he had cabled the Cuba Cane offices in New York, requesting that the company make a protest to Washington. As a follow-up to Estrada's call, the Havana office contacted Minister of the Interior Guiteras to register their concern.[39] Two of the world's largest sugar mills, Chaparra and Delicias, were the scene of strikes and violent clashes. By late October there had been eighty strikes in Cuba, most of them in the east.[40] In all, thirty-six mills were seized by workers, which represented 30 percent of Cuba's sugar production.[41]

In most respects these conflicts in the sugar sector differed little from what had transpired earlier in the year. There is no doubt that Communist Party, CNOC, and SNOIA organizers played important roles in many of these events. Yet despite the CP's persistent claims that it led these struggles, the evidence points to a more complex picture. An internal CNOC document acknowledged that most workers who participated in the occupations and strikes were not organized at all.[42] Other statements by the party after 1933 spoke about the "spontaneous" nature of the struggles.[43] The CP seemed to confuse mass mobilization with mass organization. It also seemed that the strikes had more of an effect on the party than the party had on the strikes: the struggles of 1933 provided the party with hundreds of valuable recruits, many of whom would stay in the party for the next thirty years.[44] In one notable case the party gained the support of a young worker during the occupation at the Constancia mill: Jesús Menéndez became the leader of the powerful Confederación de Trabajadores de Cuba (CTC) during the 1940s and one of the country's most popular labor leaders and communists.[45]

For all the efforts of the CP to lead the class struggles and create soviets in the countryside, however, many occupations and strikes were resolved peacefully and locally. Labor conflicts could end as quickly as they had flared up. On October 4 the *Havana Post* reported that striking workers were back on the job at the Zorrilla, Los Arabos, Tuinucú, Sagua de Tánamo, Manatí, and Victoria mills: in all cases their unions were recognized and wages improved.[46] Workers at the large Hershey mill in Matanzas had postponed their strike at the end of September in order to wait for Milton J. Hershey, the owner of the company, to arrive from Philadelphia to negotiate with them personally: on October 6 the union was recognized and higher wages were granted.[47] In Camagüey, at the Cuba Cane mill Macareno, the company signed an agreement with the workers promising to recognize the union and to pay the workers in cash and not with company store "vales."[48] Strikers at the Mabay mill in Oriente could not maintain their "soviet" because of lack of food and supplies; by October 21 they offered to return the mill to the owners. The CNOC organizers who tried to create a "soviet" at the Senado mill were expelled by striking workers. It seems that the Senado laborers were near starvation, and the strike came to a stalemate when management agreed to pay the strike committee seventy dollars per day to purchase food in exchange for the workers not damaging the mill or sacking the company store. The General Sugar Company mill Agramonte was occupied by strikers, but the workers maintained mill equipment and kept up general repairs through the occupation. Overall, there appears to have been little damage to mills during the fall strikes.[49]

The fact that many of the strikes and occupations ended rapidly—most within a few days—did not mean that the labor situation could be easily managed. On the contrary, most conflicts that were resolved in the fall of 1933 flared up again in the months and years to come. It would take years before anything resembling collective bargaining existed in Cuba. Most of the "unions" that won "recognition" in the fall of 1933 were little more than hastily formed strike committees with no legal standing and little capacity to sustain themselves as organized bodies. The correspondence of the Cuba Cane Company makes it clear that the company was willing to raise wages and recognize unions to ensure that repairs in the dead season were completed. There is no indication that the company considered these agreements to be permanent. As one mill manager explained to his superiors: "[I] conceded the increase of wages you will find in the enclosed document [a "contract" with the union] and without waiting for express authority from you, as he firmly believes that if he had waited for that authority there would have been considerable loss of property and lives."[50] What the company did acknowledge was that it had to ensure that individual mill administrators were open to talking with delegates from the worker committees, instead of simply refusing to negotiate with them. In that way, order could be maintained at each mill in accordance with local conditions. One company proposal, written in December 1933 after the most violent strikes took place, suggested that each mill have its own arbitration committee with representatives from the company and from each union. Until more systematic work is done on the history of the union movement in Cuba, little of substance can be offered on this issue. Most of the "contracts" the Cuba Cane Company signed with its workers referred to the unions as "the General Union of Workers at Manatí," "the worker's committee," and similar names. On the whole, the tone of the company's correspondence is concerned, but not panic stricken. The impression one gets from reading the company's correspondence on the 1933 strikes is that the troubles, though more serious than ever before, would pass, and things would return to normal.[51] Only after 1940 did a truly national and relatively stable union structure emerge.

The Grau coalition therefore faced a serious contradiction. On the one hand, the social legislation it promoted in early September had raised expectations among the working class and the poor. Rural and urban workers alike mobilized to obtain better labor conditions and more rights. They had done this before, but never within the context of a deep economic crisis and with a government in Havana that claimed to represent their interests. On the other hand, the government did not have the organizational capacity or the political unity to implement the desired changes. The government had the daunting task of defending the popular demands of the working class while defending its own legitimacy in the face of concerted opposition from the traditional elite, the United States, and the communist-influenced trade unions.

Nowhere was the government's dilemma more evident than in the all-important sugar industry. On September 23 the government issued a decree, signed by Grau and Guiteras, which declared that the government would work to guarantee both the sugar harvest and worker rights. After stating that the first responsibility of the government was to maintain order "within the creative plan of the revolution," the decree stated that the role of government was to balance the interests of the sugar companies with the legitimate rights of the workers. The government must therefore play an active role as a mediator between capital and labor.[52] Without a sugar harvest there would be no order; but without fair wages and unions for sugar workers there would be no harvest. A report from the British embassy noted that "the workmen at present support the government, but they will probably withdraw their support if the government cannot arrange for the harvest."[53] Twenty-seven-year-old Minister of the Interior Antonio Guiteras was designated as the man responsible for dealing with this problem.

Guiteras and the government were fighting a losing battle. On the one hand, the sugar companies were hostile to the government from the very beginning and they were not about to cooperate more than absolutely necessary. The problem for the sugar companies was that they could not be certain that the government would fall. It was therefore imperative that they keep the channels open to Grau and Guiteras in case the two sides had to work together on a more permanent basis. On the other hand, while Guiteras could talk directly to the companies, he could not meet with workers in every single mill; without a strong nationwide sugar union to negotiate with, Guiteras would have to solve the problem one mill at a time. Without a state bureaucracy behind him, the task was both politically and physically impossible. But Guiteras tried. As early as September 30, the government brokered an agreement between the Francisco Sugar Company (Cuba Cane Company mill Francisco) and the workers. In the agreement the company agreed to pay a minimum wage of one peso a day and to accept the government's overall legislation on a one peso minimum wage in the sugar sector. It included a promise that the company would accept an eight-hour day, with the understanding from the workers that some days would be longer; it agreed to pay time and a half for labor over eight hours. In addition, sanitary, water, food, and health conditions would be improved by the company, and the union at the mill would be recognized by the company.[54] The same kind of negotiations were supposed to take place at the Cuba Cane mill at Manatí on September 29, but the mill management felt that "nothing will be done in the benefit of the mills and that each mill will have to come to settlements with its workers."[55] Guiteras and his small staff tried to work out other problems in the Chaparra and Delicias sugar mills, in the railway sector, and in other parts of the sugar economy.[56] Except for the occasional temporary agreement, the ministry of interior and the ministry of labor failed to gain a foothold in the sugar economy.

In the midst of this struggle, Guiteras was making the foreign sugar companies and the Cuban elite nervous by threatening to implement land reform. By November a strong "back to the land movement" emerged among the Havana poor. The government had already expropriated land from some of the most notorious *machadista* landowners and distributed it to the poor, and there was popular expectation that more land would be granted.[57] By early December Guiteras announced his intention to implement a systematic agrarian reform law. He proposed that all land not held by clear title— he estimated the amount to be approximately 600,000 acres—be taken over by the government and handed over to the Havana poor. He then announced the government's intention to take $18 million from the state treasury and purchase another 250,000 acres for the landless. The agrarian reform would be administered by a new agricultural bank, which would also provide peasants with tools, seed, and material to build homes.[58] Once again, nothing came of this measure, but the hopes and expectations of the landless were raised by the plan and Guiteras became more popular among the Havana poor. In equal measure, he became the hated target of the elite press and the sugar companies.[59]

The situation in the city was equally complex. In Havana the strike wave had not subsided since Machado's departure. In the middle of October a bitter strike at the Havana Woolworth Store turned into a prolonged and violent struggle between the women employees and management. The Havana Electric Company workers struck, as did bakers, taxi drivers, bus drivers, street car conductors, telephone company employees, garage mechanics, and shoemakers.[60] In most cases the strikers demanded better pay, fewer hours, and the right to form unions. At the same time, business associations and merchants refused to pay taxes to the Grau government. Import houses often refused to release food, and warehouses were full of unloaded goods. Doctors and nurses were on strike.[61] Meanwhile, there was widespread hunger in Havana. On September 30, 4,500 Havana poor demanded that uncooked food be distributed to them so they could take it home to cook instead of waiting in long lines for hot meals.[62] Bread was in short supply, and the hungry and homeless were everywhere.[63] When people were faced with terrible living and working conditions, they took to the streets demanding that government legislation be implemented. Even before the eight-hour decree was publicized on September 19, armed groups of unionized workers went around to shops and factories to ensure that it was respected.[64] Workers demanded legalization of their unions, but the *machadista* judges were not about to sanction such a move. And as long as Batista was doing his best to ensure that workers were kept under control, the government's social legislation would have little impact on workers' lives.

It was precisely these pressures that forced the Guiterista wing of the government to move to the left. Not only did Guiteras directly challenge Batista's military power by encouraging the formation of popular militias, he also worked to build a base within the urban working-class movement.[65] This move placed him on a collision course with both Batista on the right and the Communist Party and CNOC on the left. Guiteras's allies in the ministry of labor, Alberto Giraudy and Armado Loret de Mola, supported his leftist ideas. Yet the Communist Party, true to the Comintern's line, condemned the entire Grau government as "bourgeois-latifundista" and "social fascist."

Their manifestos made no distinction between left and right within the government, and they lumped Guiteras and Batista together, calling them the "henchmen of reaction."[66] While the conflict between Guiteras and Batista was understandable given their clear political differences, the Guiteras-CP-CNOC confrontation presented a different set of problems. Guiteras was not anticommunist, and in late 1933 he tried to establish an alliance with the CP. Nothing came of these efforts, if for no other reason than because the Grau government was overthrown in January 1934. But in the short term the problem for the Grau coalition was that while the left hand of the government (Guiteras) tried to build bridges with the working class and the poor, the government's right hand (Batista) was knocking them down. When Batista jailed striking workers in the name of law and order, Guiteras freed them in the name of revolutionary justice and workers' rights.[67] Since most union members were not privy to the internal politics of the Grau coalition, it is understandable that there would be widespread confusion as to exactly what the government wanted to do.

Still, the attempt of the Guiteristas to obtain support of the organized working class was both an effort to create an organized popular base for the government and a threat to CNOC and party influence within the unions. The attempt by the left within the Grau coalition to build an organized base among workers can best be illustrated by examining two interrelated events. The first involved the Guiterista attempt to take over the Havana Federation of Labor (FOH). The second revolved around the government's controversial "Nationalization of Labor" decree issued on November 8.

The conflict over the Havana Federation of Labor flared up in late October when Guiteras and the minister of labor, Loret de Mola, attempted to reorganize the union. For most of its history, the FOH had been dominated by reformist and anarcho-syndicalist elements. For years the FOH and the CNOC were in a bitter rivalry over control of some Havana-based unions. By the end of the *machadato,* the FOH had lost ground to CNOC because of the rather passive role of the FOH leadership during the August events. Moreover, a small group of Cuban Trotskyists managed to gain influence within the union. As a result, there was a crisis of leadership in the union at a time when many of its rank-and-file members demanded more militant action. October and November was also a time when the fighting around the National Hotel came to a climax and the ABC–Unión Nacionalista rebellion took place: the *machadista* officers surrendered on October 3 and the government felt more secure after the military defeat of ABC-UN. Guiteras and Loret de Mola chose this conjuncture to reshape the FOH into a more militant but progovernment union. On October 10 even the communists had to admit that Guiteras and Loret de Mola were partially successful: "[T]he government is trying to build itself a base among the workers. It is not to be denied that it used the action of the soldiers in attacking the reactionary officers cleverly. It made a play at making this its own position and in this manner tried to gain the sympathy of workers and the city poor who were against the officers. To an extent this maneuver worked."[68] The ministry of labor purchased furniture and office supplies for the FOH, and the union attracted support from independent radicals who supported the government.[69] On November 2 CNOC condemned Guiteras as "the most active of the arbitrators and mediators and he is the hangman of this government."[70] The overthrow of the Grau government in January destroyed these early attempts to forge government links with the union movement. Yet this modest effort to build populist support among the working class was the first time in Cuban history a government — or at least a faction of a government — tried to carry favor with the organized working class. It would not be the last time.

At the same time, the Grau coalition began to implement the "Nationalization of Labor" decree. The purpose of this law was to ensure that at least 50 percent of all employees hired by enterprises were Cuban citizens. The motivation behind this law stemmed from years of popular frustration about Cuban labor being denied work in their own country.[71] This legislation was aimed principally at the Spanish commercial elite in Havana who tended to hire other Spaniards and not Cuban nationals. Spanish merchants and shopkeepers responded by closing their shops, *bodegas,* and trading houses.[72] The nationalization of labor decrees were popular measures, and they addressed long-standing concerns about the place of Cuban workers in their own homeland. But in the fall of 1933 they were more symbolic than real. Cuban workers were suffering massive unemployment, and though Spanish merchants and shopkeepers might have irked Cubans, most people wanted jobs. The only way to provide jobs was for Cuba to gain some control over the labor marker, both internal and external. To gain this control, it would be necessary to confront the problem that for decades sugar companies had brought in hundreds of thousands of workers from Haiti and Jamaica. To "nationalize" labor meant taking on the sugar companies, and however much Grau and his followers might have wanted to do that, they were simply too weak to do so. As we will see in Chapter 7, the issue of foreign labor migration would be confronted, but within a very different context.

The CNOC, for its part, threatened to organize a general strike against the government because it viewed the law as racist and a measure intended to break "working class unity." Many workers of Spanish origin would be hurt by the law, and the CP and CNOC valued the trade union experience of these workers.[73] Throughout November and December the Communist Party and CNOC threatened an insurrectionary strike and an armed uprising. But by the middle of December, too many of their own rank-and-file members were showing support for the government's measures. Twenty thousand people marched to the presidential palace on December 21 to show their support for the Nationalization of Labor law.[74] Ten days earlier the British embassy reported that the government had gained more support from the workers and at the same time "sap[ped] the influence of the Communists."[75] The general strike never materialized, and the government seemed to be making modest inroads into the working-class movement.

By late fall the Grau coalition was acutely aware of this new political contradiction. As the forces of old Cuba attacked them from the right, the Communists, CNOC, SNOIA, and other leftist groups challenged them from the left. Meanwhile. the people in and around the cabinet were discussing these issues in public. Grau made a statement to the press where he argued that his "government has given particular attention to all measures dictated that have had as their end the betterment of living conditions for all citizens and especially for the working classes. The series of decrees, which have transformed colonial practices, have had a beneficial impact on the republic, despite the short time they have been in place."[76]

It was the journalist Sergio Carbó who most clearly articulated the new political reality in Cuba. Carbó did not formally participate in the government, but his influence on people within and outside of the government was considerable. Carbó's journalism was an important source of information for the anti-Machado forces in the early 1930s. He bridged the gaps between the *menocalistas* of the Unión Nacionalista, the DEU, Guiteras, and Batista. Why he was able to do this is not clear, since information on his life and activity is sketchy. On November 29 the British embassy described Carbó and Batista as the two most powerful men outside of the cabinet. It was also Carbó who promoted Batista to the rank of colonel during the brief Pentarchy.[77] Carbó, in two long interviews given to the Cuban and foreign press, explained that the task of the Provisional Government was first to maintain order, second, to provide honest and efficient administration, and third, to permit all political parties to function legally and openly. Sounding remarkably like present-day liberal exponents of the idea of a clear division between "civil society" and the state, Carbó stated that "the propagation of [political] doctrines should be displayed in the streets far from the technical functioning of the administration in its daily routine in preparation for the great struggle that will take place at the Constituent Convention. There, and not elsewhere, is where the revolutionary program that we displayed on the night of September 4 should meet victory or defeat."[78]

One week later, on November 23, Carbó was more explicit: "We cannot continue in the state of disturbance and alarm in which we find ourselves today. War is no solution for peoples or for governments. Sectors and government must consider that there is another sector, more important and numerous, which is not consulted, nor is it known what it thinks, but it does think and feel. It is the public, toward which it is necessary to look and cater and which is already tiring of these disorders." Carbó concluded his remarks by saying that all the Grau government was asking was that the United States not interfere in this process.[79] If any lesson was to be learned from the previous six months, it was that a change of government was no guarantee of peace and order. Any future government would have to take into account what the popular classes thought and felt.

What did the public "think and feel" in the fall of 1933? Who was "the public" Carbó referred to? This issue, in a nutshell, was the essence of the political problem in Cuba. Each one of the political "sectors" had its own answer as to what the people *should* feel and think. And each sector had its own ideas about who "the public" was. Welles wanted to restore U.S. hegemony on the basis of the old way of doing things. Grau, Carbó, and the now former members of the DEU wanted to guide "the masses" into the nation-state's modernizing project. The Communist Party, CNOC, SNOIA, and other radical left groups wanted a "worker-soviet republic." Batista wanted "order." Antonio Guiteras and his followers generally wanted the same things as the communists, but with the important distinction that they wanted to push the government to the left from within: this division within the Cuban radical left would have dramatic long-term implications for future struggles.

Still, the Grau coalition had too many fronts to fight on. Without U.S. recognition, both political stability and the 1934 sugar harvest were in danger. In early December Grau, Carbó, and Batista were meeting with the traditional opposition groups and with Welles to try and reach a "compromise solution." It was clear to Grau that as long as he was president, there would be no U.S. recognition.[80] Meanwhile, Guiteras and his allies openly condemned any negotiations with Welles.[81] The stage was set for a major battle among all the factions. The timing was finally right for Batista to move against Grau. Welles had given Batista the green light to move against Grau in October, but the class struggles from September through November did not allow Batista to act with impunity.[82] He was forced to wait until the Grau coalition fell apart from within before he was free to move.[83] An additional factor influencing Batista's timing was the pending sugar harvest. Pressure had been mounting to bring order to the sugar sector for months. On December 3, United Fruit Vice-President and General Council William J. Jackson informed the Foreign Policy Association that "the threat of communism is very real. U.S. tariff policies have ruthlessly destroyed its [Cuba's] very life — the sugar industry of our best neighbor. . . . Cuba is economically ruined. The great mass of her people are underfed and underclothed. They are so beset with the consequent unrest that they are easy prey to communists who are flooding to Cuba. There are great and numerous strikes and seizures of property throughout Cuba by workers."[84] Jackson concluded his remarks by recommending a stabilization agreement on sugar which would guarantee Cuba's access to the U.S. market.

By late December and early January 1934 the sugar companies were confident that Batista could maintain order, but they felt a new government was needed to support the army. An official of Cuba Cane wrote that "the maintenance of order in the sugar mills no longer worries us . . . because of the disposition of the army to protect, as much as possible, the work in the fields." The official went on to say, however, that if the order was going to last, the army required legal support for its actions. Arbitrary repression was no longer sufficient.[85] Another company official wrote that it was "simply impossible to carry out the harvest under conditions similar to the year before" and that it was imperative that all the mills stabilize their workforce and that any future government be counted on to support the companies.[86] From the perspective of the sugar companies, the quotas placed on the entry of Cuban sugar into the U.S. market were not only diminishing their profit margin, but they were also the cause of social unrest on the plantations.

Earlier in December, Welles had been replaced by Jefferson Caffery. Caffery was not immediately designated as an ambassador: to do so would have been a sign that Washington recognized the Grau government. Instead, he was appointed to serve in Cuba as "personal representative of the president." On January 13 the British reported that "Cuba is becoming an armed camp. . . . A change of government without the consent of the army is unlikely. Mr. Caffery seems to be prepared to deal with Batista in order to rescue a new government based on a wider foundation, but he mentioned the necessity of obtaining an advance guarantee for foreign interests."[87] Four days later, Caffery wrote that "Batista has just sent me word that in view of the various precarious strike situation (seriously endangering enormous American properties) provoked by Guiteras . . . he has decided to declare Mendieta president this afternoon."[88] Grau's days in government were numbered. On the very day Batista told Caffery he (Batista) would oust Grau, the pro-Grau American journalist Carlton Beals identified the overriding political problem in Cuba:

> In this revolutionary moment in Cuba no means exist of determining just what is the will of the Cuban people. . . . The instrumentalities for determining the popular will do not exist and for the moment cannot be created. The popular will . . . is far more radical than the present government, and would result in a Negro-Mulatto government. Two things appear self-evident: first, the Cubans are united in their desire to purge the republic of all possible Machado elements and do not wish the return to power of the other old-line political groups and personalities which Welles was sponsoring; second, no political faction represents a popular majority. Cuba must therefore be governed by a coalition or a faction.[89]

In the middle of January 1934, Batista simply shifted support from Grau to Carlos Mendieta of the Unión Nacionalista. On January 18 Colonel Carlos Mendieta took the oath of office and became president of Cuba. Four days later, on January 22, the new government was recognized by the United States. The provisional government was thrown out of office as unceremoniously as it had assumed it. Grau went into exile in Mexico. Guiteras went underground. Workers busied themselves looking for the best working conditions for the coming harvest. While strikes continued in Havana and other cities, they were no help to the fractured Grau coalition nor any threat to Batista and Mendieta.

The day before the Mendieta-Batista government received U.S. recognition, Grau boarded a ship to Mexico. Grau's departure, however, was unlike that of any other president in the history of the country. On January 29 Grant Watson of the British embassy described the scene at the harbor:

> A crowd of his adherents gathered at the wharf and, as the vessel steamed down the harbor, they ran along the sides. They belonged to the poorer classes and were very enthusiastic. They regarded the impractical, consumptive doctor as their champion. He had been in office for only four and a half months, and yet he made reforms, some of

which will last. Students of Cuban history will remember his term because a great change came over Cuba. The rule of the sugar magnates was shaken, at any rate, for the present—perhaps forever.[90]

Two weeks earlier Watson had written, "Nationalism and socialism are rather artificial products in Cuba, but I am convinced they are factors with which we must reckon."[91] Watson's insight was remarkable, given that few people appreciated the historical significance of the final chaotic months of 1933. All of the important reforms of the Grau regime were, in fact, implemented by future governments, including the repressive Mendieta-Batista regime of 1934–35. To be sure, these reforms were not implemented in the way intended by Grau, and stability in Cuba was a long way off. The country had battered itself into a state of political exhaustion, and it would take another six years before anything resembling social peace existed on the island. A great change had indeed come over Cuba.

CHAPTER SIX

Appointed by Destiny

Fulgencio Batista and the Disciplining
of the Cuban Masses, 1934–1936

From 1934 to 1936, Cubans lived under a virtual military dictatorship headed by Fulgencio Batista. Batista remains an enigmatic figure, and it is not a simple matter to explain his political evolution. He was not an original political thinker; rather, he was a clever tactician and pragmatist who adapted quickly to changing political circumstances and ideas in order to remain in power. A scholarly biography of Batista is sorely lacking. Fulgencio Batista was born in 1901 to lower-class parents. He spent his early life working as a barber, carpenter, cane cutter, bartender, tailor, railroad worker, and army stenographer. He joined the army in 1921 and became a sergeant in 1928. In the latter role he worked for General Machado's chief of staff, General Herrera. As a sergeant, he participated in the mutiny of noncommissioned officers on September 4, 1933. Batista had been a member of the right-wing corporatist ABC Society in late 1932 and early 1933, but, in opposition to the ABC, he supported the Grau government from September 1933 to January 1934. At that point, with the support of F. D. Roosevelt's personal emissary, Sumner Welles, Batista shifted his allegiance to Carlos Mendieta. Batista ruled from behind the scenes between 1934 and 1940. In 1940 he was elected president of Cuba and served until 1944. From 1944 to 1952, Batista retained a loyal following within the army and the police, though he was never as popular as his rival, Grau San Martín. Batista's political skill rested on his ability to make alliances with people and factions who did have a mass following; this skill, coupled with his strong support within the army, guaranteed that Batista would always be a factor in Cuban politics. Batista engineered a coup against the Auténtico government of Carlos Prío Socarrás in March 1952. Thereafter, Batista and the young radicals of the 1950s, led by Fidel Castro, embarked on a prolonged struggle. After Castro's victory of 1959, Batista fled first to the Dominican Republic, then to the Portuguese Madeira Islands. Batista died in Spain in 1973.[1]

Certainly Batista held power because he controlled the army and the police. But this fact should not make us underestimate the reality that Batista saw himself as a leader of the revolution of 1933 and not as a counterrevolutionary dictator. If we fail to take this into account, we run the risk of underestimating both the importance of the 1933 revolution and of Batista as a political leader. Batista knew that Cuban politics would never be the same after 1933, and he had no intention of restoring the traditional political system. This was the great paradox of Cuban politics between 1934 and 1940. It helps explain why Batista could be both authoritarian and reformist in the course of a few years and get away with it. The Cuban leader understood that mass sentiment for reform was, in the long run, more powerful than his army and police.[2] As long as the reformist and radical opposition remained fragmented, Batista held the political initiative, something he managed to do from 1934 to 1944.

The first section of this chapter will examine first how Batista, with American political and economic support, brought "order" to Cuba; the second part will trace the defeat and decline of the Cuban left between 1934 and 1937. Overall, the central argument of this chapter is that Cuba's transition to a nominal democracy by 1940 cannot be explained without taking into account the state violence unleashed against the *clases populares* and the various opposition groups. Recent scholarship on the relationship between authoritarianism and democracy has emphasized that the line between the two is often not as clear as might be supposed. The form and degree of democratic participation cannot be adequately explained if we do not take into account the state violence that preceded the transition to democracy.[3] As we will see, Batista's corporatist ideas, backed by his repressive apparatus, made the state the central protagonist in bringing "balance" and "discipline" to Cuba's skewed social structure. This doctrine of social harmony, however, required mass repression to destroy any organizational and political autonomy the *clases populares* had managed to win for themselves over the previous years of intense popular struggle. Only when this was accomplished could Batista permit the emergence of what he called his "renovated" or "organic" democracy after 1937.

Repression and Order, 1934–1936

The story of how Batista received the backing of the United States is well documented.[4] On January 18, Colonel Carlos Mendieta took the oath of office and became president of Cuba. Shortly after, one journalist wrote that "Batista is a sort of a handy man of ambassador Caffery[5] and the chief supporter of the Mendieta government."[6] A British embassy dispatch of April 10, 1934, bluntly stated, "The government has become a dictatorship, every whit as dependent on the army as the Machado regime during the last years of its administration."[7] Colonel Batista was de facto ruler of Cuba and he would remain so for ten more years, yet, as we will see, Batista was no one's "handy man."

The Mendieta presidency proved to be a chaotic affair, with one cabinet crisis after another. The factions supporting his government—the Unión Nacionalista, the ABC Society, and politicians from the old political parties—fought publicly over cabinet postings and ministry jobs. In some cases this infighting was a simple matter of patronage. In other cases, some politicians objected to Batista and his army infringing on what they regarded as civilian territory. Such was the case with the right-wing and corporatist ABC Society, which always regarded Batista as an upstart, and they went into opposition when it became clear who held the real power in Cuba. Later, both Mendieta (1934–35) and Miguel Mariano Gómez (1936) were removed for thinking they could take their own political initiative. This intra-elite turmoil would continue for the rest of the decade, and Batista would take full advantage of the situation. Grant Watson of the British embassy wrote that "although he [Batista] has no training in national affairs, he has shown remarkable powers of assimilation, and has good advisors who have grasped the essential factors for the restoration of order. The administration is nominally in the hands of President Mendieta and his Ministers, but Colonel Batista deals with the most vital matters, and more and more people make the journey to Camp Columbia to consult him."[8]

The first priority of Batista and the Mendieta government was to bring order to Cuba. Throughout the spring of 1934 the Mendieta-Batista government was challenged by labor unrest. Unions affiliated to the Cuban National Confederation of Workers (CNOC) and the Havana Federation of Labor (FOH) were behind many of the strikes, but independent and newly organized unions were involved, too. In the first three months of 1934 there were more than 100 strikes in Cuba; the sugar sector experienced continued labor conflict; and only 30 of 178 mills were grinding by February 12, 1934.[9]

Numerous violent clashes arose between striking sugar mill workers and the rural guard. Workers were injured or killed during clashes on the Baguanos, Preston, and Tacajo plantations. In Oriente the mines at Daiquirí and Firmeza were the scenes of violent strikes throughout February and March. By early March it was practically impossible to travel to Camagüey and Oriente because of a railwaymen's strike. In response, the military took over the administration of many towns and mills.[10] Meanwhile, public school teachers refused to work; students went on strike on February 17; and on January 20, some 25,000 doctors, nurses, and chemists joined the protests.[11] In early February, 30,000 tobacco workers stopped work, virtually halting all tobacco exports. Havana and other provincial capitals were crippled by transportation strikes.[12] Newspapermen stopped work. By March 1934 some 200,000 workers were on strike.[13] Bombings and shootings continued to be nightly occurrences in Havana and other centers. The situation was so tense that one American commentator wrote there could be "civil war between the government, supported by the army, and the masses of the Cuban workers."[14]

To gain control over the situation, the government passed a series of repressive decrees. Decree Number 3, issued on February 7, 1934, required workers to give eight days' notice before they went on strike. This decree limited the right of workers not directly involved in a labor dispute to hold sympathetic strikes. Decree Number 51, issued on March 5, was intended to "defend the republic against communist agitation"; Decree Number 52 gave the government the power to expel "foreign agitators"; Decree Number 67 of March 6 suspended ten personal guarantees stipulated in the Constitution; and on March 9, any union strikes were made illegal and strike breakers were to be protected by the army and police.[15] On March 10, for example, the government brought in 500 strike breakers from the interior provinces to defeat a dock-worker strike in Havana. Protected by a contingent of police and soldiers, many of the strike breakers were members of Mendieta's Unión Nacionalista.[16]

While repressing labor unrest, the Mendieta government claimed it was not a counterrevolutionary regime but rather a continuation of the September Revolution of 1933. On January 22, 1934, Mendieta declared, "My government embraces the program of the revolution." The ABC Society, which threw its support behind Mendieta, stated on January 19 that it would support Mendieta on the condition that he "enforce the decrees of the previous [Grau] revolutionary government beneficial to the people." Grant Watson of the British embassy commented that "the socialist decrees of the late Government have been maintained."[17] Later he wrote, "The government has

made every effort to placate labor, and have undertaken to safeguard the reforms of the September revolution, but it cannot be said that they have made
much progress towards the solution of the social problems which afflict the
island."[18] For example, Mendieta's first minister of labor, Dr. Juan Antiga,
proved to be too sympathetic toward labor for his cabinet colleagues, and
he was forced to resign on March 2.[19]

Notwithstanding Watson's exaggerated use of the word "socialist" and
the claim that the government had made "every effort to placate labor," it is
true the government kept intact many of Grau's initiatives, at least on paper.
As we will see, continued labor unrest between 1934 and 1937 delayed the implementation of some of the September revolution's policies, and when they
were implemented it would be under the watchful eye of colonel Batista.
Of particular importance was the Ministry of Labor, which did not exist in
Cuba prior to its creation by the Grau regime in September 1933. In the first
months of 1934, the Mendieta government established an arbitration mechanism to resolve labor unrest. Unions were required to submit their demands
to the Ministry of Labor. Arbitration Committees were then struck at local
and national levels to discuss each conflict. The local committees comprised
three representatives from the strikers, three from the employer, and one
official from the Ministry of Labor. The local bodies would make recommen-
dations to a national committee which included three members each from
the union and company, and one member each from the Ministry of Interior,
the Ministry of Labor, and the Department of Commerce and Industry. The
secretary of labor chaired the national committee meetings.[20]

Later, in early 1935, the Mendieta government resurrected another initiative of the Grau government. Under Grau, the Ministry of Labor had organized "Labor Exchanges" in Havana province. The idea was to provide a
clearinghouse for information about available workers and to register those
seeking employment. The exchanges were intended to help workers find employment as well as to help mill owners find workers with appropriate skills
and experience. The Grau regime did not last long enough to create labor
exchanges other than in Havana province. In May 1935 the Mendieta government established labor exchanges in all five provinces. The new law stipulated that employers must advise the provincial labor exchange of all hiring
and discharging of workers. When taking on new workers, employers had to
hire laborers whose names were supplied by local labor exchanges. Unions
were required to inform the labor exchanges which of their members were
fired, hired, and rehired. Employers could not take on workers who did not
possess a labor exchange registration card and violators of this provision

were subject to fines ranging from $20 to $500. Finally, if a collective agreement existed between a union and a business, the employers had to request a list of available workers from the union before taking on nonunion labor.[21]

Despite the decrees, and despite the creation of an arbitration mechanism, labor unrest continued. The years 1934 and 1935 proved to be too unstable for the Mendieta-Batista government to implement social policies aimed at pacifying discontent among the *clases populares*. One strike would end, and another would begin. "The weakness of the Government," the British embassy reported, "is noticeable in their failure to enforce the decree of February 7. Every day a fresh strike is declared in defiance of this decree, which is treated by the workers with open contempt."[22] Government weakness was also evident with the labor exchanges, which did not begin to function adequately until after 1936. On March 12, newspapermen and Havana dock workers returned to work. The strike of telephone employees continued, but it was weakened when half their number returned to work while the other half were locked out for refusing to accept government arbitration. By mid-March most of the larger sugar mills were grinding, because "the army paid special attention to the protection of workers who were willing to work and succeeded in suppressing many disturbances."[23] In July, 5,000 Havana bus drivers struck, demanding better pay and an end to the harassment of union members by police. Postal workers went on strike, and the military took over their positions.[24] In early September students burned Batista in effigy: they chose the first anniversary of the September Revolution to attack Batista as a traitor to the people's struggle. At the same time, 256 locked-out workers from the American-owned Cuban Telephone company tried to forcefully reenter the company's building: an armed confrontation between workers and police ensued, with one policeman and two workers seriously injured. Later, management personnel joined police in firing on the laborers. The same month, employees of the Ministries of Health, Agriculture, Labor, Public Works, and Education, as well as Havana municipal workers, left their jobs to protest the killing of two students on August 31.[25] By October 1 constitutional guarantees, which had been reinstated on September 5, were again suspended in Havana and Oriente provinces because of strikes and "terrorist actions." The military occupied Havana City and Santiago de Cuba. Batista told the press, "We intend to withdraw the troops now on duty in the city as quickly as circumstances will permit, but that moment has not arrived."[26]

Batista's reference to the right moment when troops might be taken off the streets in October 1934 was similar to his attitude about the national situation generally: he would determine when the Cuban people were "ready" to assume civil authority, and only then would the army—and Batista personally—withdraw from politics. Two weeks into October Batista told J. D. Philips of the *New York Times* that "public order must be preserved at all costs." To that end, he ordered soldiers and rural guards to keep peace in villages and sugar mills. But, Batista explained, "the Cuban people do not want a dictator. Nothing would give me more pain than to see the day arrive when it would be necessary to establish a dictatorship to save the republic from chaos and anarchy." At the same time, Batista felt "personally responsible for Cuba. I believe that I have been appointed by destiny to do my utmost for the republic. To me, all figures from history who have emerged from the masses to change the course of a nation are guided by a predestined purpose." Instead of a military dictatorship, Batista's vision of a new Cuba was distinctly corporatist:

> One of the most disturbed classes in the island is labor. . . . Their demands have been heard and respected, but outside radical influence has crept in, usurping control of many syndicates and forcing many strikes. We have had an epidemic of strikes during the past year. Some of them were justifiable, others were not. In my opinion, the rights of labor must be protected, but equal protection must be extended to capital. One cannot take away rights from either. The only equitable basis is an arrangement that will permit both to operate peacefully and with benefit to themselves and to the nation. The economic situation of the island cannot improve when labor and capital are in eternal strife. We greatly need the influx of foreign capital, but, on the other hand, no exploitation of the working classes should be permitted.[27]

"Corporatism" refers to a situation "where the state plays a major role in structuring, supporting, and regulating interest groups with the object of controlling their internal affairs and relationships between them."[28] Batista, however, was still consolidating his place within the chaos of state formation after the 1933 upheavals. Corporatist leaders, moreover, tend to be pragmatists. For Batista, ideologically motivated politics was of no use as a means to bring about the reconciliation of labor and capital: "I am an idealist, but a practical one. . . . To me, all ideals are useless unless they can be put into practice, all theories are without value unless they can be applied. The group who surrounded Dr. Grau were in the majority earnest, idealistic students who lacked orientation, practicality, and knowledge of applying their theories of government."[29] Batista later acknowledged that the Grau government was a continuation of Cuba's unfinished struggle for independence and that it was the first government of truly Cuban origin in the nation's history. Like Mendieta, Batista claimed that he was continuing the work of the September revolution: "We demand the right to run our own affairs, the right of every free nation. We are not communists, we are hardly socialists, we merely want to liberate Cuba from foreign control. We do not want to frighten capital, we need capital. . . . We must raise living standards. That will also benefit the United States. Cuba was once one of America's best customers."[30]

It was becoming clear to observers of Cuban politics that Batista was not going to restore the pre-1933 status quo. For Batista, a return to pre-1933 conditions was unacceptable. A revolution had occurred, and Batista saw himself as the man who would bring "order" to the country:

> There has been a profound revolution in Cuba, with its consequent social commotions, during the last four years. That revolution was conceived and materialized within the army. Cooperation of civil elements followed, which was a result of social indiscipline. The revolution needed a figure at its head to assume responsibility. That is how it developed to me to embody the movement. . . . In a situation where the national institutions are crumbling, in which there was almost a state of anarchy, the chief of the army established contact with civil factions to reestablish social discipline. This contact initiated the reconstructive tendency classified as civil-military. . . . This cooperation of civil and military elements, which originated in that chaotic state, succeeded in reestablishing discipline in the country, making elections, and the consequent reestablishment of normality possible.

In the same statement, Batista responded to a query if the current government was "provisional": "Yes. It is provisional, lasting until the definitive structure of state is solidified through a constituent assembly."[31] In preparation for the "definitive structure of the state" and a constituent assembly, Batista wanted to bring "balance" to society. He exalted the status of the small producer, the "honest" laborer, and strove to attain a "judicious balance" among competing social classes. At the same time he defended the right of capitalists to earn "just" profits. The Cuban government, Batista declared, "has paramount interest in balancing national wealth, not in destroying it. We can neither create nor consolidate an all absorbing capitalist system, nor an anarchical, unfruitful, collectivism."[32]

Batista's ambiguous political discourse caused many at the time to wonder where to place him on the political spectrum. Earlier we saw that Batista explicitly stated that neither communism nor fascism could work in Cuba. He portrayed himself as a selfless patriot free of ideological prejudices and a "practical idealist" "above" the petty squabbles of political factions. Batista professed his admiration for U.S. president F. D. Roosevelt and his opposition to Mussolini and Hitler. At the same time he viewed himself as a nationalist who wanted economic and political independence for Cuba:

> My ideas embody the historical revolution, made necessary by the situation of the Cuban people. It is not fascism. . . . Cubans have only small industries and businesses. The revolution of the 4 of September proposes to establish the economic personality of Cuba and to suppress the habit of thinking that we cannot do things ourselves. . . . As a Cuban, not only do I believe that Cuba should be free, but it should obtain independence from economic influences. . . . I am sure that the United States would never attempt to annex Cuba. That would be impossible; it would cause a revolution worse than the struggle against Spain.[33]

In hindsight we know that Batista's political instinct was to move to the right of the ideological spectrum. But, as one contemporary observer pointed out, in the 1930s the picture was not so clear. "Batista, when he broke into the political arena, was a man of the Left. . . . With unctuous adulation, the Right seduced Batista from the Left. For some time lately, however, he has tended to hold a balance in the middle, a feat of tight-rope walking that has all Cuba guessing."[34] As early as October 14, 1934, Batista expressed his views on the nature of the Cuban crisis to the *New York Times*:

> The army has no desire to enter politics, but we have been forced to take a hand in the affairs of the nation. The entire social structure is abnormal at present. Political factions disagree violently and frequently shake the confidence of the public in the government. Small groups, without consideration of the rights of others, attempt to impose their will on the government or individuals by force. . . . When this happens, what can the army do? Our sole function is to maintain peace and order. In doing so we have come into direct conflict with many classes and have gained the enmity of people. We are accused of usurping civil authority. The army is always subordinate to civil power, but when the latter proves itself too weak to cope with the situation, then military authority must step in.[35]

Batista was not insincere about the importance of civil power. But from his perspective, "civil authority" had to be molded by the firm hand of the state; otherwise the progressive aspirations of the 1933 revolution would be undermined by "disorder." Between 1934 and 1936, however, no one cared much about Batista's ideas on civil authority and the role of the state. The "enmity of the people" was indeed directed at Batista, and it would take two more years of state repression before Batista thought Cubans "ready" to assume civil authority, and only then under the auspices of an authoritarian state under Batista's watchful eye.

From 1934 until 1936, the struggle between the dictatorship and labor continued to dominate the political scene. In March 1935 the largest general strike in Cuban history shook the nation. Estimates of the number of strikers reached 500,000.[36] From the very beginning the strike lacked both a unified leadership and an overall strategy. Throughout the month of February, students, teachers, and some trade unions actively resisted the government's suspension of civil judicial authority and formation of Military Tribunals in its place. These Military Tribunals had the power to jail people for participating in strikes, carrying out sabotage and boycotts, organizing demonstrations, handing out antigovernment propaganda, and behaving in a manner they labeled "delinquency."[37] On February 19, students at the University of Havana went on strike: they demanded the immediate abolition of military power, guarantees of individual human rights, freedom for all political prisoners, and more government support for primary, secondary, and post-secondary education.[38] Teachers and university professors soon joined the students, and by February 23 some 300,000 students, teachers and university employees were on strike across the island.[39] By late February and early March, many unions had joined the strike wave. Unions affiliated with the Cuban National Confederation of Workers (CNOC) and independent unions representing tram workers, postmen, the Cigar Makers Union, and the General Commercial Employees Union, as well as government workers from the Ministries of Justice, Agriculture, Public Works, Health, and Communications, were off work. Santiago de Cuba was completely shut down by the general strike.[40]

The general strike, however, could not maintain its momentum. Like the general strike that toppled Machado two years earlier, the 1935 strike was spontaneous and lacked unified leadership. In contrast to the events of August 1933, however, the army under Batista succeeded in breaking the strike. On March 14 some unions ordered their members to return to work, while others appealed to workers to hold firm until the government fell.[41] Batista ordered troops to drive the buses, occupy postal stations, take over the university, and protect strike breakers. All constitutional rights were suspended. Most unions were declared illegal. The Shell-Mexican Petroleum Company was instructed by Batista to rehire only those workers the company considered reliable, and the union was banned. The same happened at the United Railways of Havana, where members of the Railway Brotherhood were denied access to worksites. In the middle of March, more than 1,000 strikers were in jail and the majority of workers were back on the job.[42]

After the defeat of the 1935 strike, there could no longer be any doubt that Batista and the army were the victors in the struggle for state power. But if the forces supporting the Batista-Mendieta regime won state power, they did not yet have the *political* authority necessary to legitimize their power. The loosely knit coalition of traditional politicians, wealthy sugar planters and businessmen, and military men who owed their positions to Batista might have been united in their antipathy toward the ousted Grau government, but they had no common vision of how to rule Cuba after 1933. For all Batista's concern about promoting "harmony" between the masses and the government, he was too busy repressing the *clases populares* to concern himself with how to gain their support. Batista could not turn his attention to mass politics until he finished with mass repression.

Political developments did not permit Batista to seriously address the problem of the state's political authority until late 1936. Not only was Batista busy maintaining order in the country as a whole, but he also acted as arbitrator in the constant infighting among the governing elites. When things got out of hand, as they invariably did, "the ubiquitous Colonel Batista cracked the whip and ordered all to behave."[43] After the defeat of the general strike, the Mendieta cabinet set elections for December 15, 1935. On the surface, the old style of politics had returned to Cuba: the three presidential candidates, Miguel Mariano Gómez from the Republican Party, Mario Menocal from the Conservatives, and Dr. Manuel de la Cruz of the Liberal Party, jockeyed for position in much the same way as politicians had before 1933.[44] Largely because of Batista's backing, Gómez assumed office in May 1936. The Gómez presidency would last a year.

Gómez made the mistake of challenging Batista over the issue of civilian versus military control of the planned construction of some 2,300 rural schools. The issue of rural education was to mark Batista's first serious attempt to enter the arena of civil politics. In 1936 Batista initiated a plan to build 705 rural civic-military schools. Members of the armed forces would teach the children of peasants, workers, soldiers, and policemen practical skills such as modern agricultural techniques, reading and writing, and disease prevention.[45] Adults, too, could attend these schools. By the summer some 750 army teachers were instructing 35,000 children and 20,000 adults in areas of Cuba that had never seen a school before. In January 1937 Batista announced that an additional 1,000 schools would be constructed by the end of the year.[46]

This school program was very popular, and Batista's personal reputation grew as a result.[47] However, these schools and teachers needed to be paid for, and by the end of 1936 President Gómez and Batista clashed over who would finance the program. Originally Batista intended to support the scheme entirely from within the military budget. But, as costs increased, he demanded more money from other branches of the state. Batista encouraged Congress to pass a bill imposing a tax of nine cents per bag of sugar in order to pay for the rural education program. For his part, Gómez opposed military intervention in an area that for him clearly fell within civil jurisdiction. By December 1936 the conflict between Gómez and Batista came to a head when Gómez called Batista's measures "fascist," while Batista claimed he was only trying to improve the lot of the rural poor. Gómez, it seems, was simply following the lead of the larger sugar mill owners who objected to the tax. Yet Batista made it clear that if the sugar companies did not accept the tax, there was no guarantee that troops would protect mills and cane fields. Gómez was out of office by Christmas 1936, and the mill owners came to view the sugar tax as cheap insurance in their struggle against labor.[48]

Gómez was the last president of Cuba to seriously challenge Batista. Thereafter no one needed a reminder about who shaped important government policies. With the radical opposition muzzled and with the traditional elite politically passive, Batista could now turn his attention to implementing his political ideas.[49] On July 4, 1936, Batista outlined his political vision to the *New York Times:*

> No one can establish either fascism or communism in Cuba. They cannot live here. I believe Cuba should have a renovated democracy, under which there should be discipline of the masses and of institutions so that we can establish a progressive State under which the masses may be taught a new idea of democracy and learn to discipline themselves. I believe in a philosophy of authority, not of force. . . . There are two kinds of socialism. One means anarchy and the other functions under the discipline of the government. We must go slowly here. Government ownership may work later on in Cuba, but not now. One must be

realistic . . . we want to teach the masses that capital and labor both are necessary and should cooperate. We want to drive out utopian ideas which will not work, but which so many of our people hold.[50]

Batista was not entirely successful in driving out "utopian ideas" from Cuban politics, but, as we will see in the next section, between 1937 and 1940 he was rather successful in compelling opposition elements to be more "realistic."

Batista's success, however, is inexplicable without taking into account American policy toward Cuba after the revolution of 1933. Once again, as was the case in late 1933, it was journalist Sergio Carbó who succinctly summed up the situation in the country. On April 15, 1934, Carbó published an article entitled "The Revolution Is Dead; Save the Revolution" in the influential magazine *Bohemia*. After pointing out that the source of Cuba's ills lay in the stark social and economic inequalities in the country, Carbó went on to say that "there will never be peace nor order in Cuba, whatever coercive measures the government might use, as long as the government fails to interpret the economic sentiments of the masses, sentiments which were already set in motion by the revolution."[51] To be successful at interpreting "the economic sentiments of the masses," the Cuban economy needed to be stabilized, and this could not happen without the support of the United States. Batista, when he had said that Cuba needed to raise living standards and increase trade, clearly agreed with Carbó's analysis.

In terms of economic and diplomatic strategy, the United States implemented a rapid series of policies and initiatives throughout 1934. On March 9 the Second Export-Import Bank was established to facilitate trade between the two countries. The Jones-Costigan Act of May 1934 lowered U.S. tariffs on sugar imports and placed a series of quotas on foreign sugar entering the United States: the duty on Cuban sugar fell from 2 cents to 1.5 cents per pound. And on August 24 the duty on Cuban sugar was further reduced from 1.5 cents to 0.9 cents per pound.[52] As a result of these policies, the Cuban share of the U.S. sugar market rose from 25.4 percent in 1933 to 31.4 percent in 1937.[53] Cuban tobacco, fresh fruits, and vegetables were also permitted into the American market with reduced duties. In exchange, Cuba agreed to reduce import duties on American goods: hog lard, wheat flour, rice, automobiles, and American cigarettes received better access to the Cuban consumer market.[54] According to Secretary of State Cordell Hull, the objective of these agreements was "to restore the once flourishing trade between the two countries, now reduced to a fraction of its former amount."[55] A cornerstone of the "Good Neighbor policy" was to revive U.S. export trade as a response to the depression. In 1924 Cuba was the sixth best customer of the United States, taking in $192 million worth of U.S. exports; by 1929 that amount declined to $23 million.[56] By 1933 the value of U.S exports reached an all-time low of $22,674,000.[57] In early 1934 the U.S. secretary of agriculture explained the necessity for a new policy on Cuba:

> During the period of decline of sugar shipments to the continental United States, the purchasing power of the Cuban people was sharply reduced. This loss of Cuban buying power proceeded to a point where the island no longer provided the once substantial market it had afforded American products. Cuba formally had been an important customer for many American farm commodities, including butter, cheese, milk, pork, lard, corn, oats, wheat flour, and vegetable oils. Translated into land equivalent, the area required to produce the purchases of Cuba in 1928 was 1,738,000 acres. In that year Cuba shipped 3,125,000 short tons of raw sugar to the United States market. The purchase by Cuba of American farm products has declined as the market for Cuban sugar has been absorbed by our insular possessions. Now the area required to produce purchases by Cuba has declined to 921,033 acres. This meant that the American farmers had lost an export outlet for farm products from 817,267 acres of land, or an area larger than the entire domestic harvested acreage of beets in 1932.[58]

On March 29, Assistant Secretary of State Sumner Welles clearly outlined American policy: "What the President of the United States proposes . . . is not only an act of a good neighbor, but also of obvious self interest to the American farmer and manufacturer. We cannot regain the export trade for our own products unless we make it possible for the Cuban people to purchase them."[59]

As a consequence of these policies, economic conditions slowly improved. While Cuba secured a market for its export products, the country paid the price of increasing its dependence on the United States. Mr. Rees of the British embassy wrote to the Foreign Office that "the increased tariff preferences granted to the United States in return [for the sugar quota] cannot help but strengthen the dominant position already occupied by the United States in this market."[60] The very modest efforts at diversification attempted during the *machadato* were quickly reversed: between 1933 and 1940 the total value of U.S. imports increased from $22.6 million to $81 million; the U.S. percentage of Cuban imports for the same years rose from 53.5 percent to 76.6 percent.[61] In May 1934 the price of sugar on the New York market was

0.78 cents per pound; by the fall the price was nearly 2 cents per pound and in late 1935 the price hovered around 2.70 cents per pound.[62] As a result, the Cuban economy experienced modest economic growth, and merchants and shopkeepers reported brisk trade and sales within the country.[63]

In addition to the slow economic improvement, on May 29, 1934, Cuba was finally out from under the omnipresent Platt Amendment. The United States surrendered its right to intervene in Cuban affairs, while retaining control over the military base at Guantánamo.[64] Given the bitterness many Cubans felt about the Platt Amendment, it is striking that its abrogation met with so little rejoicing.[65] The elite press commented that the Platt Amendment had long outlived its usefulness, because the Cuban people, as with a young adult, had outgrown such paternalistic policies.[66] Referring back to Welles's arrival in the spring of 1933, the conservative *Diario del la Marina* commented, "Mr. Welles, in words that were very clear and concise, stated that if we reestablish order the State Department at Washington would grant us within a short period a sugar quota, an increase in customs differential for our sugars, the abolition of the Platt Amendment, and the revision of our reciprocity treaty."[67] On March 29, 1934, Sumner Welles, speaking to a meeting of Young Democrats, explained the attitude of the United States: "It speaks volumes for the patriotism, for the integrity, and for the genius of the outstanding leaders of today that notwithstanding the fetters that have been placed upon them since the early years of their independence, they should have so clearly demonstrated their ability to exercise their sovereign right of self-government." Welles said that the amendment "amounted to telling the Cubans how their government should be run and who should run it." Consequently, Welles argued, U.S. capital, especially in the sugar industry, "looked not to the Cuban government but to the United States government, for the adjustment of its controversies with local officials." American capital was beneficial to Cuba, and Welles concluded:

> It was in fact that the regulation and the control of such capital was de-
> termined not by the Cubans themselves, not by the government which
> they had elected . . . but by a powerful group of financial interests
> frequently potent in the councils of the government which possessed
> the right to intervene in Cuba's domestic affairs, that the inequity lay.
> *American capital invested abroad should, in fact as well as in theory, be*
> *subordinate to the authority of the people of the country where it is located.*[68]

If Cuba was to have order and capitalist development, "the authority of the people" must be nurtured and fashioned to guarantee social control from within the country, and not from the oligarchy and the United States. By implication, Cuban nationalism was not a threat to the United States as long as it did not challenge American hegemony; on the contrary, if managed properly, Cuban nationalism was the best guarantee of maintaining "civil authority." By adapting to Cuban moderate nationalism, the Good Neighbor policy was a more effective means of maintaining American hegemony than permitting the unfettered company domination of the Cuban economy that had existed under Machado and earlier. At the broadest level, this flexible approach to Cuban internal politics was the essence of "Good Neighbor" politics. The combination of the new U.S.-Cuban trade policies and the abolition of the Platt Amendment was intended to help guide Cuba out of its supposed childlike dependence on the United States.

In previous chapters it was demonstrated that Cuban middle-class nationalists identified the lack of civil authority as the central weakness of Cuban neocolonial society. The political programs of all the nationalist groups pointed to the weakness of the national state, economy, and civil institutions as the source of Cuba's persistent conflicts. In the midst of the turmoil of the September revolution, moderate nationalists expected support from the Roosevelt administration, only to be disappointed by how Roosevelt's representatives in Cuba conducted themselves. In the spring of 1933 the Good Neighbor policy was more a statement of intent than effective policy; still, given the political turmoil at the time, Roosevelt's announcement could not help but raise nationalist expectations. Grau and his followers, therefore, never appeared to understand why the U.S. State Department failed to support his government. On April 2, 1934, Grau, living in exile in Mexico, responded to Welles's speech to the Young Democrats (quoted above) by declaring that Welles's hostility to the September revolution was "inexplicable because all it did was carry out in practice what Mr. Welles recently proclaimed in his speech." The Mexican journalist interviewing Grau went on to comment, "Grau became the Roosevelt of the Cuban masses and his decrees were the New Deal to them. He made the working people, the natives, realize that their lands did not have to be developed by foreigners. He attacked the theory of the divine right of capitalists to order and to abuse. He gave to the laboring classes of Cuba the vision of a new day and a new ideal, a vision which the humble classes of Cuba will never forget."[69]

From the general political perspective of Grau San Martín and the students who supported him, Welles's attitude was "inexplicable." Grau and the students of the DEU were seemingly natural allies for Good Neighbor policy makers in Washington. Grau and the DEU were political liberals and economic nationalists, and while they were anti-interventionist, they were far from anti-American. What Grau and his supporters did not appreciate was that Welles, Caffery, and the U.S. State Department were not about to surrender the political initiative to the *clases populares,* no matter how much Cuban nationalists admired the Good Neighbor policy and the New Deal. From an American perspective, Grau's government pandered to the worst elements in Cuban society. Welles told the Young Democrats that "to carry favor among the unthinking[,] the new government [Grau] created an artificial anti-American campaign. . . . By the time December came, a condition of unprecedented chaos existed and a state verging on frank anarchy had come about. If it had not been for the support of the army, no such regime, unacceptable to the enormous majority of the people, could possibly have remained in power for more than a brief few days."[70] Batista resolved the problem of the army by changing sides. And though Welles and Grau might have shared the view that "the divine right of capitalists" was a bad thing for Cuba, Welles and his colleagues felt that the United States, and not Cubans, were the best judge of when the Cuban nation was ready for "the authority of the people." As we will see, what the Americans—and Cuban reformists, radicals, and the oligarchy alike—did not anticipate was that Batista would play a larger *political* role in this process than they could have imagined.

This seemingly "inexplicable attitude" on the part of Welles and the State Department can be explained by contrasting the evolving theoretical ideals of liberal democracy with the political reality of mass mobilization. In an age of mass mobilization, and especially between the European revolutions of 1848 and the revolutions of the early twentieth century, liberal democratic discourse clashed with the need to promote capitalist relations of production. Liberals wanted to free working populations from the fetters of pre-capitalist social relations dominated by the church, peasant communities, and slave owners, to name the most notorious targets of those who promoted free wage labor. As an alternative, people were offered the ideal of a free market and a wage labor economy that would lead to greater prosperity for all social classes. The problem was that the subordinate classes did not always wait to be "liberated" by those who claimed to speak on their behalf. Nor did people necessarily want to be wrenched from their communities and traditional ways of living. People rebelled in countless ways, and in the course of their rebellion and resistance, new ideas about the meaning of freedom emerged. Very often, subaltern ideas about freedom and democracy did not mesh with the liberal notion that wage labor and the market economy were synonymous with liberty and human progress. The "masses," therefore, could not be relied upon to be responsible citizens, at least in the short term.[71] The people needed the firm hand of the state to guide them, willingly or not, into the modern world.

It was within this broad context that the idea of "democracy" was appropriated by liberals in such a way so as to retain the idea of "popular legitimacy" and control over the state without sacrificing the economic power of the emerging capitalist classes. Politically, liberals achieved this formal separation between "politics" and "economics" by promoting capitalist economic development while simultaneously constructing constitutional mechanisms that permitted the modern state to set the terms of restricted democratic participation. These restrictions usually took the form of voting rights based on property ownership, gender discrimination, racial discrimination, and the degree of literacy of a population. By doing this, liberals could formulate ideas about what good citizenship meant and how best to translate these ideas into reality.

By the 1930s, however, the classical liberal notions of the nineteenth century were forced to compete with communist and fascist claims that these two new revolutionary ideologies were better suited to serve popular and national aspirations. Indeed, the world depression of the 1930s seemed to prove that liberal political economy had failed miserably. The Cuban revolution of 1933, like so many others in the early twentieth century, occurred within this larger context of mass mobilization and political crisis. With the collapse of the *machadato*, the dominant classes (and the United States) had lost considerable economic power and political legitimacy; at the same time, the *clases populares* and many middle-class nationalists were taking the idea of democracy in directions that the United States could not tolerate. Mass mobilization had brought forth ambiguous yet highly subversive ideas about democracy which were threatening to Cuban and foreign capitalists alike. This was the practical political problem confronting Welles, the Good Neighbor policy makers, Grau and his followers, Batista, and the post-1933 generation of politicians generally.

As we will see in the next chapter, by the late 1930s and early 1940s the struggle for democracy became synonymous with liberalism, and state intervention in society was increasingly seen as safeguarding democracy. Especially because of the trauma of World War II and the emergence of Russia as a world power, one of the dominant political issues of the time was which social system could best stake its claim to be truly representative of the people and nation. By the time of the cold war, liberalism would seize the political middle ground between dictatorship and fascism on the right and communism on the left. Western democracies increasingly proclaimed how "underdeveloped" peoples should be encouraged to vote in free and fair elections, join almost any political group, become unionists and political activists, and even have the right to protest in favor of their political rights; but these political rights could be and were often sharply restricted if mass mobilization threatened to undermine capitalist relations of production. American Good Neighbor foreign policy toward Latin America promoted these political values; yet it was equally capable of tolerating repressive regimes if the people were not ready for democracy. In Cuba, it would not be until 1940 that anything resembling a consensus was reached on these issues. In the short run, however, it fell to Fulgencio Batista to "prepare" the masses for a "renovated democracy" and constitutional government.

Groping Our Way Like a Blindman with His Cane: The Radical Opposition, 1934-1937

After the general strike of 1935, the radical opposition entered a period of defeat and ideological crisis. The roots of this ideological crisis date back to the fight against the *machadato*. In many ways the events of early 1935 marked the end of an era in Cuban politics. Since 1923 the opposition to the Plattist state had grown into a mass social and political movement that reached its high point in the summer of 1933, when General Machado was ousted. However, the ideological weaknesses of the anti-*machadista* movement existed long before the dramatic events of August 1933.

When Justo Carrillo of the Directorio Universitario Estudiantil proclaimed in early 1933 that "Machado's got to be toppled . . . *No matter who comes afterwards,*"[72] he was certainly expressing the popular will of most politically aware Cubans, but he could not have imagined that it would be Batista who would come after Machado. The moral indignation directed against the *machadato* might have been central to the demise of oligarchic rule, but the radical opposition tended to confuse mass mobilization *against* the oligarchic state with mass support *for* their programs. What was "popular," as one scholar writing on populism has pointed out, was not specific to any particular politics; rather, popular politics "represents the ideological crystallization of resistance to oppression in general."[73] The Cuban radical opposition rode the wave of popular resistance to "oppression in general" under the Plattist state, but it could not channel popular insurgency into a viable political alternative with mass support. Batista guaranteed that the radical groups would not be able to forge strong organizational ties with the masses. But opposition groups also had very little awareness of what can be called "oppression in particular": popular rebellion, especially in the countryside, was fueled by local circumstances and concrete moral and social values. As a result, such diverse groups as the ABC Society and the conservative *menocalistas* on the right, the DEU and Grau's backers in the political center, and radical leftists such as the Guiteristas and the Communist Party competed for mass support, but they all failed to establish strong organizational and ideological connections between themselves and the *clases populares*. While the opposition's collective efforts managed to destroy the Plattist state in 1933, they were unable to prevent Batista, with his control over the army and the police along with his populist rhetoric, from stealing *their* victory against Machado.

After the defeat of the 1933 revolution, four political trends represented the moderate and far left of Cuban politics. The first group were the Grauistas, who in early 1934 founded El Partido Revolucionario Cubano (Auténtico) (PRC-A). The second group formed around Grau's former minister of the interior and war, Antonio Guiteras: in May 1934, Guiteras, who went underground after the coup of January 1934, founded the political and military organization Joven Cuba (Young Cuba). A third and more diverse group of people formed smaller groups which maintained more or less cordial relations with the PRC-A and Joven Cuba. The most important of these smaller organizations were the Organización Revolucionaria Cubana Anti-imperialista (ORCA), the Izquierda Revolucionaria (IR), the Partido Agrario Nacional (PAN), and the older but small APRA-Cuba. The other organization of importance on the left was the Communist Party of Cuba. Only the PRC-A and the CP were to survive past 1936.

When Grau San Martín was in power, his main organized support came from the students of the DEU. When the DEU dissolved in October 1933, not only did Grau lose organized support, but the moderate left as a whole lost its organizational focus. In early February 1934 a large contingent of the former DEU students regrouped to form El Partido Revolucionario Cubano (Auténtico). After a series of meetings in the house of a Dr. Pablo Carrera Justíz in Havana, the PRC-A was formed by approximately 30 people, among whom were several prominent members of the old DEU. A partial list of the early leaders includes Aurelio Álvarez de Vega, Otilia André, Concepción Casteñedo de López, Félix Lancís, Francisco Polamares, Carlos Hevia, Lincoln Rodón, Carlos E. Finlay, Manuel Antonio (Tony) Varona, Antonio de Valle, Segundo Curti, Carlos Prío Socarrás, and Rubén de León. The large majority of these people were active in the DEU prior to the summer of 1933.[74] The choice of the name El Partido Revolucionario Cubano is telling: the original PRC was founded by José Martí in 1895, and the symbolic "refounding" of the party meant that the struggle for Cuba's complete independence was still to be won. The addition of the word "Auténtico" was an indication of the ideological confusion of the time. Virtually everyone, from Batista and Mendieta in government and the ABC on the right, to the Communists, CNOC, and SNOIA on the far left, was claiming to represent the "true" revolution of 1933, and the founders of the PRC-A were simply laying their own claim to represent the "authentic" revolutionary tradition of Cuba.

Ideologically, the program of the PRC-A was an amalgamation of the original DEU Manifesto-Program of 1932, American New Deal liberalism, and *aprista* influences.[75] The essential aspects of the PRC-A program included the demand for political and economic nationalization of Cuban institutions and an end to U.S. semicolonial domination. It called for agrarian reform and for the elimination of *latifundia*. The PRC-A wanted the emancipation of the Cuban working class "in accordance with the existing socialist tendency of humanity" while at the same time advocating the combined and judicious balancing of public and private property. The PRC-A's program explicitly condemned fascism and communism, emphasizing that the PRC-A was nationalist while communism was not. The PRC-A propaganda added that the program of the Grau government reflected the ideals of the party and that the PRC-A would continue to uphold those principles.[76]

Despite the persistent use of the terms "revolution" and "revolutionary," the majority of the PRC-A members were reformists. Like the DEU, the PRC-A wanted the "civic renovation" of Cuba, not a revolution. Any radical impulse the party might have shown was generated by the complete lack of a political opening between 1927 and 1936, rather than by the party's ideology. The party was founded during the peak of the postrevolutionary repression, and soon its most important leaders were in jail, underground, or in exile. Still, throughout 1934 the PRC-A issued statements advocating the creation of viable civil institutions that would check the military's growing power. The party advocated free and fair elections and the organization of a Constituent Assembly to redraft a Cuban constitution.[77] What was urgently needed, the party declared, was for the Cuban masses to regain confidence in the government. "We are not struggling for state power," one PRC-A document stated, "we simply would like to establish a state of law and order and the guarantees for full national expression."[78] This, of course, was exactly what Batista was saying; the central difference between the PRC-A position and that of the colonel was over the issue of how "a state of law and order" would be established in Cuba and who would bring this change about.

While the PRC-A did manage to expand its reach to all parts of Cuba, constant repression kept the party on the defensive. By the time of the 1935 general strike, most of its leaders were in exile and the party was racked by internal personal and political feuds.[79] Grau, who was still in Mexico in early May 1934, planned to return to Cuba to work to strengthen the party's organization. He was scheduled to arrive in Havana on May 18, and the news that he was returning was greeted with great excitement and concern. "His popularity among the masses is undoubted," reported Grant Watson of the British embassy, "but he is regarded as an enemy by the large vested interests in Cuba. His arrival may complicate a situation which is already complicated."[80] Grau did in fact return to Cuba on May 18, and his return would certainly complicate the situation, especially for Batista. Approximately 100,000 people came out to greet him. This huge demonstration, the British observed:

> was a fine example of Cubanism. . . . Dr. Grau is in the position of a sower who left before the people could judge the harvest. The people remember only his promises, and they do not know how far they can be carried into effect. They are grateful to him for his efforts to limit the competition of foreigners, to improve their conditions, and to lower the cost of living. . . . With his great popularity, Dr. Grau can become a great good or a great catastrophe for the destinies of Cuba, according to whether he and his followers adopt a policy of sound renovation or febrile impractical reforms. If he casts off the ultra-radical elements led by Guiteras, he can win over many moderate sections which now oppose him.[81]

Despite Grau's triumphant welcome, and his undoubted popularity among the masses, the PRC-A was organizationally weak and would remain so throughout its history. Batista's repression, combined with endemic disunity among its members, prevented the PRC-A from becoming the mass multiclass party it desired to be. Moreover, Grau was not the only opposition figure with mass appeal. His former colleague, Antonio Guiteras, had gained a large following among the *clases populares*. Indeed, many believed that most of the progressive measures of the September revolution were the work of Guiteras, and not Grau's moderate followers.[82] Following the defeat of January 1934, Guiteras moved further to the left, a process that had began months before the Grau regime fell. "Guiteras," the British reported, "decided that the long awaited moment had arrived when he could set up, under his own leadership, a workers' republic. Guiteras felt that he could count on the support of the labor unions, because he had helped workers form unions and obtain concessions from capitalists." After 1934, "he resolved to throw down the gauntlet to Batista and to stake all on success in civil war. . . . As Guiteras moved to the left to secure the support of the extreme labor elements, Batista moved to the right to enlist the 'forces of order.' " [83] As a consequence of this move to the left, Guiteras did not join his former comrades in the DEU and the Grau cabinet when they formed the PRC-A. While the Auténticos denied they wanted state power, Guiteras did everything he could to promote the downfall of Batista and Mendieta and to install a new and more radical government than the one he had served in under Grau.

The story of the Guiterista struggle against Batista was both heroic and tragic. Guiteras and his followers were the first to take up arms in the struggle for Cuba's total independence since the generation of 1895. His first moves in this direction were to attack the San Luis Barracks in April 1933, and as minister of the interior and war in the Grau cabinet he had encouraged the formation of popular militias to counter Batista's moves to reorganize the army. The fact that Guiteras continued to promote armed struggle after the defeat of the Grau regime, therefore, is hardly surprising. In late May 1934 Guiteras formed the political-military organization Joven Cuba to keep the militant struggle against Batista and the Cuban right wing alive.[84] One year later, on May 8, 1935, Guiteras was killed while fighting Batista's forces. Thereafter Joven Cuba lost its only leader who could keep the group together. For two more years Joven Cuba carried out terrorist attacks against the government and prominent businessmen, but, after 1936, most surviving members joined the PRC-A or formed smaller terrorist groups.

Yet, despite this mercurial and violent history, the political contribution Guiteras made to the Cuban left proved to be of lasting importance. His writings and the political program of Joven Cuba were, in addition to being more radical than Grau and his followers, far more politically sophisticated and nuanced.[85] Two documents drafted by Guiteras illustrate his political sophistication. In April 1934 Guiteras published an article in the magazine *Bohemia* analyzing the nature and weaknesses of the recently defeated Grau regime. The title of the article, "*Septembrismo,*" referred to the tendency of nearly every group to claim the heritage of the September revolution as their own. Guiteras challenged what he regarded as the demagoguery of those who claimed they were "Septembristas" when in fact they had worked against the regime. But the core of the piece was an analysis of the Grau regime itself. Guiteras pointed out that while the insurgent energy of the anti-Machado and anti-intervention movements had brought Grau's regime to power, the only basis of unity was antipathy to the *machadato*. This "doctrine of total destruction" could not provide the ideological unity necessary for revolutionary struggle in general and for maintaining state power in particular: "Our efforts from within the government to counter the mediationist sectors were difficult. But still more difficult was our gigantic effort to convert the coup of the 4 of September into an anti-interventionist revolution—and, above all—to take this anti-interventionism to its logical conclusion. . . . We failed because one can only move ahead if you can maintain a nucleus of men, ideologically firm, and powerful because of their unbreakable unity."[86]

It was precisely such ideological unity that Guiteras hoped to forge in Joven Cuba. The program of Joven Cuba outlined a broad and explicit anti-imperialist and nationalist plan for Cuba. Within Cuba the program advocated the reorganization of national and local state structures. State structures should be decentralized, and local councils, made up of labor, intellectuals, and business groups, should take over most administrative functions. The army and the police should be completely reorganized. Women must have full social, economic, and political rights. Nationalization of land and natural resources was advocated, and roads and the *bateyes* should come under municipal authority. Large land holding would be abolished and the land given to the poor and landless. The program called for the diversification of commercial and industrial activity, and cooperative productive units should be encouraged in all factories and sugar mills. The rights of workers to organize unions and work under clean and safe conditions would be guaranteed.[87]

Nothing came of this detailed political program. Joven Cuba, like all the other groups, remained on the defensive. Unlike other organizations, however, Joven Cuba fought back. Throughout 1934 and 1935 Joven Cuba exploded hundreds of bombs in Havana and other cities. They attacked the army patrolling the streets and they kidnapped prominent government and business leaders. The Cuban press paid considerable attention to what Grau said and did; but the press reports left no doubt that the elite and the army truly feared the Guiteristas.[88] It was only when the army surrounded and killed Guiteras on May 9 that Batista and the elite no longer worried about the "most feared radical in the history of Cuba."[89]

Joven Cuba fought on after the death of Guiteras. But the intense repression, combined with the loss of their only real leader, signaled the beginning of the end for the organization. Personalism and factional fighting destroyed the group from within, while Batista attacked them from without. By January 1936 a Joven Cuba internal circular admitted that "the severe problem of *caudillismo* within JC [Joven Cuba] is a persistent problem and it weakens the entire organization and the ties between the base and the leadership."[90] Five months later, the remnants of the organization were actively negotiating with the PRC-A about the possibility of joining forces. By 1937, Joven Cuba merged with the PRC-A.[91] The remaining leaders of Joven Cuba realized that "the Cuban people are tired of being cannon fodder, and they have lost faith in all the revolutionary organizations."[92]

The years 1934 to 1936 were also difficult ones for the Communist Party of Cuba. In the summer of 1934 the party acknowledged the decline in class struggle since October 1933. This decline, said one party report, "was due principally to the insufficient exposure of the Grau government to the party, which made it possible for the government, with its demagogic maneuvers, to sow illusions among certain sections of the proletariat."[93] What is striking about this statement is, given the party's earlier condemnations of the Grau government as "social fascist," the admission that the CP *should* or *could* have been closer to Grau's people was a sign the party was feeling its isolation from the masses. The party admitted that its isolation was because of its sectarian position toward the September revolution. The pact with Machado in August 1933 was another source of resentment against the party by other opposition sectors.[94]

Still, while the Communist Party moderated its position somewhat, it was not until 1935 that the party actively sought out alliances with other groups on the left and center of the political spectrum. One CP resolution declared that "[of] all the groups and the parties in Cuba, the most dangerous for the revolution are the parties of the 'left,' chiefly the Cuban Revolutionary Party of Grau . . . which, not being systematically and energetically unmasked, nor isolated from the masses, so that their influence may be broken, can canalize the mass discontent and use it for their own purposes, or, what is the same thing, divert the masses from the road of revolution in order to safeguard the bourgeois-landlord-imperialist domination."[95] It is true that the CP did not have a monopoly on sectarianism within the Cuban opposition, but the party's persistent hostility to all other groups kept them more isolated than most. An indication of just how bitter people could feel about these divisions can be seen in the words of Eduardo Chibás, the leader of the small Izquierda Revolucionaria and later a popular PRC-A leader in the 1940s, commented that "the more revolutionary a person is, the more the communists attack him. They attack the ABC more than they attack Menocal (the conservatives) and the Auténticos more strongly than the ABC. And Guiteras! they would love to eat him alive. Just because I am so attacked by these petty leaders of tropical communism, I know that I am a good revolutionary."[96]

It would not be until 1935 that the Communist Party tried to form a popular front of all the opposition groups. The immediate cause of the CP's change toward the popular-front strategy was the Seventh Congress of the Comintern in the summer of 1935. After 1935 the communist parties and their trade union cadres searched for allies in their attempt to form broad-based anti-fascist popular fronts. The Comintern's popular-front strategy, adopted at the Seventh Comintern Conference in 1935, encouraged the Cuban party to look for suitable partners in the struggle against fascism and national oligarchies.[97] As we will see in the next chapter, by 1937 a slow but steady courtship developed between the Cuban CP and their former bitter enemy turned reformist, Fulgencio Batista.

In the short run, however, the Cuban party's response to the change in tactics was accompanied by a change in analysis of Cuban reality. The Cuban delegate to the Seventh Congress, a "Comrade Marin," explained the CP's error:

> In spite of the vast sweep of the strike movement, in which the Party played a leading role, the struggle in the countryside during the same period remained weak and was of a spontaneous character. . . . In all these big struggles the proletariat succeeded to a certain extent in becoming crystallized as a class; it was able to a considerable extent [to] organize itself and create its own class and mass political party. However the basic error of the Party consisted in mechanically setting off the class interests of the proletariat against the interests of the national liberation struggle, the aims of the bourgeois-democratic, agrarian, and anti-imperialist revolution in Cuba. . . . This explains the hostile attitude taken by the Party toward the government of Grau . . . and explains the fact that the Party incorrectly characterized the so-called Cuban Revolutionary Party—a nationalist-reformist party headed by Grau—as a "fascist" party and classified as such even the national-revolutionary organization "Young Cuba" headed by Guiteras. . . . This entirely incorrect line hindered the expansion of the Party and the consolidation of its influence over the masses.[98]

As it was, the Cuban radical and reformist opposition did not succeed in forming a united front. From 1935—especially after the defeat of the March general strike—the CP entered into protracted negotiations from a united front with the PRC-A, Joven Cuba, and the other smaller groups on the left.[99] The Grauistas of the PRC-A and the Guiteristas, however, never forgave the CP for its sectarianism in the 1933–34 period, and they refused to participate in a united front with the CP. In addition, the problem of weak organization coupled with state repression did not permit any of these groups to establish firm links with the *clases populares*. The popular and mass sentiment for reform was indeed powerful, but *organizing* that sentiment was another matter entirely.

In late December 1935, Raúl Roa García of the non-Stalinist Marxist group Organización Revolucionaria Cubana Anti-imperialista (ORCA) argued that "the Cuban revolution lacks all the essential elements to bring it to victory and in the current atmosphere of gossip and *caudillismo* within all the left factions, a united front was an impossibility."[100] The radical groups were isolated from the working class and from the rural population, and their incessant infighting was pushing them farther away from the masses. "On this point," Roa wrote to a friend in the Izquierda Revolucionaria, "the organizations [of the left]—from the PRC to JC, to the CP—are groping about like a blind man with his cane."[101]

This lack of direction and constant turmoil on the left, as well as the repression from the army and police, allowed Batista to keep the opposition disoriented. As we will see in the next chapter, by 1937 the overall political and economic situation was favorable for Batista to enter the arena of civil politics without fear of serious opposition. At the same time, the radical opposition was largely tamed: *if* and *when* they entered democratic politics, it would be on Batista's terms, not their own. The three years of state violence prepared the terrain for what became known as the *pax batistiana*. This "peace" and "democracy," however, was built on a foundation of state violence and repression, as well as the deep political disillusionment on the part of the defeated opposition. Intense social mobilization, revolution, and finally defeat provided a foundation for a new form of authoritarian rule after 1937 and eventually for Cuba's transition to a constitutional democracy in 1940.

CHAPTER SEVEN

The Architect of the Cuban State

Fulgencio Batista and Populism in Cuba, 1937–1940

In the spring of 1937, Grant Watson of the British embassy observed that "Colonel Batista has attained a dominant position by his work to establish order throughout the island and this brusque transition from the role of Military Governor to that of advanced social reformer has taken people by surprise."[1] At first sight, it is understandable why the British described Batista's apparent transformation from reactionary to reformist as "brusque." Batista restored order through systematic military repression, and in 1936 there was no indication that the nature of the Cuban political process was about to change. What at first appeared to be a "brusque" change in Batista's political style reflected a shift in the political context both within Cuba and internationally. We saw in Chapter 6 that even at the height of the counterrevolutionary repression from 1934 to 1936, Batista was advocating corporatist ideas. That Batista tried to implement these ideas after order was restored should not therefore be surprising. In this sense, from 1934 to 1940 Batista was politically consistent. The young commander in chief was explicit about his role in the Cuban political process after 1933: "Many want to forget that I am the chief of a constructive social revolution, and see me as a mere watch-dog of public order. My idea of order is that of an architect rather than that of a police man. Real order is like a symmetrical edifice—it does not require propping-up to hold it in position."[2] The issue was not so much whether he would implement corporatist policies, but how and when he could put his ideas into practice.

Until January 1937, traditional political leaders who had backed Batista in the name of "order" expected they could control a poorly educated mulatto with little political experience. Because of his humble origins, Batista was largely excluded from Cuban "high society."[3] After the fight between president Gómez and the army chief, however, it became obvious who held power in Cuba. The British embassy reported that "the supporters of Colonel Batista are desirous that he should declare himself dictator, and there seems to be little doubt that it is only fear of the United States which prevents him from doing so. . . . When the Colonel drove out Miguel Gómez from the presidency, his supporters urged him to close Congress at the same time. He refused to do so, and thus his government managed to retain the recognition of Washington."[4] This assessment was correct. Washington wanted stability in Cuba, and accordingly encouraged Batista to create the conditions for constitutional government and electoral politics.[5] Two things were clear in the last half of the decade. Everyone knew that after his fight with Gómez, Batista would eventually move to become president; and everyone knew that it was Batista who guaranteed stability. The three unanswered questions were: First, how would Batista fulfill his undeclared political ambitions while maintaining order? Second, how would the United States respond to Batista's ascension to power? And third, how would the Cuban leftist and reformist groups react to Batista?

As long as Cuba was quiet and the impression of progressive reform was maintained, both the Cuban leader and the New Deal administration in Washington claimed to be achieving their goals. Despite the rather poor image of a military man like Batista holding power, especially after the *machadato,* what mattered most to Washington was the public spectacle of a Cuba moving toward elections. In early 1937 it was still not clear what strategy Batista would use in his search for political power. In February 1937 the Liberal Party asked Batista to become its leader, but he refused, saying his only role was to be commander of the military. He admitted, however, that he did "think about" becoming president of Cuba. For the time being he simply reminded people that the military would continue to play its patriotic role to guarantee civil authority.[6] Until June 1937 Batista avoided discussing political reform, but he also stated that he had no wish to form a military government. Grant Watson of the British embassy speculated, quite rightly it turns out, that "it was in order not to alienate United States public opinion that he did not mention any change of political regime."[7]

If some people were uncertain about Batista's political ambitions, many others were too busy to care. The first months of 1937 were taken up by the usual preparations for the grinding season, and political infighting among the elite took second place in the minds of sugar-industry leaders. For all the speculation about Batista's political ambitions, sugar growers were more concerned about prices, market conditions, and the maintenance of order on the sugar estates. On the issue of social control, the elite could trust Batista.

For the first time in years, the problems of labor discipline were not front and center in the minds of planters and company owners. Newspapers were full of hopeful commentaries about the upcoming sugar harvest, and there was widespread expectation the crop would reach 3 million tons for 1937.[8] In sharp contrast to previous years, the Cuban press rarely expressed concern about the labor situation. By the end of the year Cuba's most important elite newspaper, the *Diario de la Marina,* summed up the view of most large-scale sugar producers:

> The Cuban economy based upon sugar enjoys today considerable firm-ness, but its stability is not secure insomuch as it depends upon tran-sitory agreements. We must work . . . for a state of economic relations between Cuba and the United States which shall be permanent, and which will not depend eventually on the governments. . . . At the same time we must make haste to take advantage of the three or four years of relative economic improvement to create in Cuba a national economy, meeting the pending economic problems squarely and without delay.[9]

A "permanent" sugar agreement with the United States was not in the cards. Sugar producers were forced to accept yearly arrangements for the access of Cuban sugar to the U.S. market. The U.S. government had to bal-ance Cuba's interests with those of its own domestic producers and sugar growers in the Philippines. Cuban prosperity depended on the U.S. Supreme Court's decisions about treaties, tariffs, and taxes.[10] To be sure, the price of sugar was slowly rising, so the lack of a permanent treaty had become easier for Cuban producers and refiners to swallow. Better prices for sugar contrib-uted to a doubling of the value of Cuban exports between 1933 and 1939.[11] But the memory of the rock-bottom prices of 1930–33 loomed behind the shal-low optimism of the mid-1930s. Producers had seen prices fluctuate for too often to be complacent about stable price and market conditions.

If the price of sugar had improved since 1933, most other things had not changed. Despite the calming of political unrest after 1935, in early 1937 Cubans still lived under the same labor conditions and were subject to the same deprivations as before 1933. In 1937, 300,000 of a total popu-lation of 4,000,000 were out of work. Hundreds of thousands more were underemployed. The standard of living for workers remained "miserably low." [12] Middle-class Cubans were as economically insecure as during the early 1930s.[13] For the sugar industry, the problem of social control on sugar estates was a local concern or to be dealt with on a mill-to-mill basis. Prior to 1933, authorities from the central government in Havana were rarely asked to intervene to maintain order on plantations because regional *caudillos* or locally based *caciques* and rural guards were up to the task. In 1937 political leaders were still confident they could let the army, commanded by a poorly educated ex-sergeant, handle this problem while they went about their business as usual: they were mistaken.

The oligarchy's mistake was to view the problem of labor discipline as simply a policing issue. What they did not understand was that after the revolution of 1933 labor discipline became a complex political and national matter. If most of the oligarchy did not appreciate that labor relations was a political problem, Batista did. By leaving labor discipline to the army under Batista, the sugar industry—and the United States—unwittingly provided him with considerable room to maneuver. A 1937 British report, "The Labour Situation in Cuba and the British West Indies," noted that "the political and economic issues . . . remained [after 1933] inextricably mixed, with the result that successive Administrations, if they were to retain popular support, had to show that they were bent on improving the material conditions of the Cuban people, as well as on helping to restore normal constitutional government." The report continued to argue that Batista, like Grau, and in contrast to traditional politicians, understood that to hold on to power it was necessary to "remove the political grounds for economic discontent." [14] Batista's awareness of the need to change Cuban political reality in order to bring about economic stability, coupled with his control over the army, provided him with autonomy within the state. This autonomy, in turn, allowed the colonel to look for political support outside the traditional boundaries of the oligarchy. The revolution of 1933 had shaken the state to its very foundations. In the ensuing political and economic chaos, no one had clear ideas about how to rule Cuba. Political leaders had traditionally solved the problems of state among themselves without appealing for mass support. In contrast, by early 1937 Batista was free to pick up where Grau left off. Post-1933 politics had to reflect the new balance of social forces in Cuba. Instead of Grau's liberal democratic reformism, Batista's authoritarian corporatism set the terms of state formation after 1933. The organizational weakness of the *clases populares,* coupled with the marginalization of Grau's supporters, the Communists, and the left generally, permitted Batista to seize the political initiative. Batista was now free to court the support of the very people he had repressed.

In order to mobilize mass support, Batista tapped into the nationalist sentiment that had fueled popular aspirations in recent years. In early 1937

Grau's nationalization of labor decree—known as the "80 Percent Law"—was reinstated; the eight-hour day and the minimum wage were reestablished; and social security, pensions, workers' compensation, maternity leave, and paid vacations were reinstituted. One law stipulated that shops selling women's items must have 50 percent women employees.[15] Other initiatives would soon follow. The intent behind these laws was to achieve "economic balance" after thirty-five years of excessive foreign investment and a weak internal market. One government statement declared that these measures addressed "all the problems which have been disturbing the nation's peace during the past years."[16] Urban workers typically earned up to two or three dollars a day, while rural laborers were supposed to earn a minimum wage of 80 cents a day. As a result, urban workers could purchase goods, though they were usually foreign made; rural people, meanwhile, rarely earned enough to purchase more than food.[17]

While it would take several months for these government measures to take effect, the 80 Percent Law quickly raised the ire of the foreign business community and the U.S., British, and Haitian embassies. The intent behind this law was to replace foreign workers with Cubans wherever possible. The new labor law had an immediate impact. As early as February, the British report on labor conditions observed:

> [Capitalists] deplore the legislation which is making it more and more difficult for so many people to remain in Cuba. . . . Fear of breaking laws and incurring fines for that which they do not understand; the necessity of dismissing old and tired workers, and the inability to rid themselves of unsatisfactory Cuban workmen, once engaged; the army of inspectors and their accompanying corruption; the dictatorial attitude of the Ministry of Labour and its biases in favour of the working classes; all these things, it is claimed, tend to make employers restrict their enterprises instead of expanding them. . . . Foreign capital and foreign labour are thus united in their condemnation of the present Cuban policy.[18]

The degree of truth to this argument remains to be confirmed, but if the reaction of the *Havana Post*, the paper of the American community in Cuba, is any indication, foreign capitalists certainly believed it.[19] Ruby Hart Philips, the wife of *New York Times* reporter J. D. Philips, commented that "Batista, desiring the support of Cuban labor, watched passively as labor laws were tightened until it became impossible for an American to obtain employment."

The British had negotiated an agreement with the Cubans to ensure that they could retain "a reasonable number of British employees," while, to the chagrin of U.S. companies, the American government did not do the same.[20]

For urban capitalists the impact of the law most affected their skilled employees. Not only were all businesses required by law to have 80 percent Cuban employees, the government announced its intention to "nationalize" all high executive positions. Banks, credit institutions, transport companies, public utilities, newspapers, sugar mills, insurance and real estate companies, and all industrial organizations with more than ninety workers on their payroll were required to fill their executive positions with Cubans.[21] The author of the 80 Percent Law, Eduardo Suárez Rivas, explained the overall purpose of the measure. After stating that the law was meant to "balance the class structure of Cuba" by promoting the internal flow of capital, he went on to say:

> It is necessary that such capital be placed at the service of the country and not oblige the country to always be at the service of that capital. . . . The Good Neighbor Policy is intended to improve the respective conditions of each people and increase their purchasing power of consumption goods. This law attains that object, as it increases the purchasing power of Cubans and therefore fulfils the true objective of the reciprocity treaty [of 1934]. . . . The 80 percent law represents the incorporation into our social legislation of two essentially American principles: the nationalisation of the foreign worker and the increase of the purchasing power of the public consumer.[22]

Added to this strategy, taxes on foreign companies and labor were increased to pay for government programs. On March 21, 1937, the Cuban Chamber of Commerce and the American Chamber of Commerce in Cuba issued a joint statement in which they condemned the tax increases aimed explicitly at large businesses. In particular, they objected to a $3,000 annual municipal tax on all groups earning more than $3 million gross profit. A $300 annual tax on merchants selling manufactured goods was increased to $500.[23] Despite the vigorous protest by the business community, the government did not back down.

It was in rural Cuba where the labor laws had their most dramatic impact. In the sugar zones the government reduced the requirement of 80 percent Cuban employees to 50 percent. In the short term, the government knew that there was an insufficient number of Cuban workers and that foreign workers were still needed. Nonetheless, Haitian, Jamaican, and other West Indian workers became the target of a campaign of mass repatriations to their countries. On January 19, 1937, the government announced plans to expel British West Indian and Haitian workers, and the Labor Bureaus, with the backing of the Armed Forces, were to enforce this order.[24] By the end of February, three large resettlement camps in Camagüey and Oriente provinces held several thousand Haitian and Jamaican workers.[25] The British embassy complained about the treatment of their Jamaican and Barbadian subjects in these camps, though it was "a debatable point whether the British West Indians would be worse off roaming the countryside without food or shelter, or in a camp, fed and sheltered, but more or less a prisoner and probably subject to deplorable sanitary conditions."[26]

Batista ordered the Rural Guard to expel Haitian and Jamaican workers from the sugar estates, while "encouraging" mill managers to hire Cubans in their place. By March, 30,000 Haitians were repatriated, with an expected 50,000 to follow shortly. Thousands of Jamaicans, Barbadians, and other British West Indians were subject to the same measures. According to the British report on labor conditions, these expulsions were justified by the Cuban government on primarily economic terms, but, the embassy said, "there can be little doubt that there is an underlying ethnic motive also." Unemployment was as much a problem for West Indian workers as it was for Cubans: one-quarter of the estimated 40,000 British West Indians in Cuba were out of work, and the situation was far worse for the approximately 100,000 Haitian laborers. Moreover, the report argued, very few Jamaicans were cane cutters since most of that arduous work was done by Haitians and Cubans. If the Jamaicans were a social problem in Cuba it was not because they took away jobs from Cubans but because they drifted to the towns and cities precisely because there was so little work.[27]

Meanwhile, the sugar plantations that so depended on migrant labor had little choice but to use the government Labor Exchanges for their labor supply. Mills constantly petitioned the Labor Exchanges for more labor, and managers often complained that their labor needs were not being met. In Camagüey and Oriente, the Central Alto Cedro asked local exchanges for 800 workers, while the Central Boston requested 500 laborers. The Tánamo mill asked for 100 workers.[28] On January 28, the Department of Labor declared that "a notice has been sent to all Labor Boards requesting them to speed measures to send any cane laborers they may have available to the mills. . . . The Labor Department is making every effort . . . to supply an adequate number of workers in its program to handle the crop exclusively with native Cubans and thereby reduce unemployment."[29]

A "Campaign against Voluntary Idleness" was initiated in the eastern provinces to force Cubans who could not prove they were employed elsewhere to work in the mills. On February 10, 1937, police in Santiago de Cuba rounded up more than 100 men in bars and brothels: local authorities claimed the men were avoiding registering at the Labor Exchanges and they were promptly sent to nearby mills.[30] Referring to the entire 50 Percent Law, the British report on labor conditions claimed that "sugar mills are being obliged willy-nilly to refuse employment to British West Indians."[31] Because of the general labor shortage, apparently there was considerable pressure on local exchanges to register foreign workers. Many of the officials at the exchanges were friends of local mill managers or were themselves former employees of sugar companies: these personal ties were often more compelling than directives from Havana. Some mills bribed exchange officials, paying them to overlook the regulations. The Labor Ministry, however, explicitly said that foreign workers should not be registered at the exchanges. When the minister of labor discovered that some foreign workers were on exchange lists, the local authorities were told in no uncertain terms that there were to be no exceptions.[32]

Despite the overall shortage of labor, the available evidence suggests that while mill owners were displeased with the loss of cheap migrant labor, they were not willing to lobby the government to reinstate foreign-labor migration. Much of the anger directed at the labor laws focused on the law's impact on skilled American and British workers, not Haitians or British West Indians. The labor requirements of the sugar companies had to be weighed against the political realities of mass unemployment and the rise of popular nationalism. An editorial in the *Havana Post* acknowledged that "labor laws are necessary and certainly every foreigner living in the island today realizes this necessity and recognizes the equity and justice of promulgating laws which protect citizens against the possibilities of the unscrupulous exploitation of labor." The editorial went on to comment, however, that skilled Americans and British workers, many of whom had long resided in Cuba and loved the country, were the innocent victims of this legislation.[33] The British report on labor conditions concluded, "The greatest amount of evil has generally speaking not been wrought by the actual provisions of the 50 percent law, but rather by the effect of the latter in poisoning the relations between Cubans and foreigners, and thus creating a favourable atmosphere for oppression by other means."[34] Another editorial in the influential sugar-industry magazine *Revista Semanal Azucarera* noted that "in line with the avowed policy of providing work for Cubans in Cuba, the Government is laying plans for the repatriation of large numbers of West Indian laborers. Preparations for such mass repatriations have struck a snag in the Cuban mill-owner's and planter's fear of a consequent scarcity of labor for the coming sugar crop. The plan, if carried out, will therefore be on a much smaller scale than originally conceived."[35] Migrant labor continued to enter Cuba after 1937, but not in the same numbers as before. The sugar companies continued to complain about the shortage of cheap labor and the higher taxes, but they could no longer ignore the fact that unemployment was a national and deeply political problem.

Within this larger context, Batista skillfully took advantage of the options open to him. In keeping with the international trend of state-sponsored social reform, both within the United States and in Latin America, on July 25, 1937, Batista released a more systematic plan of social and economic measures. This program was published under the title *Líneas Básicas del Programa del Plan Trienal* (Three-Year Plan).[36] The announcement of the plan was not unexpected. Throughout the spring of 1937, rumors abounded about what measures Batista would include in his program. Indeed, most people had a good idea of what to expect given the deluge of legislation in the six months leading up to July. In late June the *Diario de la Marina* and the *Havana Post* devoted considerable coverage to the plan's rumored provisions. Among the measures mentioned by Batista were the recovery and survey of land owned by the state, survey of communal lands (*realengos*), abolition of large estates, a new national banking system, crop diversification, and coordination of the sugar industry through a profit-sharing mechanism among mill owners, *colonos*, and labor. Social provisions, such as health and old-age insurance, new schools and a literacy campaign, and the construction of urban and rural libraries, cultural centers for the performing arts, and sports facilities, would be included in the plan.[37] The cornerstone of the plan was the Sugar Coordination Law: as we will see shortly, Batista hoped to promote a more balanced sugar economy by organizing a profit-sharing system among producers (both large and small), labor, and the state. The state would pay for the social aspects of the plan with the anticipated revenue generated from its share of the profits.

Keeping with the facade of civil control, Batista promised that the plan would be submitted to Congress for approval. Congressional committees, all-party committees, and Cabinet ministers discussed the plan's real and rumored content throughout the spring of 1937. Watching this debate from the sidelines, Batista permitted considerable public criticism of the plan. At the same time he reminded people that he was the person ultimately responsible for the maintenance of order in Cuba: "I will be impartial but not indifferent. These words should be coordinated with my responsibilities and duties."[38] What was needed, according to Batista, "was an efficient and rigorous intervention by the state" in society to repair the damage of thirty-five years of distorted development in Cuba.[39] His goal was to build what he called an "organic democracy." According to President Laredo Bru, this "organic democracy" meant "a vast plan of reforms based on modern economic experience and aimed at procuring a state of equilibrium and justice. . . . There is no doubt that the world is going through the creation of a new public order in which individualism takes second place. The fountainhead, the basis, the medulla, of this new order is the principle of social solidarity."[40]

The considerable publicity preceding the plan's publication in late July generated widespread popular expectations. Workers and *colonos* expected that they would receive secure land tenure, a greater share of the profits from sugar sales, and more stable employment. The landless and those with insecure tenure waited to see if they would obtain binding legal titles for their holdings. The British embassy commented that the plan's provisions for land distribution to the poor and the creation of a State Agricultural Bank to provide the necessary capital outlay were eagerly awaited by Cubans. "Their enthusiasm," said the dispatch, "is due to their hope that the poorer agricultural classes will be favoured and their condition improved, and that this will lessen the discontent among field workers. Conditions in the island may then become more stable."[41]

In the long term, the hope that conditions would become stable proved false. The political fanfare surrounding Batista's Three-Year Plan was a good example of populist demagoguery: Batista promised to redistribute what was not yet produced. In the short run, however, popular expectations for reform were real, and Batista took advantage of this fact. He promised the *clases populares* what they wanted. On December 14, 1937, the Bill for the Colonisation, Reclamation, and Distribution of State Lands was passed by Congress. According to the bill, all land belonging to the state that was unoccupied or unregistered would be turned into small holdings and given to agricultural laborers. About 50,000 poor were to benefit from this measure. More than 33,000 acres were to be distributed by early 1938, with more grants to follow. Those who received land were to cultivate the land for at least six years before title deeds would be granted. Peasants squatting on unclaimed land could remain without fear of expulsion. The state was to provide $1 million for the purchase of seed, livestock, and agricultural implements. All these provisions were intended to alleviate the hardships of workers during the dead season.[42] These commitments went largely unfulfilled, mainly because of depressed economic conditions in early 1938, a poor sugar crop for the same year, lack of U.S. economic assistance, and a shift of political energies toward the elections for a future constituent assembly.[43] Cuban exports between 1937 and 1939 fell from $99 million to $60 million, while for the same period imports dropped from $53 million to $45 million. Government revenue for these years fell from $36.4 million to $31 million.[44] But, with the political commitments to the popular classes on public record, state expenditure was not curtailed and new taxes were imposed, especially on the sugar industry. Meanwhile, "Batista uses to the full his promise of the distribution of 'state' lands."[45]

Throughout the spring of 1937, the sugar companies waited to see how much the state would interfere in their business. The principle of government coordination of sugar production was not new. Since the late 1920s sugar companies had recognized that some form of state restrictions on the quantity of sugar produced was a necessity. This recognition was forced on the sugar industry by the political and economic crisis of the early 1930s. As the prominent Cuban economist and historian Ramiro Guerra y Sánchez pointed out in 1942, sugar producers received their fair share of criticism for placing their interests ahead of the nation's. He noted, however, that because of the revolutionary situation of the early 1930s, "the crisis brought its own salutary lesson . . . and gave the revolutionary ferment one of its most useful consequences." That useful consequence was the realization among sugar producers that "the internal situation and that of the foreign markets urgently called for the reorganization of the sugar industry on a new basis. The producers themselves were the first to recognise the need for such a reorganisation and were willing to collaborate actively and loyally to bring it about."[46]

The apparent willingness of producers to collaborate and their ability actually to do so were two different things. If the political pressures on the sugar industry to adapt to post-1933 conditions were real, so, too, was its desire to maximize profits with minimal political interference. It is thus understandable why, prior to any decision by state or international authorities, sugar producers were anxious about the degree and scope of restrictions on production. Such was the case with Batista's forthcoming plan. While few details about Batista's sugar policy were available before publication, it was known that Batista planned to regulate the sugar industry by establishing equitable cane quotas for both millers and small *colonos*. In addition, he wanted to institute a system of profit sharing among all producers and workers.[47] How these measures would be implemented was a matter of considerable speculation within the sugar industry and the general public.

By September 1937 the speculation was over. In mid-August Congress passed the Sugar Co-ordination Law as part of the Three-Year Plan. The law stipulated that as long as the small *colono* cultivated the land and delivered the agreed-upon quantity of cane to the appropriate mill, he would not lose his land. *Colonos* who rented land had their leases underwritten by the state.[48] The yearly crop restrictions imposed on producers, which had been a feature of the industry since the late 1920s, would continue, but only large growers would have to respect these limitations. Small *colonos,* in contrast, were allowed to keep 52 percent of their crop and sell it for their own profit. This meant that if prior to the legislation *colonos* had delivered most of their crop to a large company mill to grind and market, the new sugar law would allow them to control most of their production with the assurance of state support. Mill owners, *colonos,* unions, and the government together would work out the regulations governing the sugar industry. Arbitration boards were created to carry out this function. Another provision declared that freedom of trade at the *bateyes* should be permitted: this measure was aimed at breaking the stranglehold that many plantation stores held over workers and their communities, especially during the dead season. The objective was to promote the expansion of petty-commodity production in the countryside. The measure was also a clear populist appeal to merchants who resented the domination over rural wage earners by plantation stores. "Unbelievable as it might sound," noted an editorial in the *Revista Semanal Azucarera,* "the inhabitants of many rural districts in Cuba buy their poultry, eggs, and vegetables in city markets—an anomalous situation that would disappear under the plan here outlined."[49] Wage rates and working conditions were to be regulated, and a housing code for plantation workers was to be written.[50]

Batista's intention with the Three-Year Plan was to use profits from the sale of sugar to improve the lot of agricultural laborers and small *colonos.* The colonel was determined to save the very cultural essence of Cuba. The idea of the *colono* as the stereotypical Cuban—the symbol of *cubanidad*—was a notion popularized by nationalist writers and intellectuals in the 1920s.[51] Batista and others of his generation felt that saving the small sugar producer and saving Cuba was the same thing. This was the political and cultural logic behind Batista's "organic democracy" as laid out in the Three-Year Plan. Batista wanted to defend the status and importance of the small producer, and he promoted the idea of the equitable distribution and consumption of property and commodities. Accordingly, it was the responsibility of the state to guarantee this equity and balance. In November 1938, in a speech to the Cuban Chamber of Commerce in New York, Batista presented his notion of what political and economic "equity" and "balance" meant:

> As Chief of a revolutionary movement which brought back the renewed vigor of a dissatisfied public conscience, I feel obliged that nothing frustrate its aspiration. . . . A new conception of equity and justice has taken root in the people. It is a feeling of a generation who has faith in democracy, but which insists that it should not be deformed or led astray . . . Democratic thought recognizes the equality of rights and the same opportunities according to the capacity and ability of each individual. Proportion in capitalism should always be an unchangeable standard of security. If proportion disappears as a standard of ethics in the mission of capitalism, then it becomes converted, going back into time and in the face of progress, into feudalism. Finally, the just distribution makes for and guarantees a permanent collective well being when sustained by a satisfied public conscience.[52]

In addition to Batista's corporatist ideas, there was a deeper purpose behind the Sugar Coordination Law and the Three-Year Plan. That purpose, in the words of Guerra y Sánchez, was to "[convert] the sugar industry of Cuba into a huge national enterprise." By assuring that small, medium, and large producers would all receive an equitable share of production and profits, the legislation "will gradually create a well informed and intelligent public opinion, not only about the sugar question but also about the economy of the nation in general. Thus will be laid a more solid base for democracy in Cuba."[53] One week before the plan was officially presented to the public, an editorial in the *Revista Semanal Azucarera* argued that "the scheme is extremely important to Cuba and to her sugar industry in particular, for it lays down not only a social law tending to raise the standard of living of the poorer classes in the sugar industry, but [it] is also a precedent for schemes that may be adopted to co-ordinate other national activities."[54] The Sugar Coordination Law, therefore, was not simply promoted as an economic necessity: it was the central political objective of a populist strategy of capital accumulation. This populist strategy involved the reorientation of capitalist relations of production away from the unrestrained and unsupervised oligarchic capitalism of the previous thirty-seven years toward a state-sponsored and mediated process of capital accumulation. Batista's role in this project was decisive: not only did he bring "order" after revolution, but he also tapped into the nationalist sentiment of Cuban merchant-industrialists, *colonos,* and some large sugar growers who increasingly looked to the state for protection against both foreign domination and labor unrest. The colonel's success had long-term implications for Cuban politics. As will be seen, Batista had seized the banner of social reform from Grau and his followers, and in doing so he undermined the former president's attempts to organize a viable reformist movement between 1924 and 1940.

Given the new political situation confronted by the sugar industry, it is not surprising that the sugar law was greeted by many mill owners with hostility. Indeed, sugar producers had previously enjoyed a near complete freedom, so it is easy to see why many felt uneasy toward any form of state intervention in their affairs. The crisis in world sugar production during the late 1920s had forced most producers to grudgingly accept state regulations over the quantities of sugar produced. But their acceptance was cushioned by the idea that state regulations were an anomaly not to be repeated. Consequently, the congressional debates and public statements by Batista and his supporters leading up to the passage of the sugar law provoked sharp responses by some producers. As early as April 1937 a long and detailed internal memorandum of the Cuba Cane Sugar Company presented the main concerns of some within the sugar industry. After describing the trend in early 1937 "when sentiment was growing in favor of new social legislation to improve the lot of labor," the memorandum went on to complain:

> The social implications of this bill are evil. It means a step toward the denial of the right of free contract. It raises the question whether Cuba will no longer permit capital invested in sugar mills to get a fair return or, in fact, any return and whether the Government is going to expropriate the hacendado by loading him, through legislation, with the expenses which eat-up his share of the fruits of his industry. . . . This legislation . . . is necessarily generalized and hence often ill-suited to meet the specific needs of the varying cane zones; as [the legislation] was conceived in haste through political pressure.[55]

The reference to the different needs of various cane zones pointed to the millers' concern about the way sugar was grown in eastern as opposed to western Cuba. Growers in the western regions argued that they bore the brunt of the law because *colono* production was more prevalent in the west. *Colonos* in the west would receive state backing in their competition with the larger company plantations. In contrast, much of the eastern territory was relatively new to cane growing, and as a result there were fewer *colonos* and the large companies had little competition from small producers. The eastern mills could thus more easily absorb the costs of the legislation while western millers claimed they were being unfairly targeted.[56] A letter from the Cuban Cane Company to Arturo Antonio Bustamante, who, according to the letter, was a close friend of both Batista and President Laredo Bru, concluded by saying: "The President of the Republic, and Colonel Batista, as well as our legislators, should not listen to only one small group of *colonos* when it comes to such an important issue. Let's not kill the goose that lays the golden eggs!"[57]

In 1940, the Cuban Association of Sugar Manufacturers, looking back on the previous three years, outlined its grievances in an "Open Letter" to the new president of the Republic, Fulgencio Batista:

> The industry has been lately taxed with social and fiscal legislation arising from the revolutionary period 1933–1940, and it is permissible to state, therefore, that while a higher price [for sugar] will somewhat relieve the condition of cane planters and workers, the industry itself is on the verge of a crisis as acute as that prevailing in 1933 which . . . led to a total disruption of the politico-economic regime then in existence. . . . With so sombre a future facing Cuba's sugar industry, it could be logically expected that sugar mill owners, constituting as they do the most directly affected class, would remain united along a common front, cooperating with the Administration and other sections of our economic system in the study of formulas, ways and means to forestall, or at least mitigate, this serious threat now in the offing. Yet this grave crisis finds us, far from united, irreconcilably divided by a regime of irritating injustice and privilege that should not and cannot survive in a country ruled by democratic principles incompatible with such privileges and at a time when the Chief Executive happens to be a man born to the noble, generous bosom of Cuba's common people, who by tradition, by principle and by nature deeply resent all forms of discriminatory vassalage. We feel sure, therefore, that with the ascending sign of the Man of September the Fourth, no situation based on exception and privilege for the few, at the expense of the majority, can find support and consecration.[58]

Flattery, however, got the sugar producers nowhere. Until a thorough study of the Cuban sugar industry in the twentieth century is completed, any general conclusions about the industry's political influence within the Cuban state are provisional. We know the obvious truth that every Cuban government had a symbiotic relationship with the sugar oligarchy. But a symbiotic relationship does not imply a harmonious one. It was one thing for Batista to dominate the repressive apparatus of the state through his control of the army and the police; it was quite another matter for him to move from the shadowy background of the military into the political lime-light. By late 1937 the political pressure on the Cuban oligarchy from within Cuba and from the United States to bring an end to the provisional nature of Cuban governments was mounting. Preparations for general elections to lay the basis for a constituent assembly were made. With this objective in mind, political factions and parties set about realigning themselves for the struggles to come. Within this new context of political debate, Batista, like everyone else, needed to stake out his political territory.

Of course the military commander was already claiming the status of a social reformer when he presented his Three-Year Plan. Batista's Plan, how-ever, mentioned little in the way of political reform, concentrating instead on social and economic problems. Batista's political problem after 1937 was that Grau and his followers were still around to reclaim their role as Cuba's most advanced social reformers. One purpose of the Three-Year Plan, there-fore, was to "forestall the radical campaign which Dr. Grau San Martín is ex-pected to launch when preparations for the elections have been advanced. . . . Batista, who at one time supported him, has come to regard him as a dis-turbing element, because, as a reformer, he arouses too many passions and too much opposition. This would again imperil the maintenance of order. His three years plan [sic] is calculated therefore to take the wind out of his [Grau's] sails."[59]

It did not help Batista's political prospects as a reformer that lack of money and congressional deadlock delayed implementation of his plan. A bad sugar crop, rising unemployment, unfulfilled revenue expectations, and the reduction of government employees' salaries all fueled growing politi-cal tensions in late 1937 and early 1938. Nor did it help his reputation when people discovered that, despite the economic problems of the country, Ba-tista refused to cut military spending. An illustration of how fragile Batista's support was occurred on November 20, 1937. Batista's backers, calling them-selves the Association of the Heralds of the Three Year Plan, organized a rally in Havana's Tropical Stadium. Between 60,000 and 80,000 people at-tended the meeting. The organizers received the official backing of the De-partment of Labor, and government employees were obliged to attend the rally. Trains, cars, trams, buses, and trucks were commissioned by the gov-ernment to bring people to the stadium. Many unions, however, refused to attend, "thereby showing a considerable amount of courage." Tobacco workers, laundry workers, and many transport workers were among those who stayed away.[60] The memory of the violent repression of 1934–36 was fresh in many people's minds, and it would be an uphill battle for Batista to regain the confidence of even some sections of the working class.

Just how was Batista going to win over the working classes after three years of army violence directed at organized labor? If the colonel was to solve this problem, he would have to move quickly. With the long-delayed general elections looming in March 1938,[61] Batista needed to forge stable political alliances to assure popular support. He was faced with the ironic situation that, after having so successfully repressed the organizations of the *clases populares,* he now had to court their support if he was to legitimize his rule. He could not do this on his own authority: he needed to make alliances with people who were willing to embrace his corporatist vision of the state without demanding too much autonomy in return.

This would not be easy. Batista had made many enemies over the past four years, not least among the *clases populares* themselves. The Havana correspondent for the Italian Communist Party paper, *L'Unita,* wrote that "for most Cubans, he [Batista] personified the antination; it was he who represented fascism, even if the exigencies of North American policy demanded he join the antifascist front at an international level. Batista had massacred workers and had been responsible for the assassination of national heroes such as Antonio Guiteras." [62] This opinion, coming as it did from a communist, is striking because the writer's comrades in the Cuban Communist Party were already allied with Batista in his bid to become president of Cuba.

In Search of Allies: Batista, the Communists, and Cuban Democracy

To understand why Batista and the Communist Party of Cuba formed an alliance, it is necessary to emphasize that mass politics was a new phenomenon for all Cuban political actors, including the Communist Party. In the previous chapters we have seen that the communists, trade unions, and unaffiliated radicals who claimed to be the "vanguards" of the *clases populares* were as much the products of mass mobilization as they were the leaders. The Communist Party, the National Worker's Federation (CNOC), and the National Union of Sugar Industry Workers (SNOIA) gained valuable experience and new members in the struggles leading up to the revolution of 1933. They had no sooner established a tentative foothold in the mass movement, however, than they became the victims of Batista's repression between 1934 and 1937. The communists continued to work underground after the failed general strike of 1935, but they were no longer a significant threat to Batista or the sugar companies. The Cuban communists, their trade union organizers, and the left generally were a defeated group. What, then, were the forces which compelled Batista and the communists to forge an alliance? The answer can be found in the changing political atmosphere of the mid-1930s.

For the communists, the decision to seek an alliance with Batista fits the pattern of the worldwide turn of the communist movement toward the popular front.[63] After the Seventh Congress of the Communist International in 1935, Communist parties throughout the world sought alliances with social democratic, liberal, bourgeois democratic, or any other force they considered to be antioligarchic and antifascist.[64] In several countries, this search did not preclude looking to sections of the military as potential allies. The political logic behind this strategy was straightforward: in a world under threat from fascism, with only one socialist country (the Soviet Union) under siege and industrializing, and with reactionary forces in each country moving further to the right, the broadest possible alliances of all "progressive forces" was imperative. The dramatic events of the Spanish Civil War, the Italian fascist invasion of Ethiopia, the anti-Japanese struggle and revolution in China, and, in Latin America, the radical turn by the Cárdenas government in Mexico, strongly encouraged the idea that popular frontism was a viable and necessary strategy.

In the case of Latin America, popular fronts of one kind or another were formed in nearly every country. In Chile the Communist Party, the Socialist Party, and the Radical Party established a popular front against the "feudal oligarchy" and for the "progressive development" of Chilean capitalism. In Peru the CP and the American Popular Revolutionary Alliance (APRA) joined forces for the same purpose, as did the Colombian CP with the Liberal Party, and the Mexican communists with the moderate wing of the Party of the Mexican Revolution. In each case, the political and strategic objective was to isolate the oligarchies from the weak and politically vulnerable national bourgeoisies, while building multiclass alliances for a transition to bourgeois democratic rule. Workers' rights needed to be defended, but this struggle was framed within the context of the broader objective of attaining liberal democratic reform. At the time, the perspective of the Comintern on Latin America was that the historical situation was not ripe for socialism or revolution. Marxist orthodoxy insisted that socialism could come only after capitalism, and the analysis of communist theoreticians was that Latin America was still largely subject to feudal relations of production. The best way to fight for socialism, they argued, was to encourage liberal capitalist development as the necessary first step toward socialism.[65]

The political line of the Cuban Communist Party followed this pattern. The Cuban party had been illegal from 1934 to September 1938. We will see shortly why Batista decided to permit the party to function openly at that particular time. For the moment it is worthwhile to remember that before the party could build a popular front, the communists needed to mend some badly damaged bridges with other "progressive forces." Following the lead of the Seventh Congress of the Comintern, in 1936 the party entered discussions with other leftist and radical groups with the hope of forging greater unity among all antioligarchic groups. Nothing came of these meetings, and by late 1938 it was clear that the Cuban party was not going to form a popular front with Grau's Partido Revolucionario Cubano (Auténtico) or with any of the smaller nationalist groups. In large part these negotiations failed because of the bitter legacy of 1933. The CP had resolutely opposed Grau's government, labeling it "social-fascist" and "reactionary." Accordingly, the party, CNOC, and SNOIA had organized strikes and demonstrations against the reformist government. The change in the party's line after 1935 did nothing to assuage the resentment felt by Grau's backers. Whatever the theoretical arguments used by either side to justify their lack of unity after 1935, and despite the CP's self-criticism of its past sectarianism, the Auténticos and other independent factions could not stomach an alliance with the CP. As a result, a popular front of all progressive forces in Cuba never got off the ground.[66]

What did take place, however, was a successful alliance between the Communist Party and Fulgencio Batista. The political logic of the popular front was the same as in other countries, even if in Cuba the partners were ill matched. Batista and the CP needed allies for their respective projects, and political circumstances from 1937 to 1940 were pushing them together. On Batista's side, he needed to build a political base quickly to make the transition from military leader to a civilian leader. On the party's side, the need to find allies was not only a political duty imposed by the Comintern; there was also the reality that Cuba's closeness to the Spanish events (politically and historically) made the threat of fascism seem closer. Pro-Falangist and Francoist elements were active in Cuba, and, whatever their real strength, their presence fueled the CP's sense of urgency to form a popular front. Cuban leftists, both communist and independent, went to fight for the Spanish Republicans.[67] Added to these factors was the constant American pressure for Cuba to fall into line with the Good Neighbor policy and its emphasis on the importance of state-sponsored social reform. Within this larger context it is not surprising that some form of alliance developed.

To illustrate how this alliance developed, we need to look no further than the Communist Party's own explanation of why it supported Batista. In December 1938 the Communist Party was still looking for allies to form a popular front. According to an article published in *World News and Views*, the official organ of the Comintern, there were two possibilities on the horizon: Grau and Batista. The best prospect, the article stated, seemed to favor Grau. Juan Marinello, a leading Communist and the head of the party's legal front organization, Unión Revolucionaria (UR), had met with Grau in Miami to discuss forming a "unity party" that would include their two organizations and the smaller Partido Agrario Nacional (PAN). The objective of this "unity party" would be to bring together all progressive forces into one bloc to fight for a genuinely popular and democratic constituent assembly. The communists recognized that Grau "stands high in prestige among the Cuban population and has a reputation for sincerity . . . but he appears to be haunted by fears that he might be ruled by communists in the unity party." The article continued, "Since it has not yet been possible to form a unity party, the Communists and the Revolutionary Union want to support the movement in order to put into power a constitutional democratic government under the leadership of Grau San Martín. So long as certain putschist tendencies do not hamper this development, the present political situation promises success." [68]

Nothing came of the meeting between Marinello and Grau, nor did an alliance between the CP and the Auténticos materialize. The "putschist tendencies" mentioned in the article referred to the numerous but usually small groups of armed men loosely affiliated with the Auténticos and the Guiteristas. These groups frequently attacked Batista's police and army posts or assassinated the colonel's followers; they also tended to be violently anticommunist. An additional reason that the "unity party" between the Auténticos and communists failed was that Batista did not permit Grau and his followers to regroup in Cuba. As we saw earlier, Batista's main political competition was Grau. In January 1934 Grau had been exiled to Mexico; later he made his headquarters in Miami. As with the communists, between 1934 and 1938 Batista did not permit the Auténticos to organize openly in Cuba. As long as Batista kept the Auténticos organizationally off balance until elections could be scheduled, and if he could maintain the image of a social reformer, he would hold the political initiative. Moreover, from 1937 to 1939 the Auténticos were sharply divided along both political and personalist lines. Gradually, in response to their defeat and isolation after 1935, two wings emerged: the "realists" wanted to compromise with Batista to become legal and participate in the upcoming elections, while the "revolutionaries" thought that militant and even armed action was the only way to defeat Batista. Grau was vigorously courted by both sides, but he always seems to have been a "realist." By permitting the UR to function legally, but still keeping Grau in Miami, Batista drew one faction of the mass movement closer to him while keeping the more popular Auténticos at bay.[69]

If the article in *World News and Views* was cautiously optimistic about future relations with the Auténticos, it was equally positive about what it called Batista's recent "change of attitude." The author maintained that the reason for Batista's "progressive turn" was the economic crisis in Cuba: rising unemployment and high prices for consumer goods, coupled with failure to implement many of the Three-Year Plan initiatives, had damaged Batista's populist pretensions. "Batista," the article continued, "seems to remember the lesson taught by Machado's fall and is striking out in a new direction." The article pointed out that throughout 1938 the sugar oligarchy and Francoist/Falangist forces were more hostile to Batista.[70]

The reality was that the colonel *permitted* both the Communist party, and the working-class movement generally, to reorganize. At the end of September 1938, much to the dismay of the upper classes, Batista legalized the Communist Party. The signs that Batista was considering this move had been evident for some time. As early as January 15, 1938, Batista had met with two members of the party's politburo, Blas Roca and Joaquín Ordoqui. Following the meeting, Batista declared that the CP would receive the same legal protection as all legally recognized political groups. The colonel reiterated his view that "extremist tendencies" were "fatal for Cuba," but he emphasized that all social classes comprised "the people," and since the party represented a section of public opinion, it should be permitted to participate in drafting a new constitution. After stating that he disagreed with the communists on fundamental issues, Batista said he believed Roca and Ordoqui when they committed the party to obey the laws of Cuba.[71]

Batista's next move was equally shocking for traditional politicians. After obstructing union organizing for years, in January 1939 Batista permitted the founding meeting of the Confederation of Cuban Workers (CTC) to take place. For the past two years communists had worked long and hard for the creation of a national union body that could replace the severely weakened CNOC. The older union federation had never recovered after the defeats of 1935. Still, some 730 small and locally based unions continued to survive. Prior to January 1939 total union membership hovered around 220,000 workers.[72] How effective these unions were is unknown, but the fact that they were legal at all indicated that the political atmosphere had changed somewhat since the violent days of 1935. Union organizing in the late 1930s, however, was a thankless task. First, there was the problem of Batista's army and police who kept a sharp eye on trade unionists. Second, it was nearly impossible to build a solid union structure when most of the workforce labored in small factories, workshops, or distant sugar plantations. Sugar workers were poorly organized, though there were many small and legal unions throughout the country. A third problem was that union politics was racked by sectarianism among CP, Auténtico, and independent union organizers. All in all, in early 1938 the situation was not propitious for the union movement, and there was no indication that things would change.

So when Batista allowed 1,500 delegates to attend the CTC founding congress in January 1939, it was further proof of his populist pretensions. This move also encouraged the communists in their belief that Batista was moving to the left. As with the legalization of the Communist Party, there were prior indications that Batista was open to alliances with the unions. On May 1, 1938, President Laredo Bru had received petitions by a legally sanctioned May Day demonstration for Cuban workers to organize a national union confederation.[73] Laredo Bru, of course, would not do such a thing without Batista's approval. The colonel's willingness to entertain this initiative was dictated by his need to build inroads into the mass movement before the coming elections in November 1939. From the communist's perspective, Batista's change of direction was another indication of his "progressive" position. It was indeed a striking change in Cuban politics to see a legal mass meeting presided over by communists and international observers. Lázaro Peña, an Afro-Cuban tobacco worker and communist, was elected as the CTC general secretary.[74] Guests of honor at the congress included the secretary of labor, J. M. Portuondo Domenech, Vicente Lombardo Toledano and Fidel Velázquez from the Mexican Confederation of Workers (CTM), and Joseph Kowner from the American Confederation of Industrial Organizations (CIO).[75] From its very beginning the CTC was a state-sponsored union.

The Mexican connection to the CTC meeting was no casual act of solidarity, and it is another illustration of how Batista engineered events. In early 1938 the Mexican government, through its Chargé d'Affaires in Havana, actively supported CTM organizers in Cuba. The CTM provided money and organizational experience for the struggling Cuban union movement. The objective of the Mexican action was to secure influence in the oil distributing and refining industry in Cuba. The Mexican government, under the populist and nationalist Lázaro Cárdenas, was preparing for a major conflict with the United States over the nationalization of the oil industry in that country. Since Mexico had limited refining capability, any influence the Mexicans could gain within that strategic sector could be vital in any future confrontation with the United States. In exchange for CTM assistance, Cuban unions sent workers to Mexico to study organizational strategy. Initially, the Cuban government did not look kindly on what it regarded as Mexican interference in Cuba's internal affairs. For months, Cuba had rejected repeated requests by CTM leader Lombardo Toledano to visit Cuba. In April 1938 they issued a diplomatic protest to the Mexican government, and the Cuban police detained Cuban workers returning from Mexico.

By late 1938 the situation had changed considerably. With the Three-Year Plan seriously behind schedule, and with political tensions among Cuban political leaders reaching serious proportions because of the upcoming elections, Batista was anxious to raise his political profile as a social reformer. With this in mind, in October 1938 Batista accepted an invitation by the Mexican government to visit that country in January 1939. This gesture was frowned upon by the Cuban oligarchy: with tensions between the United States and Mexico at a high point because of the recent nationalization of the Mexican oil industry, and with Batista promoting the idea that Cuba should expand trade with Mexico to help diminish Cuban dependence on the United States, Batista's Mexican visit was seen by conservatives as a deliberate snub to the Americans. Furthermore, traditional politicians were still angry that Batista had legalized the Communist Party in September, though he assured the conservative, anti-Mexican, and pro-Francoist editor of the *Diario de la Marina*, Pepín Rivero, that communism would not be given a free hand in Cuba.[76] Still, in replying to the Mexican invitation, which promised to show the Cuban military leader "the undisputed reality of revolutionary Mexico, where the protection of the majorities rules" and "where nationalism has been adopted as the basis of constitutional aims," Batista expressed his "respectful admiration and sincere sympathy" for President Lázaro Cárdenas and his government.[77] This kind of statement made the Cuban elite very nervous about the colonel's political intentions. It was also the context in which Batista permitted the formation of the CTC.

Meanwhile, Batista was sensible enough to plan a visit to the United States before he went to Mexico. His objective was to negotiate a lower duty on Cuban sugar. He went to the United States on October 29 and returned to Havana on November 25. He failed to secure a lower duty on Cuban sugar, but he hinted that a new reciprocity treaty was in the works and he further suggested that Cuba would gain important concessions from the Americans. Nothing concrete came from Batista's visit to the United States, except that his political profile both within Cuba and abroad was raised.[78] The mass rally organized by the government to welcome Batista back to Cuba included 3,000 communists who, waving red flags and holding clenched fists in the air, chanted, "Democracy! democracy!" By playing all sides against each other, wrote Grant Watson of the British embassy, "it is impossible to foretell whether as a presidential candidate he will seek to lead the forces of the 'Centre' or those of the 'Left.' This is the great problem at the moment."[79]

Sure enough, after the commander in chief's return from Mexico, the Cuban political class did indeed have a problem on their hands. Even before his return on February 16, 1939, rumors about the colonel's rather "intemperate" speeches reached Havana. On one occasion Batista spoke about the idea of nationalizing the Cuban sugar industry. At a rally of 100,000 people in Mexico City, the Cuban leader proclaimed his support for Republican Spain and for a continent-wide antifascist front. Back in Havana, the minister of labor, Lázaro Peña from the CTC, and Blas Roca, secretary general of the Cuban Communist Party, welcomed Batista home; the speakers list also included the president of Cuba, Laredo Bru.[80] The colonel then traveled across Cuba, speaking at meetings and formal dinners organized by his backers. At one public rally organized by the CTC, Batista stated that "the Communist Party in Mexico, as well as in Cuba, and in France and the United States, where they are recognised as legal forces, instead of elements of disturbance, are acting as promoters of democracy. . . . Communism was an element of progress and democracy."[81] Such a ringing endorsement by Batista warranted a response. The Cuban CP, referring to those who still distrusted Batista, declared it would "abandon all out of date formulations that are still heard in the party. . . . The slogan of the party must be 'With Batista, Against Reaction,' meaning that we must work openly for the support of the masses to [*sic*] Batista's policies."[82]

Shortly after the Havana rally, however, Batista tried to reassure the conservative elements by saying "Mexico has not changed me" and that "capital will have all the guarantees which it needs and the workers will have the justice which they claim." He reminded people that his political philosophy was to promote balance and harmony between capital and labor; his only intention was to form a united force called the "Cuban people."[83] Such reassurances did little good, but since it was clear to all that the elections were

Batista's to win, Cuban leaders had little choice but to take sides in a political battle that would determine the overall environment in which they would do business.

When congressional elections were finally held on November 15 1939, political alignments did not correspond to ideological differences between left and right. Rather, two electoral coalitions emerged during 1939, each with its own broad vision of how to strengthen the Cuban state after the revolution of 1933. What divided politicians between 1939 and 1940 was not whether the Cuban state needed strengthening, but who would accomplish this task and what methods they would use. What united them—including the communists—was their common desire to strengthen the capitalist state by mobilizing the population in support of state-sponsored reform. One coalition believed that civil authority, as opposed to Batista's military power, should be strengthened and institutionalized. The other group comprised parties and individuals who claimed that they, too, wanted to strengthen civil power, yet they argued that Batista was the best guarantor of civil and popular power. The procivil authority coalition included the Republican Action Party of Miguel Mariano Gómez, the Democratic Republican Party led by the old conservative *caudillo* Mario Menocal, the ABC represented by Dr. Joaquín Sáenz, and the Auténticos, led by Grau San Martín. The Batistiano group included the Liberal Party, the Unión Nacionalista, the Partido Realista, and, the Communist Party. Both coalitions spoke out firmly for democracy: in a world nearing a state of war between the forces of dictatorship and democracy, and with Cuba in the United State's backyard, no Cuban political leader could afford to be labeled "antidemocratic." Indeed, promoting democracy and strengthening the state were increasingly seen as being the same thing, and no political group could strengthen the Cuban state without appealing for mass support. The congressional elections were generally considered to be fair, and Batista's group came out the loser, with 35 seats to Grau's 41. Following the defeat of his coalition, Batista graciously accepted the results. Then, on December 6, 1939, Batista announced his candidacy for president and he promised to resign from his post as army commander.

The central importance of the elections of late 1939, the presidential elections of 1940, and the Constitutional Convention of 1940 was that they represented the culmination of seven years of authoritarian rule. These events signified a new phase in the relationship between the state and society in Cuba. It is true that Batista was still the strongman of Cuba: in many ways Batista was the issue in both elections. When people spoke about military power versus civilian authority, they were speaking about Batista. At the same time, everyone knew that open military rule was no longer possible in Cuba. The *clases populares* counted for something, and the political problem facing all groups was how to mobilize and control mass support. Consequently, in his struggle to retake state power by political means, the colonel approached the Communist Party as the one group from the *clases populares* willing to support him.

Cubans concerned about the political process were very aware of this change. The British embassy reported that "though Colonel Batista has lost his controlling influence over Congress, and though the economic bodies in Cuba oppose his radical policies, he is still a social leader, that is to say, a leader of the masses, and with their support, and with his control over the army, he has the power, if he cared to exert it, to sweep aside Congress and make himself president."[84] The internal correspondence of the Cuba Cane Sugar Company reenforces the British view. One company analysis, written in September 1939, noted that while Cuban political opinion was divided between "*civilistas*" and "*militaristas*," the "vast majority" of the population was "indifferent to the political process." Then, contradicting itself, the report stated that "public opinion in Cuba is openly antimilitarist, which has usurped civilian aspirations for power." This situation, the company letter went on to say, was bad for the sugar industry; "somehow the sugar industry will have to find its way through this inexplicable confusion that constitutes Cuban politics today."[85]

By March 1940, the American ambassador in Cuba, George Messersmith, was cautiously optimistic about what he viewed as a growing conservative trend in Batista's camp. He drew this conclusion because the conservative *caudillo* Mario Menocal decided to back Batista for president. Menocal's decision displeased the communists because Menocal was part of the oligarchy they wanted to exclude from influencing Batista, but, Messersmith explained, the CP would continue to support Batista's platform of "Democracy, Social Justice, and the Defense of the National Economy." On March 31 Batista and Menocal issued a joint manifesto that, in part, declared:

> The country needs quiet and work. . . . [We are] convinced of the advantages of democracy and of its high aims we must fulfill, and we shall insist on others fulfilling, all of the duties and right which that system assures through the Constitution and the Laws, carrying out that policy with complete respect for authority, for property, and for lib-

erty, humanely interpreted. We maintain that authority does not mean that the State should become a policeman nor the individual an automaton, but that it should create discipline and civic cooperation. . . . In the social field we will not remain insensible to the real needs and just demands of the people, and in good faith we assert that the well being of the worker lies in the dignity of labor and in the possibilities of opportunities for improving his lot.[86]

By the time of the presidential elections in 1940, Messersmith was less optimistic. Writing to Undersecretary of State Sumner Welles, the ambassador said, "It doesn't make much difference who will be elected President on July 14." Grau, in Messersmith's estimation, while far less anti-American than he was in 1933, was too weak and indecisive to avoid "the worst influences around him . . . and he would be a slender reed on which to lean." Batista, meanwhile, was another problem: "the chances are that Batista will be elected, or at least in some way become president of Cuba. He is a curious individual and difficult to analyze. . . . In his conversations with me he has pretended great friendship for us and an understanding for the need for the closest cooperation in every respect. Basically, I do not believe that he likes us or ever will. He has been difficult to deal with while ruling from behind the scenes, and my guess is that the chances are that he will be much more difficult to deal with once he is president."[87] The Communists, Messersmith reasoned, were of no great concern because they were under Batista's control. Batista won the presidential election, with 800,000 votes to Grau's 575,000.

Despite these worries, however, from Washington's perspective, with the successful completion of both elections, the United States attained its long-sought-after objective of a stable and quiet Cuba. It could even describe the country as "democratic," something Washington was hard pressed to say of its own country between 1933 and 1939. The United States remained concerned about the internal economic situation and was often displeased with Cuban government intervention in the economy. But, with war raging in Europe and with its sugar supply secure, the United States could tolerate these relatively minor uncertainties.

Cuba in 1940 was a very different place from what it had been before 1933. While people held sharply divergent views on exactly how and why Cuba had changed, most everyone felt that after 1940 Cuba was a more stable, modern, and democratic country in which to live. This change in Cuban politics provided the foundation for a new cycle of crisis and transformation after 1940.

No longer were the fundamental issues of political discourse and practice centered around whether or not the state should be popular and national. Rather, from 1940 to 1959, Cuban politics focused on what being "popular" meant and which sectors of "the people" were the "true" representatives of the nation. The long struggle for social change would continue, but under very different conditions.

Conclusion

From 1920 to 1940 the practice of state power, and the forms of popular resistance to that power, had taken new directions. By the third decade of the twentieth century the oligarchic state was weakened by popular mobilization "from below" and by the insistence of the middle classes that they be included in the political life of the country. In many ways, however, before the 1930s the Cuban state did not need to be strong: it was American hegemony, exercised through the Platt Amendment, that ultimately guaranteed political order and economic stability. The Cuban political class accepted this arrangement and they were adept at using what political and economic space they had to obtain wealth and power. There was, in other words, no compelling reason why a Cuban nation state should exist before 1933.

One thing that is clear from this study is that the mechanisms of oligarchic rule proved to be very effective at maintaining control over a socially and economically unstable population. Oligarchic rule was based on the fragmentation of political power in an overwhelmingly agrarian society. While it is true that the higher levels of the oligarchic state collapsed with remarkable speed in early 1933, *caciquismo* and *caudillismo* continued to be very strong, especially in the countryside. More research is needed on how *caudillismo* and *caciquismo* functioned in Cuba. Historians of Spain have pointed out that *caciquismo* was a modern phenomenon that evolved during the last half of the nineteenth century. *Caciques* were typically not part of the established oligarchy; rather, they were a new political elite whose influence stemmed from their ties to both the central state and to the rural sector. *Caciques* were intermediaries between local communities and national political machines.[1] In Cuba, *caciquismo* evolved with particular force after the war of 1895–98.[2] As with *caciquismo* in Spain, Cuban personalistic networks of dependence and patronage functioned as a transitional form of social control within the context of the rapid destruction of precapitalist agrarian social relations and the emergence of a mass wage-labor workforce. From 1880 to 1930, Cubans witnessed the gradual abolition of slavery, the destruction of thousands of peasant communities and households due to the expansion of sugar *latifundios*, the evolution of *colono* sugar production, and the importation of hundreds of thousands of migrant workers.[3] These changes in the life and labor of rural Cubans meant that most people were neither peasants nor proletarians, but a very unstable combination of the two.[4] Especially after the extremely destructive independence wars during the last half of the nineteenth century, many poor and displaced people needed some measure of security. The sugar companies that invested in Cuba after 1898 took advantage of this vulnerable population: they paid low wages, imposed long working hours, and denied workers the right to organize unions. At the same time, Cuban and foreign capitalists did not have to worry about interference from state authorities in Havana.

It was within this context that the oligarchic state, *caciquismo*, and *caudillismo* developed. Politicians needed intermediaries to guarantee votes at election time, and landowners needed to establish control over labor. To solve these problems, aspiring politicians or company managers looked to people who had influence over local populations. Such individuals were often veterans of the independence wars who used their status within rural communities to provide their followers with land, jobs, credit, and access to wider circles of "friends" who might be of assistance when times got rough, as they invariably did.

Political rebellion before 1930 was smothered by this web of *caudillismo* and *caciquismo*. Such was the case with the Veterans' and Patriots' Rebellion of 1923–24. The Veteran's Movement certainly reflected the growing contradictions of the oligarchic state, but it would take a much more dramatic crisis to undermine oligarchic power. Such a crisis occurred when the world trade system collapsed in 1929. By the early 1930s mass mobilization, revolution, economic crisis, and the threat of foreign intervention from the United States generated widespread demands for a new and democratic country and for a Cuban nation state.

As we have seen, there was little agreement about what kind of state should replace oligarchic rule. The lack of consensus within the antioligarchic groups is understandable: mass mobilization and economic crisis fueled what one scholar has termed the "ambiguous fertility" within nationalist politics.[5] The insurgent energy of the *clases populares* and the middle classes had changed both the form and the content of political practice and discourse. After 1933, Cuban politicians had to take the supposedly "non-political" and "non-national" concerns of the popular sectors seriously. To make sense of mass insurgency, political leaders developed competing visions of how a future state should represent Cubans. These state visions could be more or less inclusionary or exclusionary, depending on which sectors of "the people" were deemed most representative of the nation.[6]

The groups that self-consciously claimed to represent "the people" had been thrown into mass politics with little or no prior experience of how to channel popular demands into effective strategies and organizational structures. Politics had erupted in rural Cuba with no prompting from students, communists, trade unionists, and radical nationalists. In late 1933, when the self-proclaimed vanguards of popular struggle found themselves holding state power, they did not have the means either to lead or to control the very people they claimed to represent. This weakness also explains why, in January 1934, the Grau coalition could so easily be pushed aside by Fulgencio Batista and his reorganized army and police. The oligarchy was equally caught off guard by a lower-rank soldier from the *clases populares* who had his own ideas about how to rule Cuba. The traditional political classes were forced to accept the unpredictable Batista as the "architect" of a postrevolutionary political settlement.

What we can learn from the Cuban experience during these critical years was how the terms of state formation in Cuba between 1933 and 1940 were set by an unlikely individual, Fulgencio Batista. The young and poorly educated sergeant-turned-colonel managed to repress, co-opt, balance, and neutralize such disparate groups as traditional politicians, sugar interests, organized labor, communists, radical nationalists, and the United States. Batista was clever enough to understand that Cuban politics would never be the same after 1933 and that "social peace" and "democracy" depended on the incorporation of the now "disciplined" *clases populares* into the political process. Yet he was also devious enough to appropriate the legacy of the revolution of 1933 for his own political ends. This explains why Batista made his alliance with the Communist Party and why he permitted the formation of the Cuban Confederation of Workers. Meanwhile, he managed to keep his main political competitors, Grau San Martín and the Auténticos, as well as the sugar companies, off balance while he implemented his populist project. Equally surprising was how the young colonel managed to confound the all-powerful United States without breaking rank with their strategic concerns in Cuba and in the region generally. The existing literature on twentieth-century Cuba tends to be so focused on explaining why there was a revolution in 1959 that these remarkable aspects of Cuba's history are often glossed over with little or no explanation about how and why Cuban politics evolved as it did. This book, I hope, will help refocus our attention on people and events that deserve to remembered and studied on their own merit and not simply in light of what happened twenty-odd years later.

Under Batista's watchful eye, the state redistributed wealth taken from capitalists' profits and used it to pay for the state's social policies. By the 1940s, the "redistributionist demagoguery" of Cuban populism was accompanied by some real, if modest, reforms.[7] As early as 1937, the British embassy observed that "on the *centrales*, the strikes of 1933–1934 gave a great impulse to a movement which had hitherto developed only slowly in agriculture. The majority of the mills now recognize syndicates of the workers and agree to deal with them. The latter have bargained successfully for wage increases and improvements in conditions, and many companies have gone so far as to sign contracts instituting a 'closed shop' of the most rigorous type."[8] Just over a decade later, an American report complained, "What started as a fair movement for the recognition of the fair rights of labor during the years just proceeding the Cuban Constitution of 1940, has since developed into a pyramid of excesses which threatens to liquidate many of the country's productive assets."[9] Another American document, written for businessmen who wanted to invest in Cuba, made the same point: "The years following 1933 witnessed the increasing influence of the labor movement in the political life of Cuba. Much advanced legislation was passed by succeeding administrations, which actively sought the support of labor. It was not until the 1940s, however, that the whole machinery of government was geared to favor labor."[10] It is, of course, an exaggeration to say that "the whole machinery of government" was on the side of labor. Cuba was a safe haven for American capital, whatever complaints investors might have had about the influence of organized labor. But it was also true that foreign capitalists could no longer act with complete impunity as they had before 1933. The Cuban Constitution of 1940 represented a political arrangement that reflected a new balance of power in the country, and foreign capitalists would have to adapt to this new reality. The importance of the 1940 consensus, as we know from subsequent history, was not found in what it actually accomplished but rather in what it promised and why those promises had to be made in the first place.

The tendency of historians to view Batista solely as a counterrevolutionary—especially in light of the revolution of 1959—has obscured the reasons behind his populist phase of 1937–40 and, I would argue, why Cuba became a formal democracy in 1940. Batista saw himself as a leader of the revolution of 1933, and though we can certainly dispute his revolutionary credentials, we should not underestimate the fact that Batista was a product of revolutionary upheaval and he saw himself as such. Batista loved to read political biographies, and one of his heroes was Napoleon Bonaparte: we do not know if Batista saw himself as a Cuban Napoleon, but we do know that he felt that it was his personal responsibility, his "destiny," to bring "order" to revolutionary "chaos." Batista was skillful at recruiting allies and satisfying their concerns while preparing the conditions for his rise to the presidency in 1940. For the first time in Cuban history, important segments of the *clases populares* were incorporated, willingly or not, into the "public domain" organized by the state. Grau's short-lived government had attempted to satisfy popular aspirations and bring democracy to Cuba, but it would be Batista, not Grau, who would become the "architect" of the post-1933 state.

In a recent article on populism in Latin America, Alan Knight described Batista in the 1930s as a "slippery populist." [11] This description is an apt one, and most of the writing on Batista for this period shares this view. What I have tried to do in this book is to explain why the Cuban leader was so "slippery." The colonel's "slipperiness," I would suggest, was not due simply to his well-known tendency to mistrust virtually everyone around him and to seize on any idea that would serve his immediate ends, but also because of the "slippery" times he lived in. Batista understood that, after 1933, political practice and discourse needed to reflect "popular" concerns and needs. He also appreciated that since Cuban political and economic life was so dominated by the United States under F. D. Roosevelt, Cuba would have to appear to be evolving toward democracy. The central issue was how, and under whose authority, "democracy" would be established. Batista and Cuba did not have the economic and political bargaining power of Lázaro Cárdenas and his Mexico; the Cuban leader would have to tread more carefully when dealing with the Americans. What was increasingly clear to many Latin Americans during the late 1930s was that, despite the rhetoric of Good Neighbor policy makers, the United States would not permit the meaning of democracy to be used against American strategic interests. The unruly peoples to the south could not be relied upon to establish democracy on their own, and they needed to be kept under the watchful eyes (and guns) of reliable dictators, at least until the people were ready to assume "responsible" political behavior.[12] Batista understood and accepted this logic, just as he was keenly aware that Cubans could not be ruled in the same way after the revolution of 1933. Consequently from 1934 to 1940, Batista was simultaneously a dictator, an American ally, a populist, and a nationalist, and he kept Cubans and Americans alike guessing as to what he might do next. By doing this so well, Batista stole the political initiative away from liberal democrats, communists, nationalist radicals, and traditional politicians. Given the political and economic turmoil of the times, it is difficult to imagine how any leader could accomplish this feat without being very slippery indeed.

Cuban politics, then, had both altered greatly and remained the same. Corruption and violence would continue to dominate the political scene. But after 1933, the popular sectors were less frightened, they had new memories and traditions of struggle, and they possessed new forms of political practice. Cubans had experienced many hardships, defeats, and some victories. Working-class and poor Cubans were still onlookers as the political elites fought over access to the state, but the idea that the state must be "popular" and represent the entire nation was now embedded in Cuban political culture. Cubans had fought for years to have the state take their demands and rights seriously, and though we know in hindsight that their expectations were denied, the seeds of a *potential* and even more radical transformation of Cuban society had been planted. To what degree this potential within Cuban political culture would be realized, and who would tap into it, is the subject of another phase of Cuban history.

The political arrangement of 1940 was therefore built on fragile foundations. It came about because of a specific combination of internal events (the crisis of oligarchic rule and the revolution of 1933) and external events (the depression and World War II). Favorable wartime conditions provided Cuban producers with a stable sugar market in the United States from 1939 to 1945. The political and economic realities of the depression, as well as the growing threat of world war, forced the United States to provide greater market access to Cuban sugar. Despite the uncertainties of regional and international politics, the investment climate in Cuba had improved for American capitalists. Before 1933, total U.S. investment in Cuba had reached $1.5 billion, and in 1933 it had fallen to barely $300 million; but in 1937, U.S. investments reached nearly twice the original amount.[13] American domestic sugar production was insufficient for wartime demand, and the Philippines, Cuba's main competitor, was too far away. As long as the threat of war lasted, Cuba was guaranteed a stable market for its sugar. Tariffs were reduced and prices improved. In the words of Jules Benjamin, "The island's sugar industry had to shift from enforced underproduction to all-out production for war."[14] The Cuban oligarchy had long clamored for a permanent sugar treaty with the United States, but the best they could get was an exceptional agreement under wartime conditions.

The income from this commerce made it possible for the Cuban elite to tolerate—and reluctantly pay for—Batista's intrusive statist policies. Wartime conditions provided Batista with the political space to promote his own brand of Cuban populism. Batista's populism took the form it did because Roosevelt's New Deal liberalism and the Good Neighbor policy did not look kindly upon overt dictatorships, especially in Cuba. Cuba's major sugar industry's magazine, *La Revista Semanal Azucarera* summed up the situation by saying that "in a troubled world where social strife is rampant, the importance to the United States of having next door a democratic, reasonably prosperous country where all the 'isms' born of dire poverty are unknown could hardly be overemphasized."[15] These words were written in March 1939, and thanks to a stable sugar market in the United States, Cuba was indeed a "reasonably prosperous country" for the next five years.

The increased revenue from sugar sales in the 1940s meant that Cuban governments had the financial means to co-opt many unionists and leftist activists within the irresistible web of state clientism. Mass organizations had to take advantage of the political space that had opened up from 1937 to 1945 to obtain better wages, improved working conditions, the right to organize, and access to jobs and state revenues. The ability of union and leftist leaders to meet these demands by the rank and file depended on their access to the state, and, from 1934 to 1944, access to the state meant access to Batista. Political credibility hinged on a leader's ability to successfully negotiate the terms of engagement between the state and one's supporters. After 1938 the Communist Party and many union leaders became adept at such negotiations. Unions won legal recognition, collective bargaining was more widespread, wages improved, and there was better job security for some workers. Union and leftist leaders could reject the temptation of state patronage, but to do so would mean obtaining nothing at all for the rank and file.[16] The political memory of the 1933 revolution was too powerful to ignore, and workers needed something in return after so many sacrifices and hardships. The only alternative was political isolation and ineffectiveness. Ironically, the Cuban left—what remained of it—gained access to the state only after their defeat and marginalization. The CP's support of Batista might have made a defeat appear to be a victory, but Batista held the political initiative, not the communists and their trade union cadre.

With the end of the world war and a return to insecure market conditions, the Batistiano political consensus quickly unraveled. Without the stable and lucrative source of state revenue from the U.S. wartime market, the economic foundation for Cuban populism fell away and the political fragility of the *pax batistiana* became obvious. After 1944, Cuban political discourse retained its populist form, but the state no longer possessed the resources, or the political credibility, to effectively manage the populist strategy of capital accumulation. Thereafter, the political and economic space that existed from 1937 to 1944 shrank at an alarming pace, especially for those who were junior partners in the populist consensus, such as the communists and organized labor. Cold-war politics would not admit state alliances with communists. After 1944, former allies in the process of state formation literally fought over the diminishing resources of the state.[17] With the umbilical cord to the state cut, some sectors found it hard to survive without state patronage. When Ramón Grau San Martín and the Auténticos were elected in 1944, the populist justifications for the inclusion of the popular sectors into the networks of state patronage no longer masked the reality of blatant corruption and pork-barrel politics. By the 1950s this situation eventually provoked another crisis within Cuban society. The stage was set for a different set of political and economic contradictions that would culminate in a new revolutionary situation.

Throughout the late 1940s and 1950s, political debate was fueled by a widespread feeling that corrupt politicians had "betrayed" and cynically manipulated the popular sentiments and expectations of 1933–40. Politicians were seen not just as parasites living off the institutions of state (this was nothing new to Cubans), but after 1940 they were also viewed as abusing a collective patrimony that belonged to the entire nation. The consensus of 1940 proved to be too fragile and state structures too weak to completely appropriate the collective memory of diverse social groups who had fought long and hard to change their conditions of existence. What made the post-1940 constitutional debates more than just rhetorical verbiage, however, was that constitutional principles could be, and were, interpreted in potentially radical ways. Grau's Auténticos would feel the strain of this popular pressure, and in 1948 Eduardo Chibás and his followers split away to form the Cuban People's Party (Ortodóxo) in an attempt to reclaim the "true" ideals of 1933 and 1940. In large measure this is what the struggles of the late 1940s and the 1950s were all about. The "symmetrical edifice" Batista was so instrumental in building proved to be too fragile, and it would eventually crumble around him.

Notes

Abbreviations

In addition to abbreviations used in the text, the following abbreviations are used in the notes.

AIH   Archivo del Instituto de Historia de Cuba
ANC   Archivo Nacional de Cuba
PRO/FO   Public Records Office, Foreign Office. British Foreign Office Documents will be cited by the initials PRO/FO, followed by the Foreign Office registration numbers, and then by the dispatch number, if provided.
FRUS, 1931   *Foreign Relations of the United States, 1931*
FRUS, 1933   *Foreign Relations of the United States, 1933*
FRUS, 1934   *Foreign Relations of the United States, 1934*

Introduction

1. The passage of the Platt Amendment in 1901 first by the American Congress and then by the Cuban Constituent Assembly denied the new Cuban republic sovereign status. The Cuban government could not enter into any treaty with foreign powers, nor could it permit its public debt to go beyond its normal ability to repay creditors. The United States was permitted to establish a naval base at Guantánamo Bay and the Cuban government conceded that the United States had the right to intervene to maintain life, property, and political order. See Pérez, *Cuba under the Platt Amendment;* and Pérez, *The War of 1898,* pp. 32–35.
2. The *machadato* refers to the regime of General Gerardo Machado y Morales. Machado ruled Cuba from 1925 to 1933.
3. The full English text of the constitution can be found in Fitzgibbon, *Constitutions of the Americas,* pp. 226–96.

4. Rayneri, "Colonel Batista and Cuba's Future," p. 51.

5. The subject of the "transition to democracy" has provoked much scholarly debate among Latin Americanists. Recently work has focused on the "Barrington Moore thesis," which argues that democracy is the result of "bourgeois revolution" against an oligarchic landed elite. Moore also contends that "authoritarian" and "fascist" regimes are typically the product of an alliance between the landed aristocracy and a weak capitalist class. See Moore, *Social Origins of Dictatorship and Democracy.* Latin Americanists have found this scheme both useful and debatable. In broad outline, historians and social scientists have challenged Moore's tendency to see such a clear distinction between the landed oligarchy and the "national bourgeoisie." As a result, the political implications of their "class interests" are equally vague. As we will see, this political ambiguity certainly existed in Cuba between 1933 and 1940. Consequently Cuba does not fit into Moore's scheme. Of course, whether or not Cuba was any more than a formal democracy after 1940 is a valid point to raise. But leaving aside the widespread disillusionment of the Cuban population after 1944 with the failure of governments to implement the 1940 constitutional provisions, there can be no doubt that from 1940 to 1944 most politically aware Cubans thought the country was more democratic than ever. Four important studies that discuss Moore's thesis in relation to Latin America are Rueschemeyer, Huber Stephens, and Stephens, *Capitalist Development and Democracy;* Huber and Safford, *Agrarian Structure and Political Power;* Yashar, *Demanding Democracy;* and Paige, *Coffee and Power.*

6. Some of the most important recent discussions of class formation in Latin America and other regions are Duncan and Rutledge, *Land and Labour in Latin America;* Cohen, Gutkind, and Brazier, *Peasants and Proletarians;* Hanagan and Stephenson, *Proletarians and Protest;* Lal, Munro, and Beechert, *Plantation Workers;* Amin and van der Lindin; *"Peripheral" Labour?;* Kluboch, *Contested Communities;* and Peloso, *Peasants on Plantations.*

7. For an academic analysis of the concept of the popular sectors, or "*el pueblo*" or "*lo popular,*" see O'Donnell, "Tensions in the Bureaucratic-Authoritarian State and the Question of Democracy," pp. 288–91.

8. Office of Strategic Services, *Political Significance and Influence of the Labor Movement,* p. 4.

9. Ibarra, *Prologue to Revolution,* pp. 55, 58.

10. Some works that provide excellent discussion of middle-class formation and identity in Latin America are Parker, *The Idea of the Middle Class;* Jiménez, "Elision of the Middle Classes and Beyond"; and Reuschemeyer et al., *Capitalist Development and Democracy,* esp. chap. 5. There is no good work that deals specifically with Cuban middle-class formation during the twentieth century. For a general description of the Cuban middle class and their occupations, see Ibarra, *Prologue to Revolution,* chap. 3; and Carvajal, "Observaciones sobre la clase media en Cuba."

11. On the issue of the proletarianization of the middle classes, see Ibarra, *Prologue to*

Revolution, pp. 57–59. On the middle classes and American culture, see Pérez, *On Becoming Cuban*.

12. Whitehead, "State Organization in Latin America," p. 9.

13. On the 1940s and 1950s, see Marqués Dolz, *Estado y economía*; Zuaznábar, *La economía cubana*; and Pérez-Stable, *The Cuban Revolution*.

14. The best treatments of Cuban class structure in the early twentieth century are Pérez, *Cuba under the Platt Amendment*, esp. chap. 9; and Ibarra, *Prologue to Revolution*, esp. chaps. 1, 2.

15. I would like to thank Professor David Parker for his insights on this point.

16. Pérez, *Cuba under the Platt Amendment*, pp. 227–28.

17. On the modern state, see Scott, *Seeing Like a State*; Wood, *The Pristine Culture of Capitalism*; Adams, "Notes on the Difficulty of Studying the State"; Paul Thomas, *Alien Politics*; and Sayer, "Everyday Forms of State Formation."

18. Two recent collections that examine how political and economic circumstances changed from the 1930s to the late 1940s are Bethell and Roxborough, *Latin America between the Second World War and the Cold War*; and Rock, *Latin America in the 1940s*. An excellent general study of the emergence of cold-war politics is Cronin, *The World the Cold War Made*.

19. For classic presentations of the modernization view, see Almond and Verba, *The Civic Culture*; and Pye and Verba, *Political Culture and Political Development*. Many of the arguments presented in these older works are being recycled and updated by such authors as Larry Diamond, Juan Linz, S. M. Lipset, Jorge Domínguez, and Samuel Huntington. These scholars use the term "civil society" in much the same way as the earlier writers used "political culture." For example, see Diamond, Linz, and Lipset, *Democracy in Developing Countries*; Huntington, *Political Order in Changing Societies*; and, more recently, Huntington, *The Clash of Civilizations*; Domínguez, *Constructing Democratic Governance*; and Diamond, *Developing Democracy*.

20. For some pioneering works taking this perspective, see Fried, *The Evolution of Political Society*; and Geertz, *The Interpretation of Cultures*. Recent work on the relationship of politics to culture are Seddon, *Relations of Production*; Godelier, *Perspectives in Marxist Anthropology*; Wolf, *Envisioning Power*; and Wolf, *Europe and the People without History*, esp. pp. 387–90; Gledhill, *Power and Its Disguises*; and Narotzky, *New Directions in Economic Anthropology*. For a highly critical analysis on the Eurocentric notion of "civil society," see Goody, "Civil Society in a Comparative Perspective."

21. For an excellent discussion of these issues within the Cuban and Puerto Rican context, see the articles in the special issue of the *Hispanic American Historical Review*, dedicated to the political and economic conjuncture of 1898.

22. The major works on the revolution of 1933 are: Tabares del Real, *La revolución del 30*; Soto, *La revolución del 33*; Roa García, *La revolución del 30 se fue a bolina*; Aguilar, *Cuba 1933*; Cairo Ballester, *La revolución del 30*; Farber, *Revolution and Reaction*; Raby, *Cuban Pre-Revolution of 1933*; Carrillo, *Cuba 1933*; Adams y Silva, *La gran men-*

tira; Lumen, *La revolución cubana;* and Charles Thomson, "Cuban Revolution: Fall of Machado," and his "Cuban Revolution: Reform and Reaction."

23. For example, see Wood, "The Long Revolution"; Aguilar, *Cuba 1933;* Blackburn, "Prologue to the Cuban Revolution"; Ruiz, *Cuba: The Making of a Revolution;* Soto, *La revolución del 33;* Suchlicki, *Cuba, from Columbus to Castro;* Bonachea and San Martín, *The Cuban Insurrection;* Liss, *Roots of Revolution;* and Smith, *Background to Revolution.*

24. See Aguilar, *Cuba 1933;* Carrillo, *Cuba 1933;* Suchlicki, *Cuba, from Columbus to Castro;* Gil, "Antecedents of the Cuban Revolution"; and Hennessy, "The Roots of Cuban Nationalism." For a recent and articulate presentation of this perspective, see Pérez-Stable, *The Cuban Revolution;* and Pérez-Stable, "Reflections on Historical Possibility."

25. Aguilar, *Cuba 1933,* pp. 231, 247.

26. Bonachea and San Martín, *The Cuban Insurrection,* p. 2.

27. Suárez, *Cuba, Castro, and Communism,* p. 13.

28. See Raby, *The Cuban Pre-Revolution of 1933;* Farber, *Revolution and Reaction in Cuba;* Soto, *La revolución del 33;* Tabares del Real, *La revolución del 30;* Liss, *Roots of Revolution,* esp. chap. 6. The most recent example of this perspective is found in Ibarra, *Prologue to Revolution,* esp. chap. 11.

29. For recent contributions on the subject of mass mobilization and political change in Cuba, see: Carr, "Mill Occupations and Soviets"; Zanetti, "The Workers' Movement and Labor Legislation"; Losanda Álvarez, "The Cuban Labor Market"; de la Fuente, "Two Dangers, One Solution"; Whitney, "What Do the People 'Think and Feel'?"; McLeod, "Undesirable Aliens"; Carr, "Identity, Class, and Nation"; Carr, "Omnipotent and Omnipresent."; and Ayala, *American Sugar Kingdom,* esp. chaps. 6–8.

30. See Joseph and Nugent, *Everyday Forms;* Chomsky and Lauria-Santiago, *Identity and Struggle;* Mallon, *Peasant and Nation;* Coronil, *The Magical State;* Nugent, *Rural Revolt in Mexico;* Joseph, LeGrand, and Salvatore, *Close Encounters of Empire;* Purnell, *Popular Movements and State Formation;* and Migdal, Kohli, and Shue, *State Power and Social Forces.*

31. Some important recent contributions on the study of subaltern politics, culture, power, and state formation are Kaplan and Pease, *Cultures of United States Imperialism;* Lloyd and Thomas, *Culture and the State;* and Lowe and Lloyd, *The Politics of Culture.*

32. Migdal, "The State in Society," p. 15.

33. Scholarship on Cuban state formation in the twentieth century is sparse, with the work of Louis Pérez Jr. and Jorge Ibarra standing out as exceptions. This gap in the historiography means that we need to know far more about exactly what kind of state the revolutionaries of the 1950s overthrew and more about Cuban political culture generally. For the most recent and stimulating analysis of Cuban cultural formation, see Pérez, *On Becoming Cuban.*

34. In addition to the works cited in note 22 above, see Pérez, *Army and Politics in Cuba;* Gellman, *Roosevelt and Batista;* and Sims, "Cuba."

35. My perspective on populism is influenced by the following works: Knight, "Populism and Neo-populism"; Simon Collier, "Trajectory of a Concept"; Schwarz, *Misplaced Ideas;* Vilas, "Latin American Populism"; Rowe and Schelling, *Memory and Modernity;* Bieber, *En torno al origén histórico;* Stein, *Populism in Peru;* Laclau, *Politics and Ideology in Marxist Theory;* and Anderle, *Algunos problemas de la evolución del pensamiento anti-imperialista.*

Chapter 1

1. For excellent general overviews of the republican period, see Ibarra, *Cuba, 1898–1921;* Ibarra, *Prologue to Revolution;* Benjamin, *The United States and Cuba;* Benjamin, *United States and the Cuban Revolution;* Pérez, *Cuba under the Platt Amendment;* Hugh Thomas, *Cuba;* Pino-Santos, *El Asalto a Cuba;* Anuario de Estudios Cubanos, *La república neocolonial;* López Seguera, *Cuba: capitalismo dependiente;* and Le Riverend, *La república.*

2. The best treatment of the historical context surrounding the Platt Amendment is Pérez, *War of 1898.*

3. For a sweeping and brilliant analysis of the complexities of Cuban national formation from the nineteenth century to 1959, see Pérez, *On Becoming Cuban.*

4. The *colono* system refers to a method of sugar production where the growers rented land, or made some kind of sharecropping agreement, with the mills. This system developed after the abolition of slavery in 1886. With the mechanization of sugar production at the end of the nineteenth century, many growers could not afford the capital outlay for the increasingly complex refining techniques. As a consequence, growers became dependent on millers to refine their sugar. Gradually, *colonos* tended to be Cubans, while many of the milling companies were foreign owned. *Colonos* could range from very wealthy growers, socially indistinguishable from mill owners, or they could be poor farmers, coming close to the social category of "peasant." The regional and social variations could be significant, with the result that the relations of production in the sugar economy were complex and often unstable. In general, *colono* production was more prevalent in western and central Cuba, where sugar production was more established and the population more settled. In the eastern provinces, on the other hand, sugar production on a massive scale developed in the first two decades of the twentieth century, with the result that mills owned large tracts of land (*latifundio*) and they hired foreign labor to harvest the cane. Poor peasants, many of whom, with no title to their lands, were forced to move to more isolated regions, and very often into the mountains. Large numbers of these poor peasants were the descendants of slaves. On *colono* production, see Ayala, *American Sugar Kingdom,* esp. chap. 5; and Dye, *Cuban Sugar in the Age of Mass Production,* esp. chap. 6.

5. On the racial and class divisions within the independence movement, see Ferrer, *Insurgent Cuba.*

6. The best works on this period of Cuban history are Pérez, *Cuba under the Platt Amendment,* esp. chaps. 3, 4; Ibarra, *Aproximaciones a Clio,* pp. 120–21; and Ibarra, *Cuba, 1898-1921,* esp. chaps. 1, 2. Much more research is required on how these personalistic networks and loyalties actually functioned, especially at a regional and local level.

7. On Gómez, see Hugh Thomas, *Cuba,* p. 504; and Ibarra, *Cuba, 1898-1921,* pp. 302–5.

8. Ibarra, *Aproximaciones a Clio,* p. 121.

9. On Menocal, see "Notes on the Leading Personalities of Cuba," April 28, 1933. PRO/FO/A/1130'1130/14. The reader will notice that I make extensive use of the British Foreign Office Papers. I do this because, while it is true that American diplomatic correspondence is far more detailed than the British, the latter often reveals greater analytical distance from events. The Americans often lost sight of the forest for the trees.

10. Pérez, *Cuba under the Platt Amendment,* pp. 150–51. The best studies of this period are Helg, *Our Rightful Share;* and Fermoselle, *Política y color en Cuba.*

11. Ibarra, *Cuba, 1898-1921,* p. 331.

12. Mañach, "Revolution in Cuba," p. 51.

13. For an excellent analysis of Cuban and American relations under the Platt Amendment, see Pérez, "Incurring a Debt of Gratitude."

14. "Memorandum on the Political Situation in Cuba and Its Effects on British Interests," Lt. H. C. Arnold-Foster, June 5, 1919, PRO/FO/141233.

15. For an excellent analysis of the political options and debates in Cuba after 1878, see Fernández, *España y Cuba;* and Pérez, "Liberalism in Cuba."

16. On the political crisis in Cuba, see the *Heraldo de Cuba,* June 15, 1922, p. 11. These events are covered in detail in Pérez, *Cuba under the Platt Amendment,* esp. chaps. 7, 8; also see Benjamin, *United States and the Cuban Revolution,* esp. chap. 3.

17. For general surveys of these changes, see Pino-Santos, *El asalto a Cuba;* Anuario de Estudios Cubanos, *La república neocolonial;* López Seguera, *Cuba: capitalismo dependiente;* Le Riverend, *La república;* García Álvarez et al., *United Fruit Co.;* García Álvarez, *La gran burguesía;* Guerra y Sánchez, *Sugar and Society in the Caribbean;* Hoernel, "Sugar and Social Change in Oriente"; Jenks, *Our Cuban Colony;* Pérez, *Cuba under the Platt Amendment;* and Ibarra, *Cuba, 1898-1921.*

18. On this issue, see Zanetti, *Los cautivos de la reciprocidad.*

19. Jenks, *Our Cuban Colony,* p. 145.

20. Ibid., p. 165.

21. Buell et al., *Problems of the New Cuba,* p. 46.

22. Primelles, *Crónica cubana, 1919-1922,* p. 62.

23. Ibid., p. 163; Ibarra, "La neocolonia," p. 11.

24. For an excellent overview of these changes, see Ibarra, *Prologue to Revolution,* esp. chap. 1; Ayala, *American Sugar Kingdom,* chaps. 1–4; Dye, *Cuban Sugar in the Age of*

Mass Production, esp. chap. 1; Aguilar, "Cuba, c. 1860-1930," pp. 255-56; and Pérez, *Cuba under the Platt Amendment,* pp. 200-203.

25. On the issue of banditry, see Pérez, *Lords of the Mountain;* and Primelles, *Crónica cubana, 1915-18.*

26. Trelles, "El progreso," pp. 313-19; Carrión, "El desenvolvimiento social de Cuba."

27. Sánchez Alonso, *Las causas de la emigración española,* pp. 116-17, 142-51.

28. República de Cuba, *Memoria de la administración del Presidente de la República Mario García Menocal,* p. 158; Álvarez Estevez, *Azúcar e inmigración,* esp. pp. 44-45; República de Cuba, Secretaría de Hacienda: Sección de Estadísticas, *Inmigración y movimiento de pasajeros en el año de 1921;* República de Cuba, Secretaría de Hacienda, Sección de Estadísticas, *Movimiento de pasajeros, años 1922-1923.*

29. For a recent analysis of the Spanish workforce in Cuba, see Alonso Valdés, "La inmigración española."

30. Hugh Thomas, *Cuba,* p. 543; Jenks, *Our Cuban Colony,* pp. 218-19.

31. Hugh Thomas, *Cuba,* p. 544.

32. Arredondo, *Cuba, tierra indefensa,* p. 333.

33. Hugh Thomas, *Cuba,* p. 557

34. República de Cuba, *Comisión Nacional de Estadísticas,* pp. 46-47.

35. Manifiesto firmado por "Los 200 operarios de Val Antuano referente a la situación que atraviesa la ciudad de Tampa y la crisis que confrontan los trabajadores tabacaleros," August 18, 1917. ANC, Fondo especial, fuera de caja, núms. 4-30. "Manifiesto de la Asociación Tabacalera," April 28, 1927, ANC, Fondo especial, fuera de caja, núms. 7-11. For an especially interesting document on the crisis in the tobacco industry, see Guillermo Serra, "Informe a la Unión de Fabricantes de Tabacos y Cigarros de la Isla de Cuba," 1929 (no month provided), ANC, Fondo especial, caja 11, núm. 99; For two excellent monograph studies, see Duarte Hurtado, *La máquina torcedora de tabaco;* and Stubbs, *Tobacco on the Periphery.*

36. Ibarra, *Prologue to Revolution,* p. 89. Ibarra points out that the census takers for these years included artisans, self-employed workers, and small-scale employers as pertaining to these sections of the working class. They were, of course, correct to do so, since stable employment in almost any section was rare, and some form of self-employment or small business was as much a necessity as it was an aspiration.

37. A good overview of the Cuban working class in this period is del Toro, *El movimiento obrero cubano.*

38. República de Cuba, Secretaría de Estado, *Adaptación de Cuba,* pp. 6-7; *Carteles* 7: 13 (July 13, 1924), p. 5; Junta Cubana de Renovación Nacional, "Manifiesto a los Cubanos," *Revista Bimestre Cubana* 18:2 (March–April 1923); Pérez, *Cuba under the Platt Amendment,* pp. 230-33.

39. Asociación de Hacendados y Colonos de Cuba, "Appeals to the American People," Braga Brothers Collection, Latin American Library, University of Florida (hereinafter Braga Collection), Record Group 11, Series 10-a-c, Manual Rionda y Pollado, Box 18, Subject Files, 1911-43.

40. Comité Organizador, *Primer Congreso Azucarero Nacional, Temas de la Comisión Comercio* (folleto) (1922), ANC, Fondo especial, caja 384.

41. "Memorandum on the Political Situation in Cuba and Its Effects on British Interests," Lt. H. C. Arnold-Foster, June 5, 1919, PRO/FO/141233.

42. See Stubbs, *Tobacco on the Periphery.* On the importance of Cuban radical nationalism and anarchism among Cubans, in southern Florida, see James, *Holding Aloft the Banner of Ethiopia,* esp. chap. 8.

43. An important study dealing with these issues for the late nineteenth century is Casanovas, *Bread, or Bullets.*

44. On Spanish immigration to Cuba, see Maluquer de Motes, *Nación e inmigración;* Carmagnani, *Emigración mediterránea;* and Sánchez Alonso, *Las causas de la emigración española.*

45. On this issue see Poyo, "Anarchist Challenge."

46. República de Cuba, Secretaría de la Presidencia, "Comunicación confidencial al Agregado Militar de la Embajada de los Estados Unidos," ANC, Fondo "Secretaría de la Presidencia," caja 12, núm. 4 (no date); Confederación Nacional Obrero Cubano (CNOC), "Pasos hacia la organización de CNOC" (1933), ANC, Fondo especial, caja 11. Also see Domoulin, *Azúcar y lucha de clases;* and Instituto de Historia de Cuba, *Historia del movimiento obrero cubano,* vol. 1.

47. It is interesting to note that General Mario Menocal's administration created a Secretariat of Labor in 1913. This Secretariat, in turn, came under the authority of the Secretariat of Justice. The purpose of the Secretariat of Labor was primarily to act as a surveillance mechanism over the growing organized workers' movement. While the Secretariat of Labor was a short-lived experiment, as we will see in Chapter 5, the revolutionaries of 1933 revived the idea, but within a different context and with very different objectives. See del Toro, *El movimiento obrero cubano en 1914,* pp. 74–76.

48. On the conditions of sugar workers during the early republic, see García, *Tiempo muerto;* Núñez Machín, *Memoria amarga;* and Domoulin, *Azúcar y luchas de clases, 1917.*

49. *Bateyes,* within the Cuban context, refer to both workers' quarters and barracks on the plantation and to the central yard of the sugar mill complex. See Dembicz, *Plantaciones cañeras.*

50. For an excellent portrayal of working-class life and conditions among Cuban sugar workers, see Carr, "Omnipotent and Omnipresent."

51. For an example of workers' demands, see *Heraldo de Cuba,* September 30, 1924, and November 6, 1924. Also see Sindicato Nacional de Trabajadores de la Industria Azucarera, *Apuntes para la historia del movimiento obrero azucarero,* ANC, Fondo especial, fuera de caja (no date; ca. 1933). The "dead season" lasted roughly from September through January.

52. "Manifiesto de la Hermandad Ferroviaria," February 20, 1924, ANC, Fondo especial, fuera de caja.

53. *Heraldo de Cuba,* November 24, 1924, p. 1.

54. *Apuntes para la historia del movimiento obrero azucarero,* n.p.

55. Manifiesto de la Hermandad Ferroviaria de Cuba, February 20, 1924, ANC, Fondo especial, fuera de caja, núms. 30–31.

56. Aguilar, *Cuba 1933,* pp. 72–73.

57. For some of the most important documents and manifestos of the early student movement, see: Olga Cabrera and Carmen Almodébar, *Las luchas estudiantiles universitarias,* esp. pp. 59–87; and Mella, *Documentos para su vida,* pp. 129–30. On the student movement generally, see Aguilar, *Cuba 1933,* pp. 73–74; González Carbajal, *Mella y el movimiento estudiantil,* pp. 12–22; Suchlicki, *University Students and Revolution in Cuba,* pp. 20–23; and Pérez, *Cuba under the Platt Amendment,* pp. 235–36.

58. Ramón de Armas, Eduardo Torres-Cuevas, and Ana Cairo Ballester, *Historia de la universidad de la Habana, 1728–1929,* 1:326–28.

59. An important study that deals with these issues for the period 1868–98 is Ferrer, *Insurgent Cuba.*

60. The major documents that express this sentiment of aggrieved nationhood are: Sociedad Económica de Amigos del País, "Llamamiento a los Cubanos," and Junta Cubana de Renovación Nacional, "Manifiesto a los Cubanos," both in *Revista Bimestre Cubana* 17:2 (1923); Ortiz, *La decadencia cubana;* Falange de Acción Cubana, "La Protesta de los trece," *Heraldo de Cuba,* April 27, 1923; Asociación de Veteranos y Patriotas, "Al poder legislativo de la República de Cuba: Manifiesto al País," August 30, 1923, ANC, Fondo donativo, caja 62; Asociación de Veteranos y Patriotas, "Por la regeneración de Cuba," September 20, 1923, ANC, Fondo donativo, caja 61; La Asociación de Buen Gobierno, "Al País," September 25, 1923, ANC, Fondo donativo, caja 61; and Asamblea Magna de Veteranos y Patriotas: Comité Ejecutivo, "Boletines publicados por el Comité Ejecutivo y Aprobado por la Asamblea," ANC, Fondo donativo, caja 63 (August 1923).

61. Representative works are Varona, *De la colonia a la república;* Trelles, "El progreso"; Carrión, "El desenvolvimiento social de Cuba"; Roig de Leuchsenring, "La colonia superviva"; Lamar-Schweyer, *La crisis de patriotismo;* Mañach, *Indagación del choteo;* Mañach, *La crisis de la alta cultura cubana;* and Maestri, *Latifundismo en la economía cubana.*

62. *La Lucha,* September 14, 1923, p. 1; *El Universal,* September 19, 1923, p. 1. Also see the speech by General Eusebio Hernández, a leader of the Veterans' movement, in *El Triunfo,* October 14, 1921, p. 1.

63. These names are taken from the following sources: *Heraldo de Cuba,* October 12, 1923; Asociación de Veteranos y Patriotas, "Patria y Libertad," (no date), ANC, Fondo donativo, caja 61; and Cairo Ballester, *El movimiento de veteranos,* esp. appendix.

64. Asociación de Veteranos y Patriotas, "Por la regeneración de Cuba," September 20, 1923, ANC, Fondo donativo, caja 61.

65. For a sample of this rhetoric, see the speeches made at the founding meeting of

the association, printed in the *Heraldo de Cuba*, August 30, 1923; for the official Proclamation of the Veterans' Association, see *Heraldo de Cuba*, September 1, 1923, p. 1.

66. *Heraldo de Cuba*, August 30, 1923, p. 1.
67. See Zanetti and García, *Sugar and Railroads*, esp. chap. 14.
68. *Heraldo de Cuba*, August 30, 1923, p. 1.
69. Ibid.
70. Mr. Hazard to Lord Curzon, Havana, June 7, 1921, PRO/FO/A/4873/165/14.
71. As early as 1919, the conservative *Diario de la Marina* attacked José Miguel's Liberals for falling under the influence of the *clases populares*. See *Diario de la Marina*, March 10 and 31, 1919, p. 1.
72. *La Discusión*, September 5, 1923, p. 1; *Heraldo de Cuba*, September 4, 1923, p. 1.
73. *Heraldo de Cuba*, October 12, 1923, p. 1.
74. For a sample of the press reports, see *El Universal*, October 1, 1923; *Heraldo de Cuba*, October 1, 1923; and *La Discusion*, October 7, 1923.
75. *El Sol*, March 25, 1924, p. 1; *Heraldo de Cuba*, March 27, 1924, p. 1; *Heraldo de Cuba*, September 29, 1924; *Heraldo de Cuba*, November 9, 1924, p. 1.

Chapter 2

The phrase "to scratch away the scab of colonialism" is taken from Rubén Martínez Villena's poem of 1923 entitled "Mensaje lírico-civil," reprinted in *Órbita de Rubén Martínez Villena*. The full stanza reads:

hace falta una carga para matar bribones
para acabar la obra de las revoluciones;

para vengar los muertos, que padecen ultraje
para limpiar la costra tenaz del coloniaje;

para poder un día, con prestigio y razón
extirpar el Apéndice de la Constitución.

The phrase "Appendix of the Constitution" refers to the Platt Amendment.

1. Kubayanda, *The Poet's Africa*, p. 37.
2. Wolf, *Envisioning Power*, p. 4.
3. The term "imagined community" comes from Anderson, *Imagined Communities*.
4. For a path-breaking study on the issues of nation, citizenship, race, and revolution in Cuba between 1868 and 1898, see Ferrer, *Insurgent Cuba*. For the twentieth century, see Brock and Castañeda Fuertes, *Between Race and Empire*; and Moore, *Nationalizing Blackness*.
5. Of course, socialist, anarchist, and Marxist ideas and movements existed in Cuba

since the last half of the nineteenth century, but such groups were small and often bitterly divided. Important figures from these early years such as Carlos Baliño and Diego Vicente Tejera influenced the younger generation of radicals in the 1920s. On the early formation of radical ideologies and groups, see Biblioteca Nacional José Martí, *Baliño;* del Toro, *El movimiento obrero cubano;* Instituto de Historia, *Historia del movimiento obrero cubano,* vol. 1, esp. parts 1, 2; Poyo, "The Anarchist Challenge"; Liss, *Roots of Revolution,* chaps. 1, 2, 3; Gómez García, *Carlos Baliño;* and Casanovas, *Bread, or Bullets.*

6. I follow Raymond Williams's view of "modernism" as the interplay of a sense of popular restlessness, cosmopolitan consciousness, and a desire to break with tradition. See Williams, *Politics of Modernism,* esp. chaps. 1, 2. On the changes taking place in Cuba, see Swan, "The 1920s."

7. Lipsitz, *Time Passages,* p. 16.

8. On Latin American modernism, see Gonzalez and Treece, *Gathering of the Voices,* esp. chaps. 1–4; Martin, *Journeys through the Labyrinth,* esp. introduction and part 1.

9. Benjamin, *United States and the Cuban Revolution,* pp. 81–84; Pérez, *Cuba under the Platt Amendment,* chap. 10; Aguilar, *Cuba 1933,* chap. 4; Smith, *United States and Cuba,* pp. 113–17.

10. For a sample of some of the optimistic editorials of the day, see *La Lucha,* August 12, 1925; "Política Nueva," in *Carteles,* March 8, 1925; "Nuestras bases económicas," *Carteles,* March 22, 1925; and "El problema del azúcar," *Carteles,* June 7, 1925.

11. For an excellent example of this writing, see Araquistaín, *La agonía antillana,* esp. chaps. 11, 13.

12. For example, Juan Marinello, "El arte y su desenvolvimiento en nuestra patria," *Social* 10:3 (March 1925); Emilio Roig de Leuchsenring, "Artistas y hombres o titiriteros y malabaristas," *Social* 17:6 (June 1929); "Editorial: Puede existir una cultura indoamericana?," *Atuei* (May 1928); Nicolás Gamolin, "Formad el Frente único," *Atuei* (December 1927); Juan Marinello, "El insoluble problema del intelectual," and Esteban Pavletich, "Nuestro frente único de trabajadores manuales e intelectuales," both in *Revista de Avance* 1:7 (June 1927); and "Trabajadores Manuales e Intelectuales" (anon.), *Venezuela Libre* 12 (June 1925).

13. Emilio Roig de Leuchsenring (1889–1964) was one of the most influential intellectuals in twentieth-century Cuba. Though he was not a Marxist, his work was dedicated to exposing the destructive effects of imperialism on Cuban society. Roig received a doctorate in civil law from the University of Havana in 1917 and went on to become one of the most popular journalists of the 1920s. In 1927 he became the official historian of the City of Havana. Roig was not a political activist (though he was a member of the Anti-Imperialist League of Cuba). He wrote with a nonacademic audience in mind. His work focused on social and cultural history, and he placed great emphasis on exposing the "false values" of colonialist culture in Cuba. Roig carried on extensive correspondence with Peruvian *apristas* and with

his friend José Carlos Mariátegui. Roig died in Havana in 1964. He professed his support for the Castro revolution of 1959. On Roig, see Cairo Ballester, *El grupo minorista*, pp. 230–32; and Liss, *Roots of Revolution*, pp. 74–83.

14. Emilio Roig de Leuchsenring, "Con el soviet ruso; en Berlín, recuerdos de viaje," *Social* 8 (August 1922), pp. 28–30.

15. Emilio Roig de Leuchsenring, "Ideales y errores," *Social* 11:9 (September 1926), p. 14.

16. "Nuestras entrevistas: Enrique José Varona," *Juventud* (March 1924), p. 30.

17. On these philosophers, see Hale, "Political and Social Ideas in Latin America."

18. Martínez Villena, "La muerte de Ingenieros," in Núñez Machín, *Rubén Martínez Villena*, pp. 357–58.

19. Fernando Ortiz (1881–1969) was one of the most influential intellectuals in twentieth-century Cuba. Ortiz was a social scientist in the broadest sense of the term, writing many books and articles about the origin and character of Cuban culture and society. Ortiz exercised a great influence over successive generations of Cubans, especially after the 1920s. Ortiz was a product of the liberal and positivist intellectual tradition in Cuba and Latin America, and he carried on extensive correspondence with writers and intellectuals from the rest of Latin America as well as Spain. As we will see below, Ortiz's notion that part of being Cuban is the *struggle to be Cuban* in the face of powerful external forces was an idea that held resonance for young Cubans in the 1920s.

20. The best biographical works on Martínez Villena are: Núñez Machín, *Rubén Martínez Villena*; and Roa García, "El fuego de semilla en el surco," in Martínez Villena, *Órbita de Rubén Martínez Villena*.

21. The most important works on Mella are Dumpierre, *Julio Antonio Mella*; Padrón, *Julio Antonio Mella y el movimiento obrero*; and González Carbajal, *Mella y el movimiento estudiantil*. For a collection of Mella's writings, see Mella, *Documentos y artículos*. On Cuban-Mexican relations during the *machadato* and Mella's assassination in Mexico, see Spenser, *The Impossible Triangle*, pp. 170–75.

22. For some of the most important works on the literary vanguards of the early 1920s, see Henríquez Ureña, *Panorama histórico de la literatura cubana*; Portuondo, *El contenido social de la literatura cubana*; Ripoll, *La generación del 23*; Ibarra, *Un análisis psicosocial del cubano*; Roig de Leuchsenring, *El grupo minorista*; Cairo Ballester, *El grupo minorista*; Pérez-Firmat, *The Cuban Condition*; González and Treece, *Gathering of Voices*; Martin, *Journeys through the Labyrinth*; and Masiello, "Rethinking Neocolonial Esthetics."

23. *Heraldo de Cuba*, May 19, 1923, p. 1.

24. Martínez Villena, "Carta a Enrique Serpa," in Núñez Machín, *Rubén Martínez Villena*, pp. 428–29.

25. Roa García, "El fuego de la semilla en el surco," p. 36.

26. *Heraldo de Cuba*, October 3, 1924, p. 1.

27. Enrique José Varona (1844–1933) was the single most important intellectual in

early republican Cuba. A philosopher firmly within the tradition of Latin American positivism, Varona's ideas came to influence successive generations of Cubans. His political ideas ran the gambit of being an *autonomista* in the 1870s and 1880s, an *independista* in the 1890s, and a Conservative Party member in the early republic, to being the mentor of Cuban youth in the 1920s. Varona was never politically radical, but his positivism allowed him to interpret the changes in the world in an optimistic way. For Varona, revolutions were almost always progressive, and he firmly believed in the progressive role of new generations. On Varona, see Guardarrama and Tussel Oropeza, *El pensamiento filosófico de Enrique José Varona.*

28. For the main resolutions of the university reform movement, see *Reportario Americano*, pp. 346–47.

29. On the university reform movement, see Suchlicki, *University Students and Revolution in Cuba*, esp. pp. 19–23; and González Carbajal, *Mella y el movimiento estudiantil*, esp. pp. 11–22.

30. Mella, "La última farsa de los políticos y patrioteros," in his *Documentos*, pp. 95–98.

31. On Haya's arrival in Havana, see *Heraldo de Cuba*, November 1, 3, and 4, 1923; *El Universal*, November 1 and 5, 1923; *Diario de la Marina*, November 3, 1923; and *La Prensa*, November 3 and 4, 1923. For Mella's comments on Haya's visit to Havana, see Julio Antonio Mella, "Víctor Raúl Haya de la Torre," *Juventud* (November–December 1923). On the Popular University José Martí, see "La Universidad Popular," *El Mundo*, November 12, 1923; "Plan de Estudios de la Universidad Popular José Martí," *El Universal*, November 19, 1923; and "Estatutos de la Universidad Popular José Martí," in *Pensamiento Crítico*. On the popular-university movement generally, see Klaiber, "Popular Universities and the Origins of Aprismo," pp. 693–715.

32. "Hablando con Julio Antonio Mella sobre la revolución universitaria," *Carteles* 3 : 50 (November 23, 1924), pp. 10, 31.

33. Entrevista con Fernando Sirgo, *Pensamiento Crítico*, pp. 28–33.

34. Mella, "Los falsos maestros," in *Documentos*, p. 119.

35. "Hablando con Julio Antonio Mella," p. 31.

36. Ibid.

37. On the need for the Popular University to be militantly anti-imperialist, revolutionary, and pro–working class, see: "Informes de la Sección de Expertos de la Policía Nacional al Secretaría de Gobernación Relativos a las clases de la Universidad Popular José Martí y La Liga Anti-imperialista de Cuba" (November 23, 1925), ANC, Fondo especial, caja 6, núm. 13. Also see "Hablando con Julio Antonio Mella," p. 31.

38. "Hablando con Julio Antonio Mella," p. 31.

39. Entrevista con Fernando Sirgo, in *Pensamiento Crítico*, pp. 28–33.

40. Mella, "Carta a Sarah Pascual," in *Documentos*, p. 256.

41. Entrevista con Fernando Sirgo, in *Pensamiento Crítico*, pp. 28–33.

42. A partial list of some of the groups founded by Mella and Martínez Villena includes: the Federation of Cuban Students (1923), the Popular University José Martí

(1924), the Veterans' and Patriots' Movement (1923), the Anti-Imperialist League (1925), the Anti-Clerical League (1925), and the Communist Party of Cuba (1925). See Cairo Ballester, *Movimiento de Veteranos y Patriotas*, pp. 58–60.

43. Ibid., p. 60.

44. Mella, "Carta a Gustavo Aldereguía," March 1926 (no day given), in *Documentos*, p. 258.

45. Ibid., p. 257.

46. Martínez Villena, "Gonfalon" (April 1927), in his *Órbita de Rubén Martínez Villena*, pp. 165–67.

47. On *aprista* populism, see Bieber, *En torno al origen histórico;* and Anderle, *Algunos problemas.*

48. Alba, *Politics and the Labour Movement*, p. 169.

49. For the Peruvian background, see Klarén, *Peru,* esp. pp. 255–62.

50. The most important works on this theme are Alexander, *Communism in Latin America;* Aguilar, *Marxism in Latin America;* Caballero, *Latin America and the Comintern;* and Löwy, *Marxism in Latin America.*

51. "Hablando con Julio Antonio Mella," p. 30.

52. Mella, "Glosas al pensamiento de José Martí," in *Documentos*, pp. 267–74.

53. Ibid.

54. Mella, "Lenin coronado," in *Documentos*, pp. 87–88.

55. Mella, "Los nuevos liberadores," in *Documentos*, p. 124. Emphasis in the original.

56. For example: "¿A dónde va Mexico?," *Revista de Avance* 1:7 (June 15, 1927); Pedro Henríquez Ureña, "Patria de la justicia," *Social* 12:7 (July 1927); Roig de Leuchsenring, "La revolución mexicana," *Social* 16:5 (May 1929); and Orestes Ferrera, "México," *Social* 11:8 (August 1926).

57. Roig, "La revolución mexicana," *Carteles* 14:5 (May 1929), pp. 28–29. On the symbolic importance of the Mexican Revolution for Latin America generally, see Spenser, *Impossible Triangle*, esp. chaps. 6, 8, 9.

58. *Venezuela Libre* 12 (June 1925), p. 4.

59. Ibid., 11 (May 1925), p. 6.

60. Ibid., 12 (June 1925), p. 5.

61. Mella, "¿Hacia dónde va Cuba?," in *Documentos*, p. 407.

62. Ibid., p. 409.

63. Ibid. Emphasis in the original.

64. Gramsci, *Selections from the Prison Notebooks*, p. 126.

65. José Carlos Mariátegui, "La 'indología' de José Vasconcelos," *Social* 13:1 (January 1928), p. 62.

66. Ibid., p. 63.

67. The most important studies of the Communist Party are Serviat, *40 aniversario;* García Montes and Alonso Ávila, *Historia del Partido Comunista;* and Goldenberg, "Rise and Fall of a Party."

68. Goldenberg, "Rise and Fall of a Party," p. 64.

69. On the early years of CNOC, see Instituto de Historia de Cuba, *Historia del movimiento obrero cubano, 1865–1958*, 1:237–44.

70. For an excellent collection of documents by working-class and other opposition groups, see Rosell, *Luchas obreras,* esp. pp. 53–143. Also see Pérez, *Cuba under the Platt Amendment,* pp. 263–64.

71. Peraza, *Machado, crímenes y horrores,* pp. 14–15. Alfredo López was a close friend of Mella.

72. Some of the most important works on this theme are Anderson, *Imagined Communities;* Balibar and Wallerstein, *Race, Nation, Class;* Al-Azmeh, *Islams and Modernities;* Chatterjee, *The Nation and Its Fragments;* Duara, *Rescuing History from the Nation;* Joseph and Nugent, *Everyday Forms of State Formation;* Mallon, *Peasant and Nation;* and Wood, *The Pristine Culture of Capitalism.*

73. Mallon, *Peasant and Nation,* p. 4.

74. Al-Azmeh, *Islams and Modernities,* esp. chap. 3.

Chapter 3

1. On the early years of the *machadato,* see Machado, *Por la Patria Libre;* Tabares del Real, "El pensamiento y el proyecto político"; Domínguez, "Seeking Permission to Build a Nation"; and Benjamin, "The Machadato and Cuban Nationalism."

2. Aguilar, *Cuba 1933,* pp. 58, 62, 101, 103; Benjamin, *United States and the Cuba Revolution,* p. 81; Pérez, *Cuba under the Platt Amendment,* p. 261.

3. Pérez, *Cuba under the Platt Amendment,* p. 269.

4. Mr. Morris to Mr. A. Henderson, Havana, July 8, 1930, PRO/FO/A/5314/2870/14.

5. "Editorial," *Unión Nacionalista,* May 25, 1927, p. 1.

6. Ambassador Guggenheim to the Secretary of State, Havana, January 20, 1931, *FRUS, 1931,* 2:45.

7. Mr. Morris to Mr. A. Henderson, Havana, October 5, 1929, PRO/FO/A/7228/6753/14.

8. Buell, "The Caribbean Situation," p. 86.

9. "Tópicos universitarios," *Unión Nacionalista,* May 18, 1927, p. 1.

10. Directorio Estudiantil Universitario, "Contra la prórroga de poderes: al pueblo de Cuba," May 30, 1927. Archivo Vilaseca, Archivo Instituto de Historia, Doc. 14S8 (hereinafter Archivo Vilaseca).

11. "Al pueblo de Cuba y los Estudiantes," November 27, 1929, ANC, Fondo especial, fuera de caja, núms. 2–26.

12. Pérez, "Cuba, 1930–1959," p. 422.

13. Dye, *Cuban Sugar in the Age of Mass Production,* p. 259.

14. Pérez, "Cuba, 1930–1959," p. 421.

15. Buell, "The Caribbean Situation," pp. 84, 85.

16. Buell, *Problems of the New Cuba,* p. 53.

17. "Informe dirigido a la Unión de Fabricantes de Tabacos y Cigarros de la Isla de

Cuba," firmado por Guillermo Serra, Presidente de la Unión de Rezagadores de la Habana (1929), ANC, Fondo especial, caja 11, núm. 99.

18. Pérez, *Cuba under the Platt Amendment*, p. 280.

19. Buell, "The Caribbean Situation," p. 85.

20. Braga Collection, Box 18, Association of Hacendados, Asociación Nacional de Hacendados de Cuba, "Una economía sana requiere un estado de equilibrio entre el costo de la materia prima, los salarios, los impuestos, y el nivel de los precios" (Havana, October 14, 1940).

21. República de Cuba, *Adaptación de Cuba*, p. 8.

22. Braga Collection, Box 33, File "Cuba Cane, Crop Restrictions," untitled letter from the *colonos* of the Eastern Cuba Sugar Corporation, Camagüey (n.d., but cover letter dated August 23, 1927).

23. Braga Collection, Box 33, File "Cuba Cane, Crop Restrictions," letter from Mr. Gerald Smith to Mr. Albert Strauss, Havana, December 13, 1927. Viriato Gutiérrez was a close friend of Machado and a powerful figure in his cabinet. He was the son-in-law of the largest Spanish-owned sugar mill owner in Cuba, Lauriano Falla Gutiérrez. He was Machado's main link with the influential Spanish colony in Cuba. See Hugh Thomas, *Cuba*, p. 573.

24. Letter from Smith to Strauss.

25. Pérez, *Cuba under the Platt Amendment*, p. 280.

26. República de Cuba, *Adaptación de Cuba*, pp. 52–54.

27. Manifiesto de la Primera Conferencia Nacional de los Obreros de la Industria Azucarera, Santa Clara, December 26–27, 1932, AIH, Fondo "Organizaciones Obreras," núm. 387.

28. Ibid. Also see Braga Collection, Box 69, Manatí, file "Rionda, Salvador, Correspondence," 1932.

29. República de Cuba, *Adaptación de Cuba*, p. 8.

30. On the conditions of rural workers during the late 1920s and early 1930s, see the fascinating first-hand account by the sugar worker García, *Tiempo Muerto*, esp. the chapters "Crisis en 1929" and "Primer encuentro con la ciudad." The collection of interviews with sugar workers in Núñez Machín, *Memoria amarga del azúcar*, is also a rich account of life during this period.

31. Mr. Morris to Mr. Henderson, Havana, April 28, 1930, PRO/FO/A/3579/2870/14.

32. Sir Broderick to Sir John Simon, Havana, December 15, 1931, PRO/FO/A/33/33/14.

33. Memorandum by the Assistant Secretary of State (White), Washington, April 10, 1931, *FRUS, 1931*, p. 51.

34. Sir Broderick to Sir John Simon, Havana, January 13, 1932, PRO/FO/A/863/33/14.

35. For example, see Guggenheim to the Secretary of State, No. 517, Havana, January 20, 1931, *FRUS, 1931*, p. 45; and Mr. Ezard to Mr. A. Henderson, Havana, May 27, 1931, PRO/FO/A/3693/36/14.

36. Guggenheim to the Secretary of State, Havana, January 16, 1931, and Guggenheim

to the Secretary of State, No. 517, Havana, January 20, 1931, both in *FRUS, 1931*, pp. 44–45.

37. Memorandum by the Assistant Secretary of State (White), Washington, April 10, 1931. *FRUS, 1931*, p. 52.

38. On the issues related to Cuban popular conceptions of modernity and progress, especially within the context of the interaction between Cuba and the United States, see Pérez, *On Becoming Cuban.*

39. Carrillo, *Cuba 1933*, p. 32. Emphasis in the original.

40. This point was emphasized to me by Segundo Curti, interview, March 1992. I would also like to thank Louis Pérez Jr. for his comments on middle- and upper-class Cubans.

41. Ibid., p. 36.

42. Fernández, *La razón del 4 de septiembre*, p. 19. Fernández was the first undersecretary of government and war in the Grau coalition of September 1933.

43. de la Osa, *Crónica del año 33*, pp. 18–20.

44. Mañach, "Revolution in Cuba," pp. 55–56. Mañach wrote extensively for literary publications and journals such as *Revista de Avance, Social,* and *Bohemia.* Later, after 1932, he became a leader of the corporatist ABC Revolutionary Society.

45. Fernando Ortiz, "¡Hay que salir al limpio!," *Bohemia* 40 (November 19, 1933).

46. Manifiesto Número 5: "A los estudiantes de la universidad," February 1930 (Havana), ANC, Fondo especial, caja 3, núm. 67. For an excellent analysis of the generational theme in Cuban politics, see Valdés, "Cuban Political Culture," pp. 207–28.

47. Manifiesto Número 6: "Al Congreso de las Universidades," February 1930 (Havana), ANC, Fondo especial, caja 3, núm. 52.

48. Mr. Morris to Mr. Henderson, Havana, April 28, 1930, PRO/FO/A/3579/2870/14.

49. Carrillo, *Cuba 1933*, p. 11.

50. Soto, *La revolución del 33*, 2:23–66.

51. Buell, "The Caribbean Situation," p. 86.

52. "Manifiesto de la Prensa al País," November 16, 1930, signed by *Diario de la Marina, El País, Bohemia, La Semana, Diario Especial, El Comercio, Heraldo Comercial, Social, Carteles, El Mundo, El Mercurio,* and *Sucesos,* ANC, Fondo especial, caja 15, núm. 69.

53. "Manifiesto-programa al pueblo de Cuba," Havana, October 23, 1930, in Pichardo, *Documentos para la historia de Cuba*, 3:458–60. The quotation "to calmly observe a crime is to commit it" is taken from José Martí.

54. *Diario de la Marina*, October 29, 1930, p. 19.

55. Buell, "The Caribbean Situation," p. 86.

56. Manifiesto-Programa, in Roberto Padrón Larrazábal, *Manifiestos de Cuba*, pp. 106–9.

57. Carrillo, *Cuba 1933*, p. 18. For an excellent overview of the historiography on Martí, see Kirk, *José Martí*, esp. chap. 1.

58. Memorandum to the Ambassador in Cuba (Guggenheim), Havana, April 10, 1931,

and Guggenheim to the Secretary of State, Havana, April 28, 1931, both in *FRUS, 1931*, 2:55-59.

59. Ibid., p. 60.

60. Sir Broderick to A. Henderson, Havana, July 31, 1931, PRO/FO/A/4893/36/14.

61. Mr. Ezard to Mr. A. Henderson, Havana, May 27, 1931, PRO/FO/A/3693/36/14.

62. On the Rebellion at Río Verde, see Sir J. Broderick to the Secretary of State for Foreign Affairs, Havana, August 25, 1931, PRO/FO/A/5371/36/14; Sir J. Broderick to the Marques of Reading, Havana, September 2, 1931, PRO/FO/A/5551/36/14; Tabares del Real, *La revolución del 30*, pp. 125-26; Soto, *La revolución del 33*, 2:89-104; Aguilar, *Cuba 1933*, pp. 111-15; and Hugh Thomas, *Cuba*, pp. 592-94.

63. Tabares del Real, *La revolución del 30*, p. 126.

64. Quoted in Tabares de Real, *Guiteras*, p. 154. For a recent work on Guiteras that uses archival material not cited in early books on Guiteras, see Briones Montoto, *Aquella decisión callada*.

65. Confederación Nacional Obrera de Cuba, *IV congreso nacional obrera de unidad sindical: resoluciones y acuerdos sobre la estructura orgánica de la CNOC* (Havana, 1933), in the Archivo del Instituto de Historia de Cuba, Fondo "Organizaciones Obreras," Documento 364:1.

66. Federación Nacional de Torcedores y CNOC, "Informe sobre la conferencia pro-unificación," December 6, 1931 AIH, Fondo "Organizaciones Obreras/CNOC," núm. 1/87/12/125.

67. CNOC, *IV Congreso Nacional Obrero de Unidad Sindical*. Also see Tabares del Real, *La revolución del 30*, p. 113.

68. Carr, "Mill Occupations and Soviets," pp. 129-58.

69. Sindicato Nacional de Obreros de la Industria Azucarera (SNOIA), "Proyecto de Resoluciones para la 11 Conferecia Nacional," June 16, 1933 (n.p.), AIH, Fondo "Registro General," núm. 35/79/75.

70. CNOC, "Programa de demandas y reglamentos de SNOIA" (July 16 and 17, 1933), AIH, Fondo "Organizaciones Obreras," núm. 386; SNOIA, "Manifiesto de la Primera Conferencia Nacional de Obreros de la Industria Azucarera" (Santa.Clara, December 26-27, 1933, Impresos CESLAM, 1933), AIH, Fondo "Organizaciones Obreras," núm 387.

71. SNOIA, "Proyecto de Resoluciones,"; SNOIA, "Manifiesto de la Primera Conferencia," December 26-27, 1933.

72. CNOC, "Pasos hacia la organización de CNOC" (folleto, n.d.), AIH, Fondo "Museo Obrero."

73. SNOIA, "Proyecto de Resoluciones."

74. Ibid.

75. Ibid.

76. Ibid.

77. Buell, *Problems of the New Cuba*, p. 285.

78. Ibid.

79. The best single work on the Ala Izquierda Estudiantil is González Carbajal, *El ala izquierda estudiantil.*
80. Manifiesto Programa del Ala Izquierda Estudiantil: A los Estudiantes y los Trabajadores de Cuba, February 1931, Archivo Vilaseca, AIH, Manifiesto 154.
81. Ibid.
82. Tabares del Real, *La revolución del 30,* pp. 113–14; Aguilar, *Cuba 1933,* pp. 116–17.
83. Gonzálaz Carbajal, *La ala izquierda estudiantil,* pp. 103–4.
84. El Ala Izquierda Estudiantil: Comunicación al Comité Central del Partido Comunista de Cuba (October 5, 1932), Archivo Vilaseca, AIH, Documento 254.
85. The ABC and its program will be discussed in detail in the next chapter.
86. El Ala Izquierda Estudiantil: Comunicación al Comité Central.
87. Ibid.
88. Sir Broderick to Sir J. Simon, Havana, December 20, 1932, PRO/FO/A/257/255/14.

Chapter 4

1. *FRUS, 1933,* pp. 309–56; Pérez, *Cuba under the Platt Amendment,* pp. 308–10; Benjamin, *United States and the Cuban Revolution,* pp. 96–98.
2. Buell, "The Caribbean Situation," p. 87.
3. Stoner, *From the House to the Street,* esp. chaps. 6, 7.
4. For a chronology of assassinations and repression under Machado, see Peraza, *Machado, crímenes y horrores de un régimen;* Carlton Beals, *Crime of Cuba;* and Philips, *Cuba, Island of Paradox.*
5. Mr. Grant Watson to Sir John Simon, Havana, July 15, 1933, PRO/FO/A/5529/255/14 Dispatch 63.
6. Beals, *Crime of Cuba,* p. 347; Benjamin, *United States and Cuba,* p. 61.
7. Mr. Border to Sir John Simon, Havana, June 7, 1933, PRO/FO/A/4710/255/14 Dispatch 56.
8. Aguilar, *Cuba 1933,* esp. chaps. 10, 11.
9. "Welles to Make First Official Mediation Move," *Havana Post,* July 1, 1933, p. 1.
10. Lamar-Schweyer, *How President Machado Fell,* p. 54.
11. This position reflected the position of the ABC Revolutionary Society. See "El ABC al Pueblo de Cuba: Manifiesto-Programa," Havana, November 1932, in Padrón Larrazábal, *Manifiestos de Cuba,* pp. 32–33. For a sophisticated and intelligent presentation of this argument, see the works by Jorge Mañach listed in the bibliography. Mañach was a principal leader of the ABC Society.
12. Philips, *Cuba, Island of Paradox,* pp. 48–49.
13. Fitzgibbon and Healey, "Cuban Elections of 1936," p. 727; Farber, *Revolution and Reaction in Cuba,* p. 53.
14. "El ABC al Pueblo de Cuba: Manifiesto-Programa," Havana, November 1932 (pamphlet); also see ABC, *Doctrina del ABC.*
15. Mañach, "Revolution in Cuba," p. 56.

16. ABC, *Doctrina del ABC*, pp. 76–77, 84–85.

17. Arredondo, *Cuba, tierra indefensa*, pp. 472–73.

18. Mr. Border to Sir John Simon, Havana, April 4, 1933, PRO/FO/A/2957/255/14; Aguilar, *Cuba 1933*, pp. 118–21.

19. "ABC Turns on Workers on the Day of Machado Fall," *Daily Worker*, August 19, 1933, p. 6. For a similar picture of events, but from a conservative perspective, see *Diario de la Marina*, August 13, 1933, p. 1.

20. Sir J. Broderick to Sir John Simon, Havana, January 13, 1932, PRO/FO/A/863/33/14.

21. Mr. Border to Sir John Simon, Havana, April 4, 1933, PRO/FO/A/2957/255/14

22. Charles Thomson, "Cuban Revolution: Fall of Machado," p. 251; Philips, *Cuba, Island of Paradox*, p. 47.

23. Philips, *Cuba, Island of Paradox*, p. 47.

24. Peraza, *Machado, crímenes y horrores*, p. 315; Charles Thomson, "Cuban Revolution: Fall of Machado," pp. 251–52; Carrillo, *Cuba 1933*, pp. 25–26.

25. Directorio Estudiantil Universatario: Al Pueblo de Cuba, July 1933 (issued publicly on August 22, 1933), in Padrón Larrazábal, *Manifiestos de Cuba*, pp. 157–72.

26. Ibid., p. 157.

27. Ibid., p. 169.

28. Carrillo, *Cuba 1933*, p. 25.

29. Directorio Estudiantil Universatario: Al Pueblo de Cuba, July 1933, in Padrón Larrazábal, *Manifiestos de Cuba*, pp. 154–55.

30. Hale, "Political and Social Ideas," p. 425.

31. Carrillo, *Cuba 1933*, p. 36.

32. Lamar-Schweyer, *How Machado Fell*, pp. 52–54.

33. Ibid., p. 37.

34. Philips, *Cuba, Island of Paradox*, pp. 17–18.

35. Directorio Estudiantil Universatario: Al Pueblo de Cuba (undated copy), Archivo Vilaseca, AIH. The Joint Resolution refers to the U.S. declaration of war on Spain in 1898.

36. It is interesting to note that General Mario Menocal also refused to participate in the mediation. I would like to thank Louis Pérez for bringing this to my attention.

37. Directorio Estudiantil Universatario: Al Pueblo de Cuba, July 16, 1933, in Padrón Larrazábal, *Manifiestos de Cuba*, p. 154.

38. Pérez, *Cuba under the Platt Amendment*, p. 301.

39. República de Cuba. *Adaptación de Cuba*, p. 12.

40. "Declaraciones del Directorio Estudiantil Universatario sobre el Decreto Presidencial No. 1298 de 24 del actual" (undated, but probably late July 1933), Archivo Vilaseca, AIH.

41. For Roosevelt's comments, see "Mensaje del Presidente Roosevelt al Pueblo de Cuba," July 2, 1933, in Rosell, *Luchas obreras contra Machado*, p. 222. Also see Williams, *Tragedy of American Diplomacy*, p. 170. For statements by Welles, see Welles,

Two Years of the "Good Neighbor" Policy, pp. 4-6, and Welles, "Address by the Honorable Sumner Welles before the Young Democratic Clubs of America," Washington, March 29, 1934, Records of the United States Department of State Relating to Political Relations between the U.S. and Latin America and the Caribbean States, 1930-1944, 67/711/3711.

42. On the ABC acceptance of the mediation, see: the Ambassador in Cuba (Welles) to the Acting Secretary of State, Havana, June 16, 1933, *FRUS, 1933,* pp. 308-9; and Charles Thomson, "Cuban Revolution: Fall of Machado," p. 251. For a defense of the ABC's acceptance of the mediation and for an indication of their fear of revolution, see Mañach, "Revolution in Cuba," esp. pp. 47-48.

43. The Ambassador in Cuba (Welles) to the Acting Secretary of State, Havana, June 16, 1933, *FRUS, 1933,* p. 309.

44. Fernández, *La razón del 4 de septiembre,* p. 31.

45. Beals, "The New Crime of Cuba," pp. 216-19.

46. Peraza, *Machado, crímenes y horrores,* p. 315; Carrillo, *Cuba 1933,* p. 46.

47. Carrillo, *Cuba 1933,* p. 24.

48. Directorio Estudiantil Universitario: Al Pueblo de Cuba, August 22, 1933, in Padrón Larrazábal, *Manifiestos de Cuba,* pp. 157-58.

49. "¿Por qué el ABC Radical no aceptó la mediación?" June 1933, Archivo Vilaseca, AIH.

50. Oscar de la Torre, "Un paso de historia revolucionario," 1934 (manuscript), Archivo Vilaseca, AIH.

51. Partido Comunista de Cuba, "Pronunciamiento del Comité Central del Partido Comunista de Cuba contra la Mediación," July 1933, in *El movimiento obrero cubano,* 2:351-61; Soto, *La revolución del 33,* 2:231-32.

52. For a sample of some of the ideas of these figures, see: Joaquín Ordoqui, "The Rise of the Revolutionary Movement in Cuba," *The Communist,* 13:12 (December 1934), pp. 1254-64; Blas Roca, "Forward to the Cuban Anti-Imperialist People's Front!," *The Communist,* 14:10 (October 1935), pp. 955-67; G. Sinani, "The New Phase in the Revolutionary Events in Cuba," *The Communist,* 12:12 (December 1933), pp. 1221-30; Communist Party of Cuba, "The Present Situation, Perspectives, and Tasks in Cuba" (Parts 1 and 2), *The Communist,* 13:9 (September 1934), pp. 875-87; "Report by Comrade Marin," in *International Press Correspondence,* 15:52 (October 10, 1935), pp. 1301-2. Also see Aguilar, *Cuba 1933,* pp. 122-24; Tabares del Real, *La revolución del 30,* pp. 112-13; and Farber, *Revolution and Reaction,* pp. 66-67.

53. See Hobsbawm, *The Age of Extremes,* esp. chaps. 3, 7; and Hart, *Coming of the Mexican Revolution,* esp. the chapter "Global Causation."

54. "Plataforma electoral del Partido Comunista de Cuba para las elecciones de 1932," in Rosell, *Luchas obreras,* pp. 188-211; Rubén Martínez Villena, "The Rise of the Revolutionary Movement in Cuba," *The Communist,* 12:6 (June 1933), pp. 566-67.

55. González Carbajal, *El ala izquierda estudiantil y su época,* pp. 102-3.

56. Except for railway and streetcar workers. The former were in conservative unions

and the latter were generally unorganized. See Buell, *Problems of the New Cuba*, pp. 188–89.

57. Ibid., p. 109.

58. Ibid., pp. 196–97.

59. Martínez Villena, "The Rise of the Revolutionary Movement in Cuba," pp. 564–65.

60. Soto, *La revolución del 33*, 2:243.

61. SNOIA, "Manifiesto de la Primera Conferencia Nacional de Obreros de la Industria Azucarera" (Impresos CESLAM, 1933), AIH, Fondo "Organizaciones Obreras," núm. 387.

62. Braga Collection, Cable received from the Latin American Trading Company, Havana, February 15, 1933, File "Manatí, labor troubles at port," Box 66.

63. Mr. Border to Sir John Simon, Havana, April 4, 1933, PRO/FO/A/2957/255/14.

64. Rovira y Garcia, "Los Soviet," pp. 221–22.

65. Ambassador in Cuba (Welles) to the Secretary of State, Havana, August 30, 1933, *FRUS, 1933*, p. 377.

66. Mr. Grant Watson to Sir John Simon, Havana, September 16, 1933, PRO/FO/A/7082/14/No.14 (confidential).

67. Ambassador Guggenheim to the Secretary of State, Havana, February 28, 1933, *FRUS, 1933*, p. 273; Mr. Border to Sir John Simon, Havana, June 7, 1933, PRO/FO/A/4710/255/14.

68. Tabares del Real, *Guiteras*, pp. 199–208.

69. Mr. Border to Sir John Simon, Havana, June 7, 1933, PRO/FO/A/4710/255/14 Dispatch 56.

70. Guiteras Holmes, *Biografía de Antonio Guiteras*, p. 5; Cabrera, *Guiteras*, p. 12.

71. Cabrera, "Introducción," in *Antonio Guiteras*, p. 14; Philips, *Cuba, Island of Paradox*, pp. 14–15.

72. Mr. Grant Watson to Sir John Simon, Havana, July 15, 1933, PRO/FO/A/6072/255/14. No. 74; *Havana Post*, August 2, 1933, pp. 1, 8; Charles Thomson, "Cuban Revolution: Fall of Machado," p. 254; Philips, *Cuba, Island of Paradox*, pp. 30–31.

73. Sinani, "New Phase in the Revolutionary Events in Cuba," p. 1222.

74. Mr. Grant Watson to Sir John Simon, Havana, September 9, 1933, PRO/FO/A/6901/255/14/No.96 (confidential).

75. Buell, *Problems of the New Cuba*, p. 182; Pérez, *Cuba under the Platt Amendment*, p. 310.

76. Charles Thomson, "Cuban Revolution: Fall of Machado," p. 254; Buell, *Problems of the New Cuba*, p. 182.

77. "Labor Conflict Grows, Trade Suffers Effects," *Havana Post*, August 4, 1933, pp. 1, 8.

78. Mr. Osborn to Sir John Simon, Havana, August 16, 1933, PRO/FO/A/6313/255/14/No.1122.

79. Charles Thomson, "Cuban Revolution: Fall of Machado," p. 254.

80. Mr. Grant Watson to Sir John Simon, Havana, August 9, 1933, PRO/FO/A/6072/255/14/No.74.

81. The Ambassador in Cuba (Welles) to the Secretary of State, Havana, August 30, 1933. *Foreign Relations, 1933*, p. 377; Mr. Grant Watson to Sir John Simon, Havana, September 9, 1933, PRO/FO/A/6901/255/No.96 (confidential).

82. Comité Ejecutivo de C.N.O.C., "Obreros de Cuba, Blancos y Negros, Nativos y Extranjeros, Adultos y Jovenes, Hombres y Mujeres, Ocupados y Desocupados," Havana, November 2, 1933, AIH, Fondo "Organizaciones Obreras (CNOC)," núm. 1, 1. It is important to note that even though this document is signed on November 2, the first couple of pages are devoted to an analysis of the previous four months. Also, see Resolution of the Second Congress of the Communist Party of Cuba, "The Present Situation, Perspectives, and Tasks in Cuba," *The Communist* 13:9 (September 1934), p. 881.

83. *Daily Worker*, August 23, 1933, p. 6; *Havana Post*, September 20, 1933, p. 1.

84. *Daily Worker*, August 26, 1933, p. 1.

85. "Demandas del Sindicato Provincial de Obreros Tabacaleros de Cienfuegos," August 28, 1933, ANC, Fondo especial, legajo 7, núm. 59.

86. Mr. Grant Watson to Sir John Simon, Havana, August 29, 1933, PRO/FO/A/6572/255/14/No.81.

87. *Daily Worker*, September 2, 1933, p. 6.

88. Unión Obrera de Oriente: a todos los trabajadores, October 2, 1933, AIH, Fondo "Organizaciones Obreras"; see also Mr. Grant Watson to Sir John Simon, Havana, August 29, 1933, PRO/FO/A/6572/255/14/No.81; and *Havana Post*, August 18, 1933, p. 1. For a fine analysis of both the Unión Obrera de Oriente and Trotskyism in Cuba in general, see Soler Martínez, "El trotskismo en Cuba."

89. See Rodríguez, "Marcos Garvey en Cuba," pp. 279–301; and Lewis, *Marcus Garvey*.

90. Comité Central de la Unión Obrera de Oriente, "A todos los trabajadores," Santiago de Cuba, October 2, 1933.

91. Mr. Grant Watson to Sir John Simon, Havana, September 9, 1933, PRO/FO/A/6901/255/14.

92. *Havana Post*, August 16 and 17, p. 1 in both editions.

93. CNOC: A los obreros de Cuba, August 15, 1933, Archivo Vilaseca, AIH, Manifiesto 8527.

94. *Havana Post*, August 19, 1933, p. 1.

95. *The Daily Worker*, August 21, 1933, p. 6.

96. *The Daily Worker*, August 26, 1933, p. 1.

97. The Ambassador in Cuba (Welles) to the Secretary of State, Havana, August 15, 1933, *FRUS, 1933*, p. 366.

Chapter 5

1. Soto, *La revolución del 33*, 2:43, 3:39.

2. The Cuban Embassy to the U.S. Department of State, Memorandum, September 7, 1933, trans. and printed in *FRUS, 1933*, pp. 399–400.

3. For a collection of all the legislation, see *La legislación auténtica.*

4. See Pérez, *Cuba under the Platt Amendment,* esp. 321–32; Aguilar, *Cuba 1933,* esp. chaps. 13–16; Tabares del Real, *La revolución del 30,* esp. pp. 140–51; Soto, *La revolución del 33,* 3:97–364; and Farber, *Revolution and Reaction,* esp. chaps. 2, 3.

5. G. Sinani, "The New Phase in the Revolutionary Events in Cuba," *The Communist* 12:12 (December 1933), pp. 1221–30; CNOC: A los obreros de Cuba, September 12, 1933, Archivo Vilaseca, AIH.

6. Sumner Welles to the Secretary of State, Havana, August 19, 1933, *FRUS, 1933,* pp. 368, 419. After suggesting September 1 as a possible date for his leaving, Welles wrote: "It is unwise not only from the point of view of our relations with Cuba but with the whole of Latin America as well for the American Embassy here to possess the measure of control over the government which it now does possess owing to the particular developments of the past two months. Caffery [the next ambassador] unquestionably will obtain all the needed influence immediately after his arrival but it will be an influence exerted behind the scenes and not apparent to the public."

7. On the fighting around the hotel, see *Diario de la Marina,* September 19, 1933, p. 1; and *Bohemia,* September 20, 1933.

8. *Havana Post,* September 6, 1933, p. 1; Philips, *Cuba, Island of Paradox,* p. 64.

9. *Havana Post,* September 5, 1933, p. 1.

10. Mr. Grant Watson to Sir John Simon, Havana, September 9, 1933, PRO/FO/A/6901/255/14/No.96 (confidential).

11. For a brief description of the cabinet members, see Acting Secretary of State of Cuba (J. R. Balmaseda) to Mr. Grant Watson, Havana, September 13, 1933, PRO/FO/A/7440/255/14. See also Pérez, *Cuba under the Platt Amendment,* pp. 321–22.

12. Guiteras Holmes, *Biografía de Antonio Guiteras,* p. 10; Tabares del Real, *Guiteras,* p. 254.

13. Tabares del Real, *La revolución del 30,* pp. 140–41.

14. *Havana Post,* September 26, 1933, pp. 1, 8.

15. Braga Collection, File "Strikes in Cuba Mensaje para el Sr. Salvador Rionda de Manatí," September 26, 1933.

16. Mr. Grant Watson to Sir John Simon, Havana, November 2, 1933, PRO/FO/A/8162/255/14/No.136 (confidential).

17. *Diario de la Marina* and *Havana Post* for October 4, 1933.

18. Mr. Grant Watson to Sir John Simon, Havana, October 4, 1933, PRO/FO/A/7580/255/14/No.114.

19. Mr. Grant Watson to Sir John Simon, Havana, November 15, 1933, PRO/FO/A/8661/255/14/No.142.

20. Tabares del Real, *La revolución del 30,* pp. 150–51; Aguilar, *Cuba 1933,* pp. 198–99.

21. *Diario de la Marina,* December 1, 1933, p. 1; *Havana Post,* December 6, 9, and 12, p. 1 in each edition; Tabares del Real, *La revolución del 30,* p. 150; Cabrera, *Antonio Guiteras,* p. 26.

22. Mr. Grant Watson to Sir John Simon, Havana, December 18, 1933, PRO/FO/A/ 9423/255/14/No.162 (confidential); *Havana Post*, December 10, 1933, p. 1.

23. For example, see *Diario de la Marina*, November 2, 1933, p. 1; *La Prensa*, November 2, 1933, p. 1; and *Havana Post*, November 3, 1933, p. 1.

24. *Havana Post*, November 5, 1933, p. 1; Carrillo, *Cuba 1933*, pp. 255–61.

25. Braga Collection, File "Manatí, Rionda, Salvador (correspondence)," 1933, Salvador Rionda to Mr. Fowler, Manatí, October 26, 1933.

26. On the rebellion and its suppression, see *Havana Post*, November 8, 9, and 10, 1933, p. 1 for each edition.

27. Grant Watson of the British embassy remarked that "while the opposition had money, their most daring spirits are either in prison or in exile and they lack trained soldiers." Watson to Sir John Simon, Havana, December 18, 1933, PRO/FO/A/ 9423/55/14/No.162 (confidential).

28. Braga Collection, File "Strikes in Cuba," "Situación obrera: Manatí y Francisco," September 28, 1933.

29. García and Zanetti, *United Fruit Co.*, pp. 256–62.

30. Rovira and García, "Los Soviet de Nazabal," pp. 221–54.

31. Soto, *La revolución del 33*, 3:142–72; Tabares del Real, *La revolución del 30*, pp. 116–36.

32. *The Daily Worker*, September 21, 1933, p. 6.

33. Braga Collection, File "Strikes in Cuba."

34. Braga Collection, File "Manatí, huelga general en Manatí," September 20, 1933.

35. Braga Collection, File "Strikes in Cuba," "Situación obrera, Manatí y Francisco."

36. Braga Collection, File "Strikes in Cuba," "Situación obrera," September 25, 1933.

37. Braga Collection, File "Manatí," "General Strike at Manatí," September 25, 1933. The signature is illegible, but the writer is from the Irving Trust Company, receiver of the Manatí Sugar Company.

38. *Havana Post*, October 2, 1933, p. 1.

39. Braga Collection, File "Strikes in Cuba," telephone message from Elia at 9:20 A.M., September 25, 1933.

40. Mr. Grant Watson to Sir John Simon, Havana, November 2, 1933, PRO/FO/A/ 8162/255/14/No.136 (confidential).

41. Pérez, *Cuba under the Platt Amendment*, p. 323.

42. CNOC, "Pasos hacia la organización del CNOC" (no date), AIH, Fondo museo obrero, 11/2/c4.

43. For example, see Comrade Marin, "Cuba," *International Press Correspondence* 15:12 (October 10, 1935); and Fabio Grobart, "El movimiento obrero cubano entre 1925 a 1933," in *Pensamiento Crítico*.

44. For a sample of a wide range of interviews with sugar workers, many of whom were recruited to the party in the early 1930s, see Núñez Machín, *Memoria amarga del azúcar;* and García, *Tiempo muerto*.

45. Soto, *La revolución del 33*, 2:243.

46. *Havana Post,* October 4, 1933, p. 1.

47. *Havana Post,* October 6, 1933, p. 1.

48. Braga Collection, File "Strikes in Cuba," Mr. V. A. Estrada to the Francisco Sugar Company, New York, September 20, 1933.

49. Mr. Grant Watson to Sir John Simon, Havana, October 21, 1933, PRO/FO/A/7892/255/14/No.130.

50. Braga Collection, File "Manatí, Rionda, Salvador, Correspondence, General Strikes at Manatí," September 29, 1933.

51. Braga Collection, File "Strikes in Cuba: Cuestión obrera en los ingenios, (confidencial)," Havana, December 12, 1933.

52. "Texto íntegro del decreto que acaba de ser promulgado," Decreto, *Diario del la Marina,* September 24, 1933, p. 1.

53. Mr. Grant Watson to Sir John Simon, Havana, October 21, 1933, PRO/FO/A/7892/255/14/No.130.

54. Braga Collection, File "Strikes in Cuba," República de Cuba, Secretaría de Gobernación, Acta, September 30, 1933.

55. Braga Collection, File "Manatí, Rionda, Salvador, Correspondence," Huelga general en Manatí, September 29, 1933.

56. See the reports in the *Havana Post* for September 26, October 2, October 29, November 22, and December 26, p. 1 for each edition.

57. Mr. Grant Watson to Sir John Simon, Havana, December 11, 1933, PRO/FO/A/9400/255/14/No.155.

58. *Havana Post,* December 15, 1933, p. 1.

59. Mr. Grant Watson to Sir John Simon, Havana, December 11, 1933, PRO/FO/A/9400/255/14/No.155.

60. *Diario de la Marina,* October 18–November 8; *Havana Post,* October 18–November 8; *Daily Worker,* October 18, 23, and 25, November 3 and 15.

61. *Diario de la Marina,* September 17, 1933, p. 1; *Havana Post,* September 17, 1933, p. 1.

62. *Havana Post,* October 1, 1933, p. 1.

63. Mr. Grant Watson to Sir John Simon, Havana, September 26, 1933, PRO/FO/A/7253'255/14/No.110.

64. *Havana Post,* September 17, 1933, p. 1.

65. Tabares del Real, *Guiteras,* pp. 282–85.

66. *Bandera Roja* (October 20, 1933), p. 1; CNOC, "A la clase obrera de Cuba," September 12, 1933, Archivo Vilaseca, Manifiesto 11-s-27, AIH; CNOC, "Obreros de Cuba—blancos y negros—nativos y extranjeros—adultos y jovenes—hombres y mujeres—ocupados y desocupados," La Habana, November 2, 1933, AIH, Fondo "Organizaciones obreras, CNOC," núm. 1, 87/61, 1-5.

67. *Havana Post,* December 9 and 14, 1933, p. 1 for each edition.

68. *The Daily Worker,* October 10, 1933, p. 6.

69. Farber, *Revolution and Reaction in Cuba,* p. 50.

70. CNOC, "Obreros de Cuba—blancos y negros."

71. For the full text of the law, see "Nacionalización del Trabajo," Decreto 2583, Nomber 8, 1933, firmado por Alberto Giraudy, Secretaría del Trabajo, in Viego Delgado, *La legislación auténtica,* pp. 26-27.

72. See the text of the law, which makes mention of the Spanish elite in Cuba but does not mention Haitians or Jamaicans in the sugar industry. According to the British Embassy, the Haitian and Jamaican workers were unaffected by the law because "no one else wanted to do the work [cut cane]." Mr. Grant Watson to Sir John Simon, Havana, January 2, 1934, PRO/FO/A/350/29/14/No.1.

73. For news on the build-up to the strike call, see the *Diario de la Marina,* October 29–November 8, 1933. Also see the *Havana Post* for the same dates; and see the *Daily Worker,* October 25 and November 3, 1933, p. 6 for each edition. For the condemnation of the law by the CP, see CNOC, "Obreros de Cuba—blancos y negros."

74. *Havana Post,* December 22, 1933, p. 1.

75. Mr. Grant Watson to Sir John Simon, Havana, December 11, 1933, PRO/FO/A/9400/255/14/No. 155.

76. *Diario de la Marina,* December 16, 1933, p. 1; *Havana Post,* December 17, 1933, pp. 1, 5.

77. Mr. Grant Watson to Sir John Simon, Havana, November 29, 1933, PRO/FO/A/9014/255/14/No.148 (confidential). On Batista's promotion, see Adam y Silva, *La gran mentira,* pp. 71-71; and Tabares del Real, *La revolución del 30,* p. 142.

78. *Havana Post,* November 14, 1933, p. 1.

79. *Havana Post,* November 23, 1933, pp. 1, 2.

80. Sumner Welles to the Acting Secretary of State, Havana, December 9, 1933, *FRUS, 1933,* pp. 536-37.

81. *Havana Post,* December 23, 1933, p. 1.

82. Sumner Welles to the Secretary of State, Havana, October 4, 1933, *FRUS, 1933,* p. 470. In the same volume see Welles's references to Batista throughout the month of October for an indication of how Welles courted Batista's support and vice versa. On Batista and the growing influence of the army, see Pérez, *Army Politics in Cuba;* and Benjamin, *United States and Cuba,* pp. 164-65.

83. Tabares del Real, "Fulgencio Batista," p. 16, and "Reflexiones sobre el surgimiento," p. 15. I would like to thank Dr. Tabares del Real for providing me with these papers and for giving me permission to refer to them. Also see Philips, *Cuba, Island of Paradox,* p. 142.

84. *Havana Post,* December 3, 1933, p. 1.

85. Braga Collection, File "Internal Correspondence, April 1933 to May 1935," Cuba Trading Company to Aurelio Portuondo, January 10, 1934.

86. Braga Collection, File "Francisco, Rionda, 1927-1937," Folder 1, Francisco, trabajadores, January 26, 1934. For some more general comments, see Hugh Thomas, *Cuba,* p. 691; and Benjamin, *United States and the Cuban Revolution,* p. 92.

87. Mr. Grant Watson to Sir John Simon, Havana, January 13, 1934, PRO/FO/A/833/29/14/No.5 (confidential).

88. The Personal Representative of the President (Caffery) to the Acting Secretary of State, Havana, January 17, 1934, *FRUS, 1934,* p. 103.
89. Beals, "American Diplomacy in Cuba," p. 68.
90. Mr. Grant Watson to Sir John Simon, Havana, January 29, 1934, PRO/FO/A/1127/29/14/No.13 (confidential).
91. Mr. Grant Watson to Sir John Simon, Havana, January 13, 1934, PRO/FO/A/833/29/24/No.5 (confidential).

Chapter 6

1. For biographical sketches of Batista, see Chester, *A Sergeant Named Batista;* Tardiff and Mabunda, *Dictionary of Hispanic Biography;* and Alexander, *Biographical Dictionary of Latin American and Caribbean Political Leaders.* A useful sketch of Batista's regime of 1952–58 is Domínguez, "The Batista Regime in Cuba."
2. Of course Batista failed to understand this change in Cuban political culture in March 1952.
3. See, for example, Huber and Safford, *Agrarian Structure and Political Power.*
4. Charles Thomson, "Cuban Revolution: Reform and Reaction," p. 269; Hugh Thomas, *Cuba,* chap. 53; Aguilar, *Cuba 1933,* chap. 16. The events leading to Batista's ouster of Grau and his relations with the U.S. embassy in Havana can be followed in *FRUS, 1934,* pp. 95–109.
5. Ambassador Caffery replaced "Special Representative" Welles on December 8, 1933.
6. Porset, "Cuba's Troubled Waters," pp. 353–54.
7. Mr. Grant Watson to Sir John Simon, Havana, April 10, 1934, PRO/FO/A/3177/29/14 (confidential).
8. Mr. Grant Watson to Sir John Simon, Havana, March 29, 1935, PRO/FO/A/3517/228/14/No.31 (confidential). Camp Columbia was an important military barracks outside of Havana.
9. Charles Thomson, "Cuban Revolution: Reform and Reaction," p. 270.
10. Mr. Grant Watson to Sir John Simon, Havana, March 5, 1934, PRO/FO/A/2191/29/14 No.34 (confidential).
11. Mr. Grant Watson to Sir John Simon, Havana, January 29, 1934, PRO/FO/A/1127/29/14/No.13 (confidential).
12. Hackett, "Restive Cuban Labor," p. 81.
13. Charles Thomson, "Cuban Revolution: Reform and Reaction," p. 270.
14. Hackett, "Restive Cuban Labor," p. 81.
15. Buell, *Problems of the New Cuba,* pp. 202–8; Charles Thomson, "Cuban Revolution: Reform and Reaction," p. 270; Porset, "Cuba's Troubled Waters," p. 353; Mr. Grant Watson to Sir John Simon, Havana, March 13, 1934, PRO/FO/A/2448/29/14/No.40 (confidential).
16. Hackett, "Labor Crisis Averted in Cuba," p. 215.

17. Mr. Grant Watson to Sir John Simon, Havana, January 29, 1934, PRO/FO/A/1127/29/14/No.13 (confidential).

18. Grant Watson to Sir John Simon, Havana, February 19, 1934, PRO/FO/A/1841/29/14 No. 24 (confidential).

19. *Diario de la Marina,* March 3, 1934, p. 1; Mr. Grant Watson to Sir John Simon, Havana, March 5, 1934, PRO/FO/A/2191/29/14 No.34 (confidential).

20. Antonio Penichet, "Huelgas 'lícitas' y huelgas 'ilícitas,'" *Bohemia* 27:17 (May 13, 1934), p. 59; Porset, "Cuba's Troubled Waters," p. 353; Farber, *Revolution and Reaction,* pp. 45–46.

21. H. P. Crawford, "The Labor Laws of Cuba," in *General Legal Bulletin of the Department of Commerce and the Bureau of Foreign and Domestic Commerce* (October 24, 1935, Washington), pp. 2–3.

22. Mr. Grant Watson to Sir John Simon, Havana, March 5, 1934, PRO/FO/A/2191/29/14/No.34 (confidential).

23. Mr. Grant Watson to Sir John Simon, Havana, March 26, 1934, PRO/FO/A/2656/29/14/No.48 (confidential).

24. Hackett, "Cuba and the Good Neighbor Policy," pp. 88–89.

25. Hackett, "Continued Unrest in Cuba," pp. 215–16.

26. Batista quoted in J. D. Philips, "Cuba Suspends Civil Guarantees in Chief Provinces to Fight Reds," *New York Times,* October 2, 1934, p. 1.

27. Batista quoted in J. D. Philips, "Batista Links His Destiny with Cuba's," *New York Times Magazine,* October 14, 1934, p. 12.

28. Mericle, "Corporatist Control of the Working Class," p. 303.

29. Batista quoted in Philips, "Batista Links Destiny," p. 12.

30. Batista quoted by Beals, "New Machado of Cuba," p. 153.

31. *Havana Post,* January 15, 1937, pp. 1, 7.

32. "Colonel Batista Explains New Land Program," *Havana Post,* July 4, 1937, pp. 1, 12.

33. Batista quoted in *Havana Post,* January 15, 1937, p. 7.

34. Rayneri, "Colonel Batista and Cuba's Future," p. 51.

35. Philips, "Batista Links Destiny," pp. 3, 14.

36. Charles Thomson, "Cuban Revolution: Reform and Reaction," p. 273; Sánchez Arango, "The Recent General Strike in Cuba," p. 14; *Havana Post,* esp. February 23–March 14, 1935; Herring, "Cuba's General Strike," p. 192; Farber, *Revolution and Reaction,* pp. 47–48.

37. Sánchez Arango, "The Recent General Strike in Cuba," p. 12.

38. "Student Strike Made National Issue by Heads," *Havana Post,* February 19, 1935, pp. 1, 2.

39. "Two Secretaries Resign in Face of Student Row," *Havana Post,* February 23, 1935, pp. 1, 2.

40. "Trams, Mailmen, Join in Strike; Others Prepared," *Havana Post,* March 8, 1935, p. 1.

41. "General Strike Cracks; Many Federal Workers Return; Others Jailed," *Havana*

Post, March 14, 1935, p. 1; Herring, "Cuba's General Strike," p. 192; Charles Thomson, "Cuban Revolution: Reform and Reaction," p. 274.

42. Mr. Grant Watson to Sir John Simon, Havana, March 16, 1935, PRO/FO/3/A 036/228/14/No.28 (confidential); Mr. Grant Watson to Sir John Simon, Havana, March 27, 1935, PRO/FO/A 3517/228/14/No.31 (confidential); Mr. Grant Watson to Sir John Simon, Havana, March 29, 1935, PRO/FO/A/3517/228/14/No.31 (confidential); "Government Will Try Leaders of General Strike; 12 Face Death," *Havana Post*, March 15, 1935, p. 1.

43. Herring, "Cuba's Election Campaign," p. 603.

44. For a description of the 1936 campaign, see Fitzgibbon and Healy, "Cuban Elections of 1936," pp. 724–35.

45. For an excellent summary of how the civil-military schools worked, see "Civic-Military Schools," *Havana Post* (Tourist Edition), August 29, 1937, Section 2.

46. "1,500 Rural Schools Seen," *Havana Post*, January 28, 1937, pp. 1, 12.

47. Hugh Thomas, *Cuba*, p. 704; Gellman, *Roosevelt and Batista*, p. 147.

48. *Nation* (Editorial), December 26, 1936, p. 746; Hugh Thomas, *Cuba*, pp. 703–4.

49. For a perceptive analysis of Batista's ability to play one side against the other, see Mañach, *El militarismo en Cuba*, esp. pp. 17–18. Another insightful analysis is a long letter that Pablo de la Torriente Brau of the Ala Izquierda Estudiantil wrote to Raúl Roa García in June 1936. The letter is entitled "Algebra y política."

50. Russell B. Porter, "Dual Regime Denied by Batista," *New York Times*, Sections 2 and 3, July 5, 1936, pp. 1, 2.

51. Sergio Carbó, "La revolución se muere; salvemos la revolución," *Bohemia* 27 (April 15, 1934), pp. 32–33, 42 (quotation on p. 33).

52. Guerra y Sánchez, "Sugar: Index of Cuban-American Cooperation," p. 216.

53. Pérez, "Cuba, 1930–1959," p. 437.

54. Popper, "The Latin American Policy of the Roosevelt Administration," p. 274.

55. Quoted in Hackett, "Cuba and the Good Neighbor Policy," p. 88.

56. Charles Thomson, "Cuban Revolution: Fall of Machado," p. 250.

57. Guerra y Sánchez, "Sugar: Index of Cuban-American Cooperation," p. 6.

58. Quoted by Sumner Welles in "Address by the Honorable Sumner Welles before the Young Democratic Clubs of America," March 29, 1934, Records of the U.S. Department of State Relating to Political Relations between the U.S. and the Latin American and Caribbean States, 1930–1944, 711/37/135.

59. Ibid., n.p.

60. Mr. Rees to Sir John Simon, Havana, August 30, 1934, PRO/FO/A/7290/29/14/No.115.

61. Pérez, "Cuba, 1930–1959," p. 438.

62. Charles Thomson, "Cuban Revolution: Reform and Revolution," p. 273.

63. Mr. Rees to Sir John Simon, Havana, June 25, 1934, PRO/FO/A/5531/29/14/No.91 (confidential).

64. The text of the treaty can be found in the U.S. Department of State, *Treaty Information*.

65. On the lack of public rejoicing, see Mr. Grant Watson to Sir John Simon, Havana, June 6, 1934, PRO/FO/A/5056/4318/14/No.80 (confidential).

66. For example, see the editorials in *Diario de la Marina* for May 29, June 1 and 2, 1934. Also see the editorial in *El Mundo*, May 29; and *Ahora*, editorial, May 30.

67. *Diario de la Marina*, June 4, 1934, p. 1.

68. Sumner Welles, "Address" (emphasis added).

69. *La Prensa* (Mexico), April 2, 1934. The article was included in the Records of the U.S. Department of State, 1930–1944, 711/37/155.

70. Welles, "Address."

71. For a broad perspective on these issues, see the two works by Wood, *Democracy Versus Capitalism* and *The Pristine Culture of Capitalism*. Also see Wallerstein, *End of the World as We Know It*, esp. chap. 6, "Liberalism and Democracy."

72. Carrillo, *Cuba 1933*, p. 37.

73. Laclau, *Politics and Ideology in Marxist Theory*, p. 167.

74. This list was taken from de Leon, *El origen del mal*, p. 309.

75. The ideological influences of *aprismo* were emphasized to me in two personal interviews, one each with DEU and PRC-A founder Segundo Curti and with APRA-Cuba founder Enrique de la Osa, in Havana in July 1994. Both men stressed the intellectual influence of *aprismo* among radical nationalists during the 1920s, 1930s, and 1940s. De la Osa joined the PRC-A, along with the rest of his small party. *Aprismo*'s organizational strength was never strong in Cuba, but its political influence on young people and intellectuals was strong. APRA-Cuba founder de la Osa reinforced the point (personal interview, Havana, July 1, 1994).

76. Partido Revolucionario Cubano (Auténtico), *Doctrina Auténtica*. Also see de León, *El origen del mal*, p. 310.

77. For example, see the PRC-A manifesto "Al Pueblo de Cuba," in *El Pais*, August 11, 1934, and another manifesto published in the newspaper *El Crisol*, September 3, 1934, p. 1.

78. Manifiesto del PRC-A, "Poder Civica y Poder Militar," *El Crisol*, September 11, 1934; Mr. Grant Watson to Sir John Simon, Havana, May 9, 1934, PRO/FO/A/4099/29/14/No.67 (confidential).

79. De León, *El origen del mal*, pp. 312–13; Farber, *Revolution and Reaction in Cuba*, p. 62.

80. Mr. Grant Watson to Sir John Simon, Havana, May 9, 1934, PRO/FO/A/4099/29/14/No.67 (confidential).

81. Mr. Grant Watson to Sir John Simon, Havana, May 24, 1934, PRO/FO/A/4665/29/14/No.74 (confidential).

82. Tabares del Real, *Guiteras*, pp. 267–340.

83. Mr. Grant Watson to Sir John Simon, Havana, January 29, 1934, PRO/FO/A/1127/29/14/No.13 (confidential).

84. On the founding of Joven Cuba, see Tabares del Real, *Guiteras*, pp. 434–39.

85. The best compilation of Guiteras's writings is Cabrera, *Antonio Guiteras*.

86. Antonio Guiteras, "Septembrismo," *Bohemia* 26:2 (April 1, 1934), pp. 30, 32, 38.

87. The program of Joven Cuba is published in Cabrera, *Antonio Guiteras*, pp. 183–98.

88. For a sample of the press reports, see *El Crisol*, September 4, 5, and 14, 1934; *El Pais*, August 3, 6, 7, 8, 9, and 11; and *Havana Post*, January 5, 9, and 17, 1935.

89. *Havana Post*, May 9, 1935, p. 1.

90. Joven Cuba, Comisión de Organización y Propaganda: A todas las Organizaciones de Joven Cuba (circular), January 1936, Archivo Vilaseca, AIH, Documento 11S17.

91. De León, *El origen del mal*, p. 315.

92. Joven Cuba, Carta de Pepe Velasco a Eduardo, May 25, 1936, Archivo Vilaseca, AIH, Documento 13S17; and Joven Cuba, Comité Ejecutivo, Región de Oriente, June 1936, Archivo Vilaseca, AIH (no number).

93. Resolution of the Second Congress of the Communist Party of Cuba, "The Present Situation, Perspectives, and Tasks in Cuba" (Part 1), 13:9 *The Communist* (September 1934), p. 880.

94. For the party's self-criticism on the pact with Machado, see Manuel Ventura, "The Second Party Congress of the CP of Cuba," *International Press Correspondence, World News and Views* 14:34 (June 15, 1934), p. 910.

95. Resolution of the Second Congress of the Communist Party of Cuba, "The Present Situation, Perspectives, and Tasks in Cuba," (Part 2) *The Communist* 13:11 (November 1934), p. 1157.

96. Quoted in Baeza Flores, *La cadenas vienen de lejos*, p. 111. Chibás, after 1948, became the most popular political leader in Cuba. He was an unflinching opponent of corruption, and he led the Partido del Pueblo Cubano-Ortodóxo from 1948 until his suicide in 1951. On Chibás, see Conte Agüero, *Eduardo Chibás*, and Alávez, *Eduardo Chibás*.

97. See the lead article "The Seventh World Congress of the Communist International: Discussion on the Report of Comrade Dimitrov," in the Comintern's journal *World News and Views: International Press Correspondence* 15:62 (November 21, 1935).

98. "Report of Comrade Marin," p. 1302.

99. The record of these negotiations can be found in the Archivo Vilaseca located in the Archives of the Cuban Institute of History. While nothing came of the negotiations, the exchange of letters, articles, and manifestos provides a fascinating insight into how the Cuban left fought to come to terms with their defeat and the rise of Batista's authoritarian reformism.

100. Raúl Roa García, "Carta a Juan Antonio Rubio Padilla," December 31, 1935, Archivo Vilaseca, AIH, Documento 29S28.

101. Raúl Roa García, "Carta a Ramiro Valdés Daussá," September 16, 1935, Archivo Vilaseca, AIH, Documento 1S16. Raúl Roa García was later to become Castro's minister of foreign relations in the 1960s and early 1970s. He was to have a forma-

tive influence on the young radicals who joined the 26 of July Movement and the Revolutionary Directorate in the 1950s.

Chapter 7

1. Mr. Grant Watson to Mr. Eden, Havana, June 30, 1937, PRO/FO/A/4946/65/14.
2. Batista quoted in *Havana Post*, June 23, 1937, p. 10.
3. Chester, *A Sergeant Named Batista*, pp. 1-25; Hugh Thomas, *Cuba*, p. 845.
4. Mr. Grant Watson to Mr. Eden, Havana, June 21, 1937, PRO/FO/A/4790/65/14/ No.95.
5. Gellman, *Roosevelt and Batista*, pp. 146-54; Benjamin, *United States and the Cuban Revolution*, p. 96; Farber, *Revolution and Reaction*, p. 83.
6. "Colonel Batista Refuses Bid for President," *Havana Post*, February 27, 1937, p. 1.
7. Mr. Grant Watson to Mr. Eden, Havana, June 30, 1937, PRO/FO/A/4946/65/14/ No.98.
8. See various editions of the *Diario de la Marina* and the *Havana Post* for the months of January and February 1937. Also see the U.S. Department of Commerce, *Investment in Cuba*, p. 36.
9. *Diario de la Marina*, November 20, 1937, p. 1.
10. For a selection of Cuban commentaries and views on U.S. sugar policy and legislation, see Mendoza, *Revista Semanal Azucarera*, esp. pp. 71-101. Also see Hugh Thomas, *Cuba*, p. 707.
11. Bulmer-Thomas, *Economic History of Latin America*, p. 212.
12. Mr. Rees to Mr. Eden, Havana, February 20, 1937, Enclosure, Document 21, "The Labour Situation in Cuba and the British West Indies," PRO/FO/A/1864/65/14 (hereinafter "Labour Situation in Cuba"), n.p.
13. Two useful studies on this issue are Carvajal, "Observaciones sobre la clase media en Cuba"; and Raggi Ageo, "Contribución al estudio de las clases medias en Cuba."
14. "Labour Situation in Cuba."
15. "Labor Law Must Be Enforced," *Havana Post*, May 22, 1937, p. 1.
16. "Codify Labor Laws Is Plea," *Havana Post*, April 6, 1937, p. 1.
17. This argument was presented by Labor Secretary Portuondo. See "Labor Secretary Analyses Cuba's Economic Troubles," *Havana Post*, March 4, 1937, p. 1.
18. "Labour Situation in Cuba."
19. See the editorials in the *Havana Post*, May 13 and May 16, 1937.
20. Philips, *Cuba, Island of Paradox*, pp. 183-84.
21. "High Posts for Cubans," *Havana Post*, March 27, 1937, pp. 1, 12; Mr. Grant Watson to Mr. Eden, Havana, June 1, 1937, PRO/FO/A/4239/65/14/No.86.
22. "New Saviour of Cuba Backs Payroll Bill," *Havana Post*, May 15, 1937, pp. 1, 10.
23. "Chambers of Commerce Protest New Taxes," *Havana Post*, March 22, 1937, p. 1.
24. *Havana Post*, January 20, 1937, p. 1; *Havana Post*, January 28, 1937, p. 12.

25. "Labour Situation in Cuba"; *Havana Post,* February 23, 1937, p. 1; *Havana Post,* April 6, 1937, p. 1.

26. "Labour Situation in Cuba."

27. Mr. Grant Watson to Mr. Eden, Havana, July 22, 1937, PRO/FO/A/5610/65/14/ No.108.

28. "Sugar Mills Ask Labor Exchanges for Field Help," *Havana Post,* January 28, 1937, p. 12.

29. Ibid.

30. "Labour Situation in Cuba"; "Idle in Camagüey Forced to Work," *Havana Post,* February 11, 1937, p. 1.

31. "Labour Situation in Cuba."

32. Ibid.

33. "A Showdown" (editorial), *Havana Post,* May 13, 1937, pp. 1, 10.

34. "Labour Situation in Cuba."

35. "Los antillanos," *Revista Semanal Azucarera* (October 22, 1937), p. 59.

36. *Líneas Básicas del Programa del Plan Trienal.*

37. *Diario de la Marina,* June 20 and 27, 1937, p. 1 in both editions. Also see *Havana Post,* June 23 and June 25, 1937, p. 1 for both editions.

38. Batista quoted in Mr. Grant Watson to Mr. Eden, Havana, June 1, 1937, PRO/FO/A/ 4239/65/14/No.86.

39. "Colonel Batista Explains His New Land Program," *Havana Post,* July 1, 1937, pp. 1, 12.

40. "Laredo Bru Imports OK to New Program," *Havana Post,* June 23, 1937, pp. 1, 10. The term "organic democracy" was credited to Batista by President Laredo Bru. It was also a term commonly used by other corporatist leaders in Latin America and by the ideologues of Francoist Spain after 1939.

41. Mr. Grant Watson to Mr. Eden, Havana, July 22, 1937, PRO/FO/A/5610/65/14/ No.108.

42. Mr. Grant Watson to Mr. Eden, Havana, December 27, 1938. PRO/FO/A/262/ 262/14/No.178; Hugh Thomas, *Cuba,* pp. 708–9.

43. Gellman, *Roosevelt and Batista,* p. 162.

44. Mr. Grant Watson to Viscount Halifax, Havana, August 30, 1939, PRO/FO/A/5823/ 165/14/No.96.

45. Mr. Grant Watson to Mr. Eden, Havana, December 2, 1937, PRO/FO/A/9019/65/ 14/No./171.

46. Guerra y Sánchez, "Sugar: Index of Cuban-American Cooperation," p. 751.

47. Pérez-Stable, *The Cuban Revolution,* p. 43. A small *colono* was classified as someone who usually produced fewer than 30,000 *arrobas* (330 tons) of sugar. See Hugh Thomas, *Cuba,* p. 708.

48. Hugh Thomas, *Cuba,* p. 708.

49. "Free Colonos" (editorial), *Revista Semanal Azucarera,* (April 16, 1938).

50. Guerra y Dében, "Recent Evolution of the Sugar Industry."

51. The best-known work taking this perspective is, of course, Guerra y Sánchez, *Sugar and Society in the Caribbean*. Also see Lamar-Schweyer, *La crisis del patriotismo;* Maestri, *Capitalismo y anticapitalismo;* Maestri, *Latifundismo en la economía cubana;* Mañach, *La crisis de la alta cultura en Cuba;* and Mañach, *Indagación del choteo.*

52. Braga Collection, File "Batista, Fulgencio," Speech by Fulgencio Batista to the Cuban Chamber of Commerce in the United States, New York, November 6, 1938.

53. Guerra y Sánchez, "Sugar: Index of Cuban-American Cooperation," pp. 752–53.

54. "Cuba's Trienal Plan," *Revista Semanal Azucarera* (July 17, 1937).

55. Braga Collection, Box 31, File "Colonos of Manatí, Francisco, and Elia," "In Regard to a Proposed Law Regulating the Relations Between the Hacendados and the Colonos," April 13, 1937.

56. Ibid.

57. Braga Collection, Box 31, File "Colonos of Manatí, Francisco, and Elia," Letter from Cuba Cane Company, signed "H.F.," to Antonio Arturo Bustamante, April 30, 1937. It is clear in the letter that Bustamante was a close friend of both Batista and Rafael Montalvo, then secretary of state.

58. Braga Collection, Box 18, File "Asociación Nacional de Hacendados de Cuba," Asociación Cubana de Fabricantes de Azúcar, "Open Letter," Havana, November 6, 1940. The letter was widely published in both Spanish and English. The quotation is taken from the English version.

59. Mr. Grant Watson to Mr. Eden, Havana, June 30, 1937, PRO/FO/A/4946/65/14/No.98.

60. Mr. Grant Watson to Mr. Eden, Havana, December 2, 1937, PRO/FO/A/9019/65/14/No.171.

61. They were delayed again until general elections for a constituent assembly were held in November 1939, with presidential elections to follow in February 1940.

62. Quoted in Löwy, *Marxism in Latin America,* p. 72.

63. The most important studies of the Batista-Communist alliance are García Montes and Alonso Ávila, *Historia del Partido Comunista de Cuba,* esp. chaps. 9, 10; Hugh Thomas, *Cuba,* esp. chap. 60; Goldenberg, "The Rise and Fall of a Party," pp. 61–80; Farber, *Revolution and Reaction,* esp. pp. 84–87; and Sims, "Cuban Labor and the Communist Party," pp. 43–58.

64. See the lead article "The Seventh World Congress of the Communist International: Discussion on the Report of Comrade Dimitrov," *World News and Views: International Press Correspondence* 15:62 (November 21, 1935).

65. Important studies of this period are Aguilar, *Marxism in Latin America;* Munick, *Revolutionary Trends in Latin America;* and Caballero, *Latin America and the Comintern.*

66. For the party's position on why the negotiations with the PRC-A and other groups failed, see Marcos Díaz (Blas Roca), *El PRC y los Frentes Populares.* For the party's

self-criticism, see Manuel Ventura, "The Second Party Congress of the CP of Cuba," *World News and Views* 14:34 (June 15, 1934); and "Report of Comrade Marin," *World News and Views* 15:62 (November 21, 1935).

67. Hugh Thomas, *Cuba*, p. 703. For the relations between Cuba and Spain during the Civil War, see Hennessy, "Cuba."

68. Abed Brooks, "Perspectives," *World News and Views* 18:60 (December 24, 1938), p. 60.

69. On these events, see de León, *El origen del mal*. For the acts of violence and police raids against the PRC-A, see Mr. Grant Watson to Mr. Eden, Havana, November 18, 1937, PRO/FO/A/8603/65/14/No.168. Also see Roa García, *15 Años Después*, p. 219.

70. This point is supported by the British embassy: see Grant Watson to Viscount Halifax, Havana, May 26, 1938, PRO/FO/A/4618/262/14/No.52.

71. *Diario de la Marina*, September 16, 1938, p. 1; Mr. Buxton to Viscount Halifax, Havana, September 22, 1938, PRO/FO/A/7743/262/14/No.93.

72. Tellería Toca, *Congresos obreros en Cuba*, pp. 293–94.

73. Mr. Grant Watson to Viscount Halifax, Havana, May 10, 1938, PRO/FO/A/4411/262/14/No.47 (confidential).

74. Sims, "Cuba," p. 221.

75. R. A. Martínez, "The Latin American Significance of the Cuban Democratic Upsurge," *World News and Views* 19:18 (April 1939), p. 367; Tellería Toca, *Congresos Obreros en Cuba*, p. 302.

76. Mr. Grant Watson to Viscount Halifax, Havana, May 26, 1938, PRO/FO/A/4618/262/14/No.52.

77. Batista quoted in Mr. Grant Watson to Viscount Halifax, Havana, November 1, 1938, PRO/FO/A/9688/8684/14/No.118 (confidential).

78. Gellman, *Roosevelt and Batista*, pp. 167–68.

79. Mr. Grant Watson to Viscount Halifax, Havana, December 1, 1938, PRO/FO/A/9688/8684/14/No.118 (confidential).

80. William Z. Foster, "The Congress of the CP of Cuba," *World News and Views* 19:7 (February 1939), p. 147; Mr. Grant Watson to Viscount Halifax, Havana, March 4, 1939, PRO/FO/2109/1586/14/No.28 (confidential).

81. Batista quoted in R. A. Martínez, "The Latin American Significance of the Cuban Democratic Upsurge," p. 368.

82. Martínez, "The Latin American Significance," p. 368.

83. Mr. Grant Watson to Viscount Halifax, Havana, March 4, 1939, PRO/FO/2109/1586/14/No.28 (confidential).

84. Mr. Grant Watson to Viscount Halifax, Havana, April 5, 1939, PRO/FO/A/2969/1586/14/No.43.

85. Braga Collection, Box 33, File "Cuba, Political Conditions," Carta, "Situación política," September 18, 1939.

86. George Messersmith to the Secretary of State, Havana, April 1, 1940, Records of the U.S. Department of State, 1930–1944, 711/379/148.

87. George Messersmith to Undersecretary of State Sumner Welles (personal and confidential), Havana, July 12, 1940, Records of the U.S. Department of State, 1930–1944, 711/379/148.

Conclusion

1. For an excellent analysis of *caciquismo* within the Spanish context, see Moreno Luzón, *Romanones,* esp. pp. 445–48. Also see Álvarez Junco, "Rural and Urban Popular Cultures," pp. 83–82, and his "History, Politics, and Culture," pp. 70–74; Carr, *Spain,* pp. 366–79; and Shubert, *A Social History of Modern Spain,* pp. 185–86, 188–89.
2. See Pérez, *Cuba under the Platt Amendment,* esp. chap. 6.
3. For an excellent recent analysis of the Cuban sugar economy between between 1868 and 1898, see Iglesias García, *Del ingenio al central.* For the years 1898–1930s, see Dye, *Cuban Sugar,* esp. chap. 1; and Ayala, *American Sugar Kingdom,* chaps. 1–4.
4. On this issue, see Frucht, "A Caribbean Social Type"; Mintz, *Worker in the Cane;* Mintz, *Caribbean Transformations;* Scott, *Slave Emancipation in Cuba;* and most recently Dye, *Cuban Sugar,* esp. the intro. and chap. 1; and Ayala, *American Sugar Kingdom,* esp. chap. 6.
5. The term "ambiguous fertility" is taken from Davidson, *Africa in Modern History,* p. 374.
6. The most important treatment of these issues for the late nineteenth century is Ferrer, *Insurgent Cuba.*
7. Vilas, "Latin American Populism," pp. 398–407.
8. "Labour Conditions in Cuba."
9. International Bank for Reconstruction and Development, *Report on Cuba,* p. 138.
10. U.S. Department of Commerce, *Investment in Cuba,* p. 21.
11. Knight, "Populism and Neo-populism," p. 231.
12. An excellent study of American policy and attitudes toward democracy in Latin America and elsewhere is Schmitz, *Thank God Their on Our Side,* especially the section on Batista, pp. 73–83.
13. *Revista Semanal Azucarera,* p. 59.
14. Benjamin, *United States and the Cuban Revolution,* p. 100.
15. *Revista Semanal Azucarera,* p. 59.
16. For an excellent overview of how Cuban politics worked in the 1940s, see Sims, "Cuba's Organized Labor." Also see U.S. Office of Strategic Services (OSS), *The Political Significance and Influence of the Labor Movement.*
17. Stokes, "National and Local Violence in Cuban Politics," pp. 57–63. Stokes comments: "Organized use of force in urban areas in Cuba is seen primarily in connection with party factions, the university, and the labor unions" (p. 57), and "Force is a technique for mobilizing political power and organizing and changing governments. . . . Force is also used to influence the appointment of personnel, the formulation of policy, and the adjudication of competing interests" (p. 62).

Bibliography

Archival Sources and Government Publications

Gainesville, Florida, U.S.A.
Latin American Library, University of Florida
  Braga Brothers Collection

Havana, Cuba
Archivo Nacional de Cuba
  Fondo Donativo
  Fondo Presidencial
  Fondo Especial
Archivo Instituto de Historia de Cuba
  Fondo Museo Obrero
  Fondo Organizaciones Obreras
  Archivo Vilaseca

London, United Kingdom
Public Records Office
  British Foreign Office Papers, London

Government Publications
Cuba

República de Cuba. *Adaptación de Cuba a las condiciones económicas actuales.* Havana: Imprenta Rambla y Bouza, 1930.

República de Cuba. *Comisión Nacional de Estadísticas y Reformas Económicas.* Havana: Imprenta Rambla y Bouza, 1928.

República de Cuba. *Memoria de la Administración del Presidente Mario García Menocal.* Havana: Editorial Rambla y Bouza, 1921.

República de Cuba, Secretaría de Hacienda, Sección de Estadísticas. *Inmigración y movimiento de pasajeros en el año de 1921.* Havana: Imprenta La Propagandista, 1921.

República de Cuba, Secretaría de Hacienda, Sección de Estadísticas. *Movimiento de pasajeros, años 1922-1923.* Havana: Imprenta Rambla y Bouza, 1925.

United States

Foreign Relations of the United States, 1931. Vol. 2. Washington, D.C.: U.S. Government Printing House, 1946.

Foreign Relations of the United States, 1933. Diplomatic Papers. Vol. 5. Washington, D.C.: U.S. Government Printing House, 1952.

Foreign Relations of the United States, 1934. Diplomatic Papers. Vol. 5, *The American Republics.* Washington, D.C.: U.S. Government Printing Office, 1952.

Office of Strategic Services. Latin American Section. Report Number 39. *Crisis in the Cuban Government.* August 7, 1942.

Records of the United States Department of State Relating to Political Relations between the U.S. and the Latin American and Caribbean States, 1930–1944. Microfilm, reels 67 and 68.

United States Department of Commerce. *Investment in Cuba: Basic Information for United States Businessmen.* Washington D.C.: U.S. Government Printing Office, 1957.

United States Department of State, *Treaty Information.* Bulletin Number 56, May 31, 1934. Washington D.C.: U.S. Government Printing House, 1934.

United States Office of Strategic Services (OSS). *The Political Significance and Influence of the Labor Movement in Latin America. A Preliminary Survey: Cuba.* R&A, No. 3076.1. Washington, D.C., September 18, 1945.

Newspapers and Periodicals

Atui
Bandera Roja
Bohemia
Carteles
The Communist
El Crisol
Cuba Contemporánea
The Daily Worker
Diario de la Marina
La Discusión
Havana Post
Heraldo de Cuba
Juventud
Línea
La Lucha

The Nation
New York Times
El País
Pensamiento Crítico 39 (April 1970). Número Especial.
Revista Bimestre Cubana
Revista de Avance
Social
El Sol
El Triunfo
Unión Nacionalista
Venezuela Libre
World News and Views: International Press Correspondence

Books and Articles

Abad, L. V. de. *Azúcar y caña de azúcar: Ensayo de orientación cubana.* Havana: Editorial Mercantil Cubana, 1945.

ABC. *El ABC en la mediación.* Havana: Mazo, Caso y Cía, 1934.

———. *Doctrina del ABC.* Havana: Publicaciones del Partido ABC, 1942.

Abrams, Philip. "Notes on the Difficulty of Studying the State (1977)." *Journal of Historical Sociology* 1:1 (March 1988): 58–89.

Adam y Silva, Ricardo. *La gran mentira: 4 de septiembre de 1933.* Havana: Editorial Lex, 1947.

Agüero, Luis Conte. *Eduardo Chibás: El adalid de Cuba.* Mexico City: Editorial Jus, 1955.

Aguilar, Luis E. "Cuba, c. 1860–1930." In *Cuba: A Short History,* edited by Leslie Bethell, 21–55. Cambridge: Cambridge University Press, 1992.

———. *Cuba 1933: Prologue to Revolution.* Ithaca, N.Y.: Cornell University Press, 1972.

———, ed. *Marxism in Latin America.* Philadelphia: Temple University Press, 1978.

Alavez, Elena. *Eduardo Chibás: En la hora de la ortodoxia.* Havana: Editorial de Ciencias Sociales, 1994.

Al-Azmeh, Aziz. *Islams and Modernities.* London: Verso, 1993.

Alba, Víctor. *Politics and the Labor Movement in Latin America.* Stanford, Calif.: Stanford University Press, 1968.

Alexander, Robert. *Communism in Latin America.* New Brunswick, N.J.: Rutgers University Press, 1957.

———, ed. *Biographical Dictionary of Latin American and Caribbean Political Leaders.* New York: Greenwood Press, 1988.

Almond, Gabriel, and Sydney Verba. *The Civic Culture.* Princeton, N.J.: Princeton University Press, 1963.

Alonso Valdés, Coralia. "La inmigración española como fuerza de trabajo: 1800–1933." Paper presented at the Latin American Studies Association XXII International Congress, Miami, Florida, March 16–18, 2000.

Álvarez Estévez, Rolando. *Azúcar e inmigración en Cuba, 1900–1940.* Havana: Editorial de Ciencias Sociales, 1988

Álvarez Junco, José. "History, Politics, and Culture, 1875–1936." In *The Cambridge Companion to Modern Spanish Culture,* edited by David T. Gies, 67–85. Cambridge: Cambridge University Press, 1999.

———. "Rural and Urban Popular Culture." In *Spanish Cultural Studies: An Introduction,* edited by Helen Graham and Jo Labanyi, 82–9. Oxford: Oxford University Press, 1995.

Amin, Shahid and Marcel van der Lindin, eds. *"Peripheral" Labour?: Studies in the History of Partial Proletarianization.* Cambridge, England: Cambridge University Press, 1997.

Anderle, Adam. *Algunos problemas de la evolución del pensamiento anti-imperialista en*

Cuba entre las dos guerras mundiales: Comunistas y apristas. Szeged: Acta Historica, Tomus LII, 1975.

Anderson, Benedict. *Imagined Communities: Reflections on the Origin and Spread of Nationalism*. London: Verso, 1991.

Anuario de Estudios Cubanos. *La república neocolonial*. 2 vols. Havana: Editorial de Ciencias Sociales, 1979.

Araquistaín, Luis. *La agonía antillana: El imperialismo yanqui en el mar Caribe*. Madrid: Espada Calpe, S.A., 1928.

Arrendondo, Alberto. *Cuba, tierra indefensa*. Havana: Editorial Lex, 1945.

Arrighi, Giovanni. *The Long Twentieth Century: Money, Power, and the Origins of Our Times*. London: Verso, 1994.

Asociación Nacional de Hacendados de Cuba. *El tratado de reciprocidad de 1934: Sus efectos sobre la economía nacional*. Havana: Asociación Nacional de Hacendados de Cuba, 1939.

Ayala, César J. *American Sugar Kingdom: The Plantation Economy of the Spanish Caribbean, 1898-1934*. Chapel Hill: University of North Carolina Press, 1999.

Baeza Flores, Alberto. *Las cadenas vienen de lejos: Cuba, América Latina y la libertad*. Mexico City: Editorial Letras, 1960.

Balibar, Etienne and Immanuel Wallerstein. *Race, Nation, Class: Ambiguous Identities*. London: Verso, 1991.

Beals, Carlton. "American Diplomacy in Cuba." *Nation* 138 (January 17, 1934): 68–70.

———. *The Crime of Cuba*. Philadelphia: J. P. Lippencott, 1933.

———. "The New Crime of Cuba." *New Republic* 83 (July 3, 1935): 216–19.

———. "New Machado in Cuba." *Nation* 141 (August 7, 1935): 152–54.

Becker, Marc. *Mariátegui and Latin American Marxist Theory*. Athens, Ohio: Centre for International Studies, 1993.

Benjamin, Jules R. "The Machadato and Cuban Nationalism, 1928-1932". *Hispanic American Historical Review* 55 (February 1975): 66–91.

———. *The United States and Cuba: Hegemony and Dependent Development, 1880-1934*. Pittsburgh: Pittsburgh University Press, 1977.

———. *The United States and the Origins of the Cuban Revolution: An Empire of Liberty in the Age of National Liberation*. Princeton, N.J.: Princeton University Press, 1990.

Berman, Marshall. *All That Is Solid Melts into Air: The Experience of Modernity*. London: Penguin Books, 1982.

Berquist, Charles. *Labor in Latin America: Comparative Essays on Chile, Argentina, Venezuela, and Colombia*. Stanford, Calif.: Stanford University Press, 1986.

Bethell, Leslie, and Ian Roxborough, eds. *Latin America between the Second World War and the Cold War, 1944-1948*. Cambridge: Cambridge University Press, 1992.

Biblioteca Nacional José Martí. *Baliño: Apuntes históricos sobre sus actividades revolucionarias*. Havana: Biblioteca Nacional José Martí, 1967.

Bieber, Leon. *En torno al origen histórico e ideológico del ideario nacionalista populista en Latinoamérica*. Berlin: Colloquium Verlag, 1982.

Blackburn, Robin. "Prologue to the Cuban Revolution." *New Left Review* 12 (October 1963): 52–91.

Bonachea, Ramón, and Marta San Martín. *The Cuban Insurrection, 1952-1959.* New Brunswick N.J.: Transaction Books, 1974.

Briones Montoto, Newton. *Aquella decisión callada.* Havana: Editorial de Ciencias Sociales, 1998.

Buell, Raymond Leslie. "The Caribbean Situation: Cuba and Haiti." *Foreign Policy Reports* 8 (June 21, 1933): 82–92.

Buell, Raymond Leslie, et al. *Problems of the New Cuba.* New York: Foreign Policy Association, 1935.

Bulmer-Thomas, Victor. *The Economic History of Latin America since Independence.* Cambridge: Cambridge University Press, 1994.

Buttari Gaunaurd, J. *Boceto crítico histórico.* Havana: Editorial Lex, 1954.

Caballero, Manuel. *Latin America and the Comintern, 1919-1943.* Cambridge: Cambridge University Press, 1986.

Cabral, Amilcar. *Unity and Struggle: Speeches and Writings.* trans. Michael Wolfers. London: Heinemann, 1980.

Cabrera, Olga. *Guiteras: La época, el hombre.* Havana: Editorial de Arte y Literatura, 1974.

———. *Los que viven por sus manos.* Havana: Editorial de Ciencias Sociales, 1985.

———. *El movimiento obrero cubano en 1920.* Havana: Instituto Cubano del Libro, 1969.

———, ed. *Antonio Guiteras: su pensamiento revolucionario.* Havana: Editorial de Ciencias Sociales, 1974.

Cabrera, Olga, and Carmen Almovódar, eds. *Las luchas estudiantiles universitarias, 1923-1934.* Havana: Editorial de Ciencias Sociales, 1975.

Cairo Ballester, Ana. *El Grupo Minorista y su tiempo.* Havana: Editorial de Ciencias Sociales, 1978.

———. *El Movimiento de Veteranos y Patriotas.* Havana: Instituto Cubano del Libro, 1976.

———. *La revolución del 30 en la narrativa y el testimonio cubanos.* Havana: Editorial Letras Cubanas, 1993.

Callinicos, Alex. *Theories and Narratives: Reflections on the Philosophy of History.* Durham, N.C.: Duke University Press, 1995.

Carmagnani, Marcello. *Emigración mediterránea y América: Formas y transformaciones, 1860-1930.* Oviedo: Fundación Archivo de Indianos, 1994.

Carr, Barry, "Identity, Class, and Nation: Black Immigrant Workers, Cuban Communism, and the Sugar Insurgency, 1925-1934." *Hispanic American Historical Review* 78:1 (February 1998): 83–116.

———. "Mill Occupations and Soviets: The Mobilization of Sugar Workers in Cuba, 1917-1933." *Journal of Latin American Studies* 28 (1996): 129–58.

———. "Omnipotent and Omnipresent: Labor Shortages, Worker Mobility, and Employer Control in the Cuban Sugar Industry, 1910-1934." In *Identity and Struggle* at the Margins of the Nation-State: The Laboring Peoples of Central America and the Hispanic Caribbean,* edited by Aviva Chomsky and Aldo Lauria-Santiago, 260–91. Durham, N.C.: Duke University Press, 1998.

Carr, Raymond. *Spain, 1808–1975.* London: Oxford Clarendon Press, 1982.

Carrillo, Justo. *Cuba 1933: Students, Yankees and Soldiers.* Trans. Mario Llerena. New Brunswick, N.J.: Transaction Publishers, 1994.

Carrión, Miguel. "El desenvolvimiento social de Cuba en los últimos veinte años." *Cuba Contemporánea* 27 (September 1921): 5–27.

Carvajal, Juan F. "Observaciones sobre la clase media en Cuba." In *La clase media en México y Cuba: Cuatro colaboraciones,* edited by Theo R. Crevenna. Washington. D.C.: Panamerican Union, 1950.

Casanovas, Joan. *Bread, or Bullets: Urban Labor and Spanish Colonialism in Cuba, 1850–1898.* Pittsburgh: University of Pittsburgh Press, 1998.

Chatterjee, Partha. *The Nation and Its Fragments: Colonial and Postcolonial Histories.* Princeton, N.J.: Princeton University Press, 1993.

———. *Nationalist Thought and the Third World.* Minneapolis: University of Minnesota Press, 1986.

Chester, Edmund A. *A Sergeant Named Batista.* New York: Holt, 1954.

Chomsky, Aviva, and Aldo Lauria-Santiago, eds. *Identity and Struggle at the Margins of the Nation-State: The Laboring Peoples of Central America and the Hispanic Caribbean.* Durham, N.C.: Duke University Press, 1998.

Cohen, Robin, Peter C. W. Gutkind, and Phylis Blazier, eds., *Peasants and Proletarians: The Struggles of Third World Workers.* New York: Monthly Review Press, 1979.

Collier, Simon. "Trajectory of a Concept: 'Corporatism' in the Study of Latin American Politics." In *Latin America in Comparative Perspective: New Approaches to Methods and Analysis,* edited by Peter H. Smith, 135–62. Boulder, Colo.: Westview Press, 1995.

Coronil, Fernando. *The Magical State: Nature, Money and Modernity in Venezuela.* Chicago: University of Chicago Press, 1997.

Crawford, H. P. "The Labor Laws of Cuba." In *General Legal Bulletin of the Department of Commerce and the Bureau of Foreign and Domestic Commerce.* Washington, D.C., October 24, 1935.

Crevenna, Theo R., ed. *La clase media en México y Cuba: Cuatro colaboraciones.* Washington, D.C.: Unión Panamericana, 1950.

Cronin, James E. *The World the Cold War Made: Order, Chaos, and the Return of History.* New York and London: Routledge, 1996.

Davidson, Basil. *Africa in World History.* London: Allen Lane, 1978.

———. *The Black Man's Burden: Africa and the Curse of the Nation State.* New York: Times Books, 1992.

———. "On Revolutionary Nationalism: the Legacy of Cabral." *Race and Class* 27: 3 (Winter 1986): 21–45.

de Armas, Ramón, Eduardo Torres-Cuevas and Ana Cairo Ballester. *Historia de la Universidad de la Habana.* 2 vols. Havana: Editorial de Ciencias Sociales, 1984.

de Armas, Ramón, Francisco López Segrera and Germán Sánchez Otero. *Los partidos políticos burgueses en Cuba neocolonial, 1899-1952.* Havana: Editorial de Ciencias Sociales, 1985.

de la Fuente, Alejandro. "Two Dangers, One Solution: Immigration, Race, and Labor in Cuba, 1900-1930." *International Labour and Working Class History* 15 (Spring 1997): 30-49.

de la Osa, Enrique. *Crónica del año 33.* Havana: Editorial de Ciencias Sociales, 1989.

———. *En Cuba: Primer tiempo, 1943-1946.* Havana: Editorial de Ciencias Sociales, 1990.

de la Torriente Brau, Pablo. "Álgebra y política." *Islas* 10: 2 (April–June, 1968): 227-268.

de León, Rubén. *El origen del mal: Cuba, su ejemplo.* Miami, Fla.: Service Offset Printers, 1964.

del Toro, Carlos. *Algunos aspectos económicos, sociales y políticos del movimiento obrero cubano (1933-1958).* Havana: Instituto Cubano del Libro, 1974.

———. *El movimiento obrero cubano en 1914.* Havana: Instituto Cubano del Libro, 1969ᵃ

Dembicz, Andrzej. *Plantaciones cañeras y poblamiento en Cuba.* Havana: Editorial de Ciencas Sociales, 1989.

Diamond, Larry. *Developing Democracy: Toward Consolidation.* Baltimore, Md.: Johns Hopkins University Press, 1999.

Diamond, Larry, Juan Linz, S. M. Lipset, eds. *Democracy in Developing Countries: Latin America.* Boulder, Colo.: Lynne Rienner Publishers, 1989.

Díaz, Marcos (Blas Roca). *El PRC y los frentes populares.* Havana: Ediciones Populares, 1938.

Diop, Cheikh Anta. *Civilization or Barbarism: An Authentic Anthropology.* New York: Lawrence Hill Books, 1981.

Dirks, Nicolas B., ed. *Colonialism and Culture.* Ann Arbor: University of Michigan Press, 1992.

Domínguez, Jorge. "The Batista Regime in Cuba." In *Sultanistic Regimes,* edited by H. E. Chehabi and Juan J. Linz, 113-31. Baltimore, Md.: Johns Hopkins University Press, 1998.

———. *Constructing Democratic Governance: Latin America and the Caribbean in the 1990s.* Baltimore, Md.: Johns Hopkins University Press, 1996.

———. "Seeking Permission to Build a Nation: Cuban Nationalism and the U.S. Response under the First Machado Presidency." *Cuban Studies/Estudios Cubanos* 16 (1986): 33-48.

Duara, Prasenjit. *Rescuing History from the Nation: Questioning Narratives of Modern China.* Chicago: University of Chicago Press, 1995.

Duarte Hurtado, Martín. *La máquina torcedora de tabaco: las luchas en torno de su implantación en Cuba.* Havana: Editorial de Ciencias Sociales, 1973.

Dumoulin, John. *Azúcar y lucha de clases, 1917.* Havana: Editorial de Ciencias Sociales, 1980.

Dumpierre, Erasmo. *Julio Antonio Mella: Biografía.* Havana: Instituto Cubano del Libro, 1975.

Duncan, Kenneth, and Ian Rutledge, eds. *Land and Labour in Latin America: Essays on the Development of Agrarian Capitalism.* Cambridge: Cambridge University Press, 1977.

Dye, Alan. *Cuban Sugar in the Age of Mass Production: Technology and the Economics of the Sugar Central, 1899-1929.* Stanford, Calif.: Stanford University Press, 1998.

Eagleton, Terry. *Ideology: An Introduction.* London: Verso, 1990.

Fanon, Frantz. *Black Skin, White Masks.* New York: Grove Press, 1968.

————. *The Wretched of the Earth.* New York: Grove Press, 1963.

Farber, Samuel. *Revolution and Reaction in Cuba: From Machado to Castro, 1933-1960.* Middletown, Conn.: Wesleyan University Press, 1976.

Fermoselle, Rafael. *Política y color en Cuba: la guerrita de 1912.* Montevideo: Ediciones Géminis, 1974.

Fernández, Áurea Matilde. *España y Cuba: revolución burguesa y relaciones coloniales.* Havana: Editorial de Ciencias Sociales, 1988.

Fernández, Enrique. *La razón del 4 de septiembre.* Havana: La Revolución Cubana, Número 1, 1935; 2d ed., 1950.

Fernández Retamar, Roberto. *Caliban and Other Essays.* Translated by Robert Baker. Minneapolis: University of Minnesota Press, 1989.

Ferrer, Ada. *Insurgent Cuba: Race, Nation, and Revolution, 1868-1898.* Chapel Hill: University of North Carolina Press, 1999.

Fitzgibbon, Russell H. *The Constitutions of the Americas.* Chicago: University of Chicago Press, 1948.

Fitzgibbon, Russell H., and H. Max Healey. "The Cuban Elections of 1936." *American Political Science Review* 30:4 (August 1936): 724-35.

Flores Galindo, Alberto. *La agonía de Mariátegui: La polémica con el Komintern.* Lima: DESCO, 1980.

Foncueva, José Antonio. *Escritos de José Antonio Foncueva.* Edited by Ricardo Luis Hernández Otero. Havana: Editorial Letras Cubanas, 1985.

Freeman Smith, Robert, ed. *Background to Revolution.* New York: Knopf, 1966.

Freyre de Andrade, Leopoldo. *La intervención gobernamental en la industria azucarera cubana.* Havana: Leopoldo Freyre de Andrade, 1931.

Fried, Morton H. *The Evolution of Political Society: An Essay in Political Anthropology.* New York: Random House, 1967.

Frucht, Richard. "A Caribbean Social Type: Neither 'Peasant' nor 'Proletarian.'" In *Black Society in the New World,* edited by Richard Frucht, 98-104. New York: Random House, 1971.

García, Francisco. *Tiempo muerto: Memorias de un trabajador azucarero.* Havana: Instituto del Libro, 1969

García Álvarez, Alejandro. *La gran burguesía comercial en Cuba, 1899-1920.* Havana: Editorial de Ciencias Sociales, 1990.

García Álvarez, Alejandro, and Oscar Zanetti, eds. *United Fruit Company: Un caso del dominio imperialista en Cuba.* Havana: Editorial de Ciencias Sociales, 1976.

García Montes, Jorge, and Antonio Alonso Ávila. *Historia del partido comunista de Cuba.* Miami, Fla.: Editorial Universal, 1970.

Geertz, Clifford. *The Interpretation of Cultures.* New York: Basic Books, 1973.

Gellman, Irwin F. *Roosevelt and Batista.* Albuquerque: University of New Mexico Press, 1973.

Gil, Federico. "Antecedents of the Cuban Revolution." *Continental Review* 6 (Summer 1962): 373–93.

Gledhill, John. *Power and Its Disguises: Anthropological Perspectives on Politics.* London: Pluto Press, 1994.

Godelier, Maurice. *Perspectives in Marxist Anthropology.* London: Cambridge University Press, 1977.

Goldenberg, Boris. "The Rise and Fall of a Party: The Cuban CP (1925–59)." *Problems of Communism* 19:4 (July–August 1970): 61–80.

Gómez García, Carmen. *Carlos Baliño: Primer pensador marxista cubano.* Havana: Editorial de Ciencias Sociales, 1985.

González, Mike, and David Trece. *The Gathering of the Voices: The Twentieth-Century Poetry of Latin America.* London: Verso, 1992.

González Carbajal, Ladislao. *El ala izquierda estudiantil y su época.* Havana: Editorial de Ciencias Sociales, 1974.

———. *Mella y el movimiento estudiantil.* Havana: Editorial de Ciencias Sociales, 1977.

Goody, Jack. "Civil Society in a Comparative Perspective." Chap. 5 in *Food and Love: A Cultural History of East and West.* London: Verso, 1998.

Gramsci, Antonio. *An Antonio Gramsci Reader: Selected Writings, 1916-1935.* Edited by David Forgacs. New York: Schocken Books, 1988.

———. *Selections from the Prison Notebooks.* Edited and translated by Quintin Hoare and Geoffrey Nowell Smith. New York: International Publishers, 1971.

Grau San Martín, Ramón. *La revolución cubana ante América.* Mexico City: Ediciones del Partido Revolucionario Cubano, 1934.

Guardarrama, Pablo, and Edel Oropeza. *El pensamiento filosófico de Enrique José Varona.* Havana: Editorial de Ciencias Sociales, 1987.

Guerra y Deben, José Antonio, "Recent Evolution of the Sugar Industry." Appendix to Ramiro Guerra y Sánchez, *Sugar and Society in the Caribbean.* New Haven, Conn.: Yale University Press, 1964.

Guerra y Sánchez, Ramiro. "Sugar: Index of Cuban-American Cooperation." *Foreign Affairs* 20 (July 1942): 743–56.

———. *Sugar and Society in the Caribbean.* New Haven, Conn.: Yale University Press, 1964.

Guiteras Holmes, Calixta. *Biografía de Antonio Guiteras.* Havana: Municipio de la Habana, 1960.

Gutiérrez y Sánchez, Gustavo. *El problema ecónomico de Cuba: Sus causas, sus posibles soluciones.* 2 vols. Havana: Molina y Cía, 1931.

Hackett, Charles W. "Continued Unrest in Cuba." *Current History* 42 (November 1934): 215–17.

———. "Cuba and the Good Neighbor Policy." *Current History* 41 (October 1934): 88–90.

———. "Labor Crisis Averted in Cuba." *Current History* 40 (May 1934): 214–15.

———. "Restive Cuban Labor." *Current History* 40 (April 1934): 80–82.

Halaebsky, Sandor, and John Kirk, eds. *Cuba in Transition: Crisis and Transformation.* Boulder, Colo.: Westview Press, 1992.

Hale, Charles. "Political and Social Ideas in Latin America, 1870–1930." In *The Cambridge History of Latin America.* Volume 4, edited by Leslie Bethell, 367–441. Cambridge: Cambridge University Press, 1986.

Hanagan, Michael, and Charles Stephenson, eds. *Proletarians and Protest: The Roots of Class Formation in an Industrializing World.* New York: Greenwood Press, 1986.

Hardt, Michael, and Antonio Negri. *Labor of Dionysus: A Critique of the State-Form.* Minneapolis: University of Minnesota Press, 1994.

Hart, John Mason. *The Coming and Process of the Mexican Revolution.* Berkeley: University of California Press, 1987.

Helg, Aline. *Our Rightful Share: The Afro-Cuban Struggle for Equality, 1886–1912.* Chapel Hill: University of North Carolina Press, 1995.

Hennessey, Alistair. "Cuba." In *The Spanish Civil War, 1936–1939: American Hemispheric Perspectives,* edited by Mark Falcoff and Frederick B. Pike, 101–58. Lincoln: University of Nebraska Press, 1982.

Hennessy, C. A. M. "The Roots of Cuban Nationalism." *International Affairs* (July 1963): 345–59.

Henríquez Ureña, Max. *Panorama histórico de la literatura cubana.* New York: Las Américas, 1963.

Herring, Hubert. "Cuba's Election Campaign." *Current History* 41 (February 1935): 603.

———. "Cuba's General Strike." *Current History* 42 (May 1935): 192.

Hispanic American Historical Review 78:4 (November 1998). Special Issue on 1898.

Hobsbawm, Eric. *The Age of Extremes: The Short Twentieth Century, 1914–1991.* London: Michael Joseph, 1994.

Hoernel, Robert. "Sugar and Social Change in Oriente, 1898–1946." *Journal of Latin American Studies* 8:2 (1976): 215–48.

Huber, Evelyne, and Frank Safford, eds. *Agrarian Structure and Political Power: Landlord and Peasant in the Making of Latin America.* Pittsburgh: University of Pittsburgh Press, 1995.

Huntington, Samuel. *The Clash of Civilizations and the Remaking of World Order.* New York: Simon and Schuster, 1996.

———. *Political Order in Changing Societies.* New Haven, Conn.: Yale University Press, 1968.

Ibarra, Jorge. *Un análisis psicosocial del cubano, 1898–1925.* Havana: Editorial de Ciencias Sociales, 1985.

————. *Aproximaciones a Clio.* Havana: Editorial de Ciencias Sociales, 1979.

————. *Cuba, 1898-1921: Clases sociales y partidos políticos.* Havana: Editorial de Ciencias Sociales, 1992.

————. "La neocolonia, estructura socioeconómica y desenvolvimiento cultural." Unpublished paper, Havana, 1992.

————. *Prologue to Revolution: Cuba, 1898-1958.* Boulder, Colo.: Lynne Rienner Publishers, 1998.

Iglesias García, Fe. *Del ingenio al central.* San Juan: Editorial de la Universidad de Puerto Rico, 1998.

Instituto de la Historia de Cuba y del Movimiento Comunista y de la Revolución Socialista de Cuba. *Historia del movimiento obrero cubano.* 2 vols. Havana: Editoria Política, 1985.

International Bank for Reconstruction and Development. *Report on Cuba.* Washington, D.C.: International Bank for Reconstruction and Development, 1951.

James, Winston. *Holding Aloft the Banner of Ethiopia: Caribbean Radicalism in Early Twentieth Century America.* London: Verso, 1998.

Jenks, Lyland H. *Our Cuban Colony.* New York: Vanguard, 1928.

Joseph, Gilbert, and Daniel Nugent, eds. *Everyday Forms of State Formation: Revolution and Negotiation of Rule in Modern Mexico.* Durham, N.C.: Duke University Press, 1994.

Joseph, Gilbert M., Catherine C. LeGrand, and Ricardo D. Salvatore, eds. *Close Encounters of Empire: Writing the Cultural History of U.S.-Latin America Relations.* Durham, N.C.: Duke University Press, 1998.

Kaplan, Amy, and Donald E. Pease, eds. *Cultures of United States Imperialism.* Durham, N.C.: Duke University Press, 1993.

Kimmel, Michael S. *Revolution: A Sociological Interpretation.* Philadelphia: Temple University Press, 1990.

Kirk, John. *José Martí: Mentor of the Cuban Nation.* Gainesville: University Presses of Florida, 1983.

Klaiber, Jefferey. "The Popular Universities and the Origins of Aprismo, 1921-1924." *Hispanic American Historical Review* 55:4 (November 1975): 693-715.

Klarén, Peter Flindell. *Peru: Society and Nationhood in the Andes.* New York and Oxford: Oxford University Press, 2000.

Klubock, Thomas Miller. *Contested Communities: Class, Gender, and Politics in Chile's El Teniente Mine, 1904-1951.* Durham, N.C.: Duke University Press, 1998.

Knight, Alan. "Populism and Neo-populism in Latin America, Especially Mexico." *Journal of Latin American Studies* 30:Part 2 (May 1998): 223-48.

Kubayanda, Jasaphat. *The Poet's Africa: Africanness in the Poetry of Nicolas Guillen and Aime Cesaire.* New York: Greenwood Press, 1990.

Laclau, Ernesto. *Politics and Ideology in Marxist Theory.* London: New Left Books, 1977.

Lal, Brij V., Doug Munro, and Edward D. Beechert, eds. *Plantation Workers: Resistance and Accommodation.* Honolulu: University of Hawaii Press, 1993.

Lamar-Schweyer, Alberto. *La crisis del patriotismo.* Havana: Editorial Martí, 1929.

————. *How President Machado Fell*. Havana: La Casa Montalvo Cárdenas, 1938.

Larrain, Jorge. *The Concept of Ideology*. Athens: University of Georgia Press, 1979.

————. *Ideology and Cultural Identity: Modernity and the Third World Presence*. Cambridge: Polity Press, 1994.

Larsen, Neil. *Reading North by South: On Latin American Literature, Culture and Politics*. Minneapolis: University of Minnesota Press, 1995.

Laugiault, Robin. "Virgin Soil: The Modernization of Social Relations on a Cuban Sugar Estate: The Francisco Sugar Company, 1898–1921." Ph.D. diss., University of Florida, 1994.

Lemelle, Sidney, and Robin D. G. Kelly, eds. *Imagining Home: Class, Culture and Nationalism in the African Diaspora*. London: Verso, 1994.

Le Riverend Brussone, Julio E. *La república: Dependencia y revolución*. Havana: Editorial de Ciencias Sociales, 1971.

Levine, Daniel H., ed. *Constructing Culture and Power in Latin America*. Ann Arbor: University of Michigan Press, 1993.

Lewis, Rupert. *Marcus Garvey: Anti-colonial Champion*. London: Karia Press, 1987.

Líneas Básicas del Programa del Plan Trienal. Havana: Carasa y Cía, 1937.

Lipsitz, George. *Time Passages: Collective Memory and American Popular Culture*. Minneapolis: University of Minnesota Press, 1990.

Liss, Sheldon. *Roots of Revolution: Radical Thought in Cuba*. Lincoln: University of Nebraska Press, 1987.

Lloyd, David, and Paul Thomas. *Culture and the State*. New York: Routledge, 1998.

López Civeira, Francisca. *La crisis de los partidos políticos burgueses en Cuba, 1925–1958*. Havana: Ministerio de Educación Superior, 1990.

López-Seguera, Francisco. *Cuba: Capitalismo dependiente y subdesarrollo*. Havana: Editorial de Ciencias Sociales, 1972.

Losanda Álvarez, Abel F. "The Cuban Labor Market and Immigration from Spain, 1900–1930." *Cuban Studies* 25 (1996): 147–64.

Lowe, Lisa, and David Lloyd, eds. *The Politics of Culture in the Shadow of Capital*. Durham, N.C.: Duke University Press, 1997.

Löwy, Michael, ed. *Marxism in Latin America from 1909 to the Present*. Atlantic Highlands, N.J.: Humanities Press, 1992.

Lukács, Georg. *History and Class Consciousness*. Translated by Rodney Livingstone. London: Merlin Press, 1971.

Lumen, Enrique. *La revolución cubana, 1902–1934*. Mexico City: Ediciones Bota, 1934.

Machado, Gerardo. *Por la patria libre*. Havana: Imprenta de F. Verdugo, 1926.

McLeod, Marc C. "Undesirable Aliens: Race, Ethnicity, and Nationalism in the Comparison of Haitian and British West Indian Immigrant Workers in Cuba, 1912–1939." *Journal of Modern History* 31:3 (Spring 1998): 599–623.

Maestri, Raúl. *Capitalismo y anticapitalismo*. Havana: Editorial Atalaya, 1939.

————. *Latifundismo en la economía cubana*. Havana: Editorial Martí, 1929.

Mallon, Florencia. *Peasant and Nation: The Making of Postcolonial Mexico and Peru.* Berkeley: University of California Press, 1995.

Maluquer de Motes, Jordi. *Nación e inmigración: Los españoles en Cuba, siglos XIX-XX.* Oviedo, Asturias: Júcar, 1992.

Mañach, Jorge. *La crisis de la alta cultura cubana.* Havana: Editorial Lex, 1925.

———. *Historia y estilo.* Havana: Editorial Minerva, 1944.

———. *Indagación del choteo.* Havana: Editorial Martí, 1929.

———. *El militarismo en Cuba.* Havana: Seoane, Fernández y Cía, 1939.

———. *Pasado vigente.* Havana: Editorial Tropical, 1939.

———. "Revolution in Cuba." *Foreign Affairs* 1 (October 1933): 46–56.

Marcuse, Herbert. *Reason and Revolution: Hegal and the Rise of Social Theory.* 2d ed. New York: Humanities Press, 1968.

Mariátegui, José Carlos. *El hombre methanal.* Lima: Biblioteca Amide, 1987.

———. *Seven Interpretive Essays on Peruvian Reality.* Austin: University of Texas Press, 1971.

Marinello, Juan. *Ensayos.* Havana: Editorial Arte y Literatura, 1977.

Martin, Gerald. *Journeys though the Labyrinth: Latin American Fiction in the Twentieth Century.* London: Verso, 1989.

Martínez Villena, Rubén. *Órbita de Rubén Martínez Villena.* Esbozo biográfico de Raúl Roa García. Havana: Editorial La Unión, 1964.

Marx, Karl, and Friederich Engels. *The German Ideology.* New York: International Publishers, 1976.

Masiello, Francine. "Rethinking Neo-Colonial Esthetics: Literature, Politics, and Intellectual Community in Cuba's Revista de Avance." *Latin American Research Review* 28 (1993): 3–31.

Mella, Julio Antonio. *Documentos para su vida.* Havana: UNESCO, 1964.

———. *Mella: Documentos y artículos.* Havana: Editoria Política, 1975.

Mendoza, Luis G., ed. *Revista Semanal Azucarera.* Havana: Bolsa de la Habana, 1945.

Mericle, Kenneth S. "Corporatist Control of the Working Class: Authoritarian Brazil since 1964." In *Authoritarianism and Corporatism in Latin America,* edited by James M. Malloy, 303–18. Pittsburgh: Pittsburgh University Press, 1977.

Mészáros, István. *Beyond Capital: Towards a Theory of Transition.* New York: Monthly Review Press, 1995.

———. *Marx's Theory of Alienation.* 3d ed. London: Merlin Press, 1972.

———. *The Power of Ideology.* New York: New York University Press, 1989.

Middlebrook, Kevin. *The Paradox of Revolution: Labor, the State, and Authoritarianism in Mexico.* Baltimore, Md.: Johns Hopkins University Press, 1994.

Migdal, Joel, Atul Kohli, and Vivienne Shue, eds. *State Power and Social Forces: Domination and Transformation in the Third Worlds.* Cambridge: Cambridge University Press, 1994.

Mintz, Sidney. *Caribbean Transformations.* Chicago: Aldine Publishers, 1974.

———. *Worker in the Cane: A Puerto Rican Life History*. New Haven, Conn.: Yale University Press, 1960.

Moore, Barrington. *Social Origins of Dictatorship and Democracy*. Boston: Beacon Press, 1966.

Moreno Luzón, Javier. *Romanones: Caciquismo y política liberal*. Madrid: Alianza Editorial, 1998.

Munick, Ronaldo. *Revolutionary Trends in Latin America*. Montréal: Centre for Developing Area Studies, Occasional Monograph Series, Number 17, 1984.

Narotzky, Susana. *New Directions in Economic Anthropology*. London: Pluto Press, 1997.

Nelson, Lowry. *Rural Cuba*. New York: Octagon Books, 1970.

Nugent, Daniel, ed. *Rural Revolt in Mexico: U.S. Intervention and the Domain of Subaltern Politics*. Durham, N.C.: Duke University Press, 1998.

Núñez Machín, Ana, ed. *Memoria amarga del azúcar*. Havana: Editorial de Ciencias Sociales, 1981.

———. *Rubén Martínez Villena: Hombre y época*. Havana: Editorial de Ciencias Sociales, 1974.

O'Donnell, Guillermo. "Tensions in the Bureaucratic-Authoritarian State and the Question of Democracy." In *The New Authoritarianism in Latin America*, edited by David Collier, 285–318. Princeton, N.J.: Princeton University Press, 1979.

Ortiz, Fernando. *Cuban Counterpoint: Tobacco and Sugar*. Translated by Harriet de Onis. New York: Random House, 1970.

———. *Órbita de Fernando Ortiz*. Edited by Julio Le Riverend. Havana: Colección Órbita, Unión de Escritores y Artistas de Cuba, 1973.

———. *Las responsabilidades de los Estados Unidos en los males de Cuba*. Washington, D.C.: Cuban Information Bureau, 1932.

Padrón, Pedro Luis. *Julio Antonio Mella y el movimiento obrero*. Havana: Editorial de Ciencias Sociales, 1980.

Padrón Larrazábal, Roberto, ed. *Manifiestos de Cuba*. Sevilla: Universidad de Sevilla, 1975.

Paige, Jeffery. *Coffee and Power: Revolution and the Rise of Democracy in Central America*. Cambridge, Mass.: Harvard University Press: 1997.

Partido Demócrata Republicano. *Problemas constitucionales*. Havana: Ediciones Atenas, 1939.

Partido Revoluciónario Cubano (Auténtico). *Doctrina Auténtica: Posición del Partido Revolucionario Cubano (Auténtico) en la política de Cuba*. Havana: Ediciones del Partido Revolucionario Cubano (Auténtico), 1936.

Partido Socialista Popular. *Los socialistas y la realidad cubana: Informes, resoluciones y discursos*. Havana: Ediciones del PSP, 1944.

Peloso, Vincent C. *Peasants on Plantations: Subaltern Strategies of Labor and Resistance in the Pisco Valley, Peru*. Durham, N.C.: Duke University Press, 1999.

Peraza, Carlos G. *Machado, crímenes y horrores de un régimen*. Havana: Cultural S.A., 1933.

Pérez, Louis A., Jr. *Army and Politics in Cuba, 1898-1958*. Pittsburgh: Pittsburgh University Press, 1976.

———. "Cuba, 1930-1959." In *The Cambridge History of Latin America*. Volume 7, edited by Leslie Bethell, 419-55. Cambridge: Cambridge University Press, 1990.

———. *Cuba under the Platt Amendment*. Pittsburgh: University of Pittsburgh Press, 1986.

———. *Essays on Cuban History: Historiography and Research*. Gainesville: University Presses of Florida, 1995.

———. "Incurring a Debt of Gratitude: 1898 and the Moral Sources of United States' Hegemony in Cuba." *American Historical Review* 104:2 (April 1999): 356-98.

———. "Liberalism in Cuba: Between Reaction and Revolution, 1878-1898." In *Liberals, Politics and Power: State Formation in Nineteenth Century Latin America*, edited by Vincent C. Peloso and Barbara A. Tenenbaum, 259-77. Athens: University of Georgia Press, 1996.

———. *Lords of the Mountain: Social Banditry and Peasant Protest in Cuba, 1878-1919*. Pittsburgh: University of Pittsburgh Press, 1989.

———. *On Becoming Cuban: Identity, Nationality, and Culture*. Chapel Hill: University of North Carolina Press, 1999.

———. *The War of 1898: The United States and Cuba in History and Historiography*. Chapel Hill: University of North Carolina Press, 1998.

Pérez-Firmat, Gustavo. *The Cuban Condition*. Cambridge: Cambridge University Press, 1989.

Pérez-Stable, Marifeli. *The Cuban Revolution: Origins, Course and Legacy*. New York: Oxford University Press, 1993.

———. "Reflections on Historical Possibility: Cuba, 1956-1961." In *Challenging Authority: The Historical Study of Contentious Politics*, edited by Michael P. Hanagan, Leslie Page Moch, and Wayne Te Brake, 167-81. Minneapolis: University of Minnesota Press, 1998.

Philips, Ruby Hart. *Cuba, Island of Paradox*. New York: MacDowell, Oblolensky, 1959.

Pichardo, Hortensia, ed. *Documentos para la historia de Cuba*. 3 vols. Havana: Editorial de Ciencias Sociales, 1973.

Pino-Santos, Oscar. *El asalto a Cuba por la oligarquía financiera yanqui*. Havana: Editorial de Ciencias Sociales, 1973.

Popper, David H. "The Latin American Policy of the Roosevelt Administration." *Foreign Policy Reports* 10 (December 19, 1934): 270-80.

Porset, Clara. "Cuba's Troubled Waters." *Nation* 138 (March 28, 1934): 353-54.

Portuondo, José Antonio. *El contenido social de la literatura cubana*. Mexico City: Colegio de México, Centro de Estudios Sociales, 1944.

Poyo, Gerald E. "The Anarchist Challenge to the Cuban Independence Movement, 1885-1890." *Cuban Studies* 15:1 (Winter 1985): 29-42.

Primelles, Leon. *Crónica cubana, 1915-1918*. Havana: Editorial Lex, 1955.

———. *Crónica cubana, 1919-1922*. Havana: Editorial Lex, 1957.

Purnell, Jennie. *Popular Movements and State Formation in Revolutionary Mexico: The Agraristas and Cristeros of Michoacán.* Durham, N.C.: Duke University Press, 1999.

Pye, Lucian, and Sidney Verba, eds. *Political Culture and Political Development.* Princeton, N.J.: Princeton University Press, 1965.

Raby, David. *The Cuban Pre-Revolution of 1933: An Analysis.* Glasgow: Institute of Latin American Studies, 1975.

Raggi Ageo, Carlos Manuel. "Contribución al estudio de las clases medias en Cuba." In *La clase media en México y Cuba,* edited by Theo R. Crevenna. Washington, D.C.: Panamerican Union, 1950.

———, ed. *Condiciones económicas y sociales de la República de Cuba.* Havana: Editorial Lex, 1944.

Rayneri, Rene. "Colonel Batista and Cuba's Future," *Current History* 50 (April 1939): 51.

Reportario Americano (San José, Costa Rica) 3 (February 13, 1922): 346–47.

Riera Hernández, Mario. *Historial obrero cubano, 1574-1965.* Miami, Fla.: Rema Press, 1965.

Ripoll, Carlos. *La generación del 23 en Cuba y otros apuntes sobre el vanguardismo.* New York: Las Américas, 1968.

Roa García, Raúl. *15 años después.* Havana: Editorial Librería Selecta, 1950.

———. *Retorno a la alborada.* 2 vols. Las Villas: Universidad de Las Villas, 1964.

———. *La revolución del 30 se fue a bolina.* Havana: Instituto Cubano del Libro, 1969.

Roca, Blas. *Las experiencias de Cuba.* Mexico City: Editorial Popular, 1939.

———. *Por la igualdad de todos los cubanos.* Havana: Ediciones Sociales, 1939.

———. *¿Qué es Unión Revolucionaria Comunista?* Havana: Ediciones Sociales, 1942.

———. *15 de Marzo: análisis y perspectivas.* Havana: Ediciones Populares, 1942.

———. *El triunfo popular en las elecciones.* Havana: Ediciones Populares, 1946.

Roca, Blas, and Lázaro Peña. *La colaboración entre obreros y patrones.* Havana: Ediciones Sociales, 1945.

Rock, David, ed. *Latin America in the 1940s: War and Postwar Transitions.* Berkeley: University of California Press, 1994.

Rodríguez, Pedro Pablo. "Marcos Garvey en Cuba." *Anales del Caribe* 78–79 (1987–88): 279–301.

———. "El pensamiento nacional burgués durante los primeros años republicanos: El caso José Commallonga." Unpublished manuscript, Havana.

Roig de Leuchsenring, Emilio. "La colonia supervive: Cuba y los veinte años de la república." *Cuba Contemporánea* 36 (December 1924): 249–61.

———. *El grupo minorista de intelectuales y artistas habaneros.* Havana: Oficina del Historiador de la Ciudad de la Habana, 1961.

Rosell, Mirta, ed. *Luchas obreras contra Machado.* Havana: Editorial de Ciencias Sociales, 1973.

Rovira, Violeta, and Ethel García. "Los Soviet Hormiguero y Parque Alto de la Provincia de Las Villas." *Islas* 11:4 (October–December 1968): 241–50.

Rowe, William, and Vivian Schelling. *Memory and Modernity: Popular Culture in Latin America*. London: Verso, 1991.

Rueschemeyer, Dietrich, Evelyne Huber Stephens, and John D. Stephens. *Capitalist Development and Democracy*. Chicago: University of Chicago Press, 1992.

Ruiz, Ramón Eduardo. *Cuba: The Making of a Revolution*. Amherst: University of Massachusetts Press, 1968.

Said, Edward W. *Culture and Imperialism*. New York: Knopf, 1993.

Sánchez Alonso, Blanca. *Las causas de la emigración española, 1880-1930*. Madrid: Alianza Editorial, 1995.

Sánchez Arango, Aurelio. "The Recent General Strike in Cuba." *Three Americas* (Mexico City) 1:4 (June 1935).

Sayer, Derek. "Everyday Forms of State Formation: Some Dissident Remarks on 'Hegemony'." In *Everyday Forms of State Formation: Revolution and Negotiation of Rule in Modern Mexico*, edited by Gilbert Joseph and Daniel Nugent, 367-77. Durham, N.C.: Duke University Press, 1994.

Schmitz, David F. *Thank God They're on Our Side: The United States and Right-Wing Dictatorships, 1921-1965*. Chapel Hill: University of North Carolina Press, 1999.

Schutte, Ofelia. *Cultural Identity and Social Liberation in Latin American Thought*. New York: State University of New York Press, 1993.

Schwarz, Roberto. *Misplaced Ideas: Essays on Brazilian Culture*. London: Verso, 1992.

Scott, James C. *Seeing Like a State: How Certain Schemes to Improve the Human Condition Have Failed*. New Haven, Conn.: Yale University Press, 1998.

Scott, Rebecca. *Slave Emancipation in Cuba: The Transition to Free Labor, 1860-1899*. Princeton, N.J.: Princeton University Press, 1985.

Seddon, David, ed. *Relations of Production: Marxist Approaches to Economic Anthropology*. London: Frank Cass, 1974.

Serviat, Pedro. *40 aniversario de la fundación del partido comunista de Cuba*. Havana: Editorial EIR, 1965.

Shubert, Adrian. *A Social History of Spain*. London: Routledge, 1996.

Sims, Harold D. "Collapse of the House of Labor: Ideological Divisions in the Cuban Labor Movement." *Cuban Studies* 21 (1991): 123-47.

———. "Cuba." In *Latin America between the Second World War and the Cold War, 1944-1948*, edited by Leslie Bethell and Ian Roxborough, 217-42. Cambridge: Cambridge University Press, 1992.

———. "Cuban Labor and the Communist Party, 1937-1958: An Interpretation." *Cuban Studies* 15:1 (Winter 1985): 43-58.

———. "Cuba's Organized Labor, from Depression to Cold War." *MACLAS Latin American Essays* 11 (1997): 45-62.

Smith, Robert. *The United States and Cuba: Business and Diplomacy, 1917-1960*. New York: Bookman Associates, 1960.

Soler Martínez, Rafael. "El trotskismo en Cuba." Ph.D diss., Universidad de Oriente, Santiago de Cuba, 1997.

Soto, Lionel. *La revolución del 33.* 3 vols. Havana: Editorial de Ciencias Sociales, 1977.

Spenser, Daniela. *The Impossible Triangle: Mexico, Soviet Russia, and the United States in the 1920s.* Durham, N.C.: Duke University Press, 1999.

Stein, Steve. *Populism in Peru.* Madison: University of Wisconsin Press, 1980.

Stokes, William S. "National and Local Violence in Cuban Politics." *Southwestern Social Science Quarterly* 34:2 (September 1953): 54–65.

Stoner, K. Lynn. *From the House to the Street: The Cuban Women's Movement for Legal Reform.* Durham, N.C.: Duke University Press, 1991.

Stubbs, Jean. *Tobacco on the Periphery: A Case Study of Cuban Labour History.* Cambridge: Cambridge University Press, 1985.

Suárez, Andrés. *Cuba, Castro, and Communism, 1959–1966.* Cambridge, Mass.: MIT Press, 1967.

Suchlicki, Jaimi. *Cuba, from Columbus to Castro.* New York: Scribner's Sons, 1974.

———. *University Students and Revolution in Cuba, 1920–1968.* Miami, Fla.: University of Miami Press, 1969.

Swan, Harry. "The 1920s: A Decade of Intellectual Change in Cuba." *Revista Interamericana* 8:2 (Summer 1978): 275–88.

Tabares del Real, José. "Fulgencio Batista: la forja y ascenso de un caudillo." Unpublished paper, Havana, 1991.

———. *Guiteras.* Havana: Editorial de Ciencias Sociales, 1973.

———. "El pensamiento y el proyecto político de Gerardo Machado y Morales." Unpublished paper, Havana, 1991.

———. "Reflexiones sobre el surgimiento y la evolución de la dualidad de poderes en Cuba." Unpublished paper, Havana, 1991.

———. *La revolución del 30: Sus dos últimos años.* Havana: Editorial de Ciencias Sociales, 1973.

Tardiff, Joseph C., and L. Mpho Mabunda, eds. *Dictionary of Hispanic Biography.* Washington, D.C.: Gale Research, 1996.

Tellería Toca, Evelio. *Congresos obreros en Cuba.* Havana: Instituto Cubano del Libro, 1973.

Thomas, Hugh. *Cuba, or the Pursuit of Freedom.* London: Eyre & Spottiswoode, 1971.

Thomas, Paul. *Alien Politics: Marxist State Theory Retrieved.* New York: Routledge, 1994.

Thompson, E. P. *The Making of the English Working Class.* New York: Vintage Books, 1963.

Thomson, Charles. "The Cuban Revolution: The Fall of Machado." *Foreign Policy Reports* 11:21 (December 18, 1935): 250–60.

———. "The Cuban Revolution: Reform and Reaction." *Foreign Policy Reports* 11:22 (January 1, 1936): 262–76.

Thomson, John B. *Ideology and Modern Culture: Critical Social Theory in the Era of Mass Communication.* Stanford, Calif.: Stanford University Press, 1990.

Torre, R. S. de la. "The Situation in Cuba." *New International* 2:6 (October 1935).

Touraine, Alain. *Critique of Modernity.* Oxford: Blackwell, 1995.

Trelles, Carlos M. "El progreso (1902 a 1905) y el retroceso (1906 a 1922) de la República de Cuba." *Revista Bimestre Cubana* 18 (1924): 313-19.

Valdés, Nelson P. "Cuban Political Culture: Between Betrayal and Death." In *Cuba in Transition: Crisis and Transformation,* edited by Sandor Halebsky and John M. Kirk, 207-28. Boulder, Colo.: Westview Press, 1992.

Varona, Enrique José. *De la colonia a la república.* Havana: Sociedad Editorial Cuba Contemporánea, 1919.

Vázquez Gallego, Antonio. *La consolidación de los monopolios en Camaguey en la década del 20.* Havana: Instituto Cubano del Libro, 1975.

Viego Delgado, Sénen, ed. *La legislación auténtica.* Cortesia de Sénen Viego Delgado a los electores de Las Villas, 1940.

Vignier, E., and G. Alonso. *La corrupción política administrativa en Cuba, 1944-1952.* Havana: Editorial de Ciencias Sociales, 1973.

Vilas, Carlos M. *Between Earthquakes and Volcanoes: Market, State and Revolution in Central America.* New York: Monthly Review Press, 1995.

———. "Latin American Populism: A Structural Approach." *Science and Society* 56:4 (Winter 1992-93): 389-420.

Waleerstein, Immanuel. *The End of the World as We Know It: Social Science for the Twenty-First Century.* Minneapolis: University of Minnesota Press, 1999.

Welles, Sumner. *Two Years of the "Good Neighbor Policy."* Washington, D.C.: U.S. Government Printing House, 1935.

Whitehead, Laurence. "State Organization in Latin America since 1930." In *The Cambridge History of Latin America.* Volume 6, edited by Leslie Bethell, 3-95. Cambridge: Cambridge University Press, 1994.

Whitney, Robert. "What Do the People 'Think and Feel'?: Mass Mobilisation and the Cuban Revolution of 1933." *Journal of Iberian and Latin American Studies* 3:2 (December 1997): 1-31.

Williams, Raymond. *The Politics of Modernism: Against the New Conformists.* London: Verso, 1989.

Williams, William A. *The Tragedy of American Diplomacy.* 2d ed. New York: Dell Press, 1962.

Wolf, Eric R. *Envisioning Power: Ideologies of Dominance and Crisis.* Berkeley: University of California Press, 1999.

———. *Europe and the People without History.* Berkeley: University of California Press, 1982.

Wood, Denis B. "The Long Revolution: Class Relations and Political Conflict in Cuba, 1868-1968." *Science and Society* 34:1 (Spring 1970): 1-41.

Wood, Ellen Meiksins. *Democracy versus Capitalism: Renewing Historical Materialism.* Cambridge: Cambridge University Press, 1995.

———. *The Pristine Culture of Capitalism: A Historical Essay on Old Regimes and Modern States.* London: Verso, 1991.

Yashar, Deborah J. *Demanding Democracy: Reform and Reaction in Costa Rica and Guatemala, 1870s–1950s.* Stanford, Calif.: Stanford University Press, 1997.

Zanetti Lecuona, Oscar. *Los cautivos de la reciprocidad.* Havana: Ministerio de Educación Superior, 1989.

———. "The Workers' Movement and Labor Legislation in the Cuban Sugar Industry." *Cuban Studies* 25 (1996): 183–205.

Zanetti, Oscar, and Alejandro García, *Sugar and Railroads: A Cuban History, 1837–1959.* Translated by Franklin W. Knight and Mary Todd. Chapel Hill: University of North Carolina Press, 1998.

Zuaznábar, Ismael. *La economía cubana en la década del 50.* Havana: Editorial de Ciencias Sociales, 1989.

Index